Entertaining with
MARY BERRY
AND **LUCY YOUNG**

CONTENTS

FOREWORD

We've worked together for 30 years and have written cook books on a vast range of subjects. One of the many joys of publishing them is the feedback we get from you, our readers. We take your comments extremely seriously. And if there's one request that's kept on coming, it's for a book to serve numbers—a party book, with recipes for anything from a family get-together in the kitchen to a full-on feast. It's an area we feel well qualified to write on—in our personal lives as well as in our professional lives, there's nothing we like so much as cooking for family, friends, and neighbors—no matter the number.

At the same time, we're well aware of the worries that many of you have about cooking for more than six. "What can I make for so many people?" "How can I keep the food hot and will there be enough?"—these are the sorts of question we're asked, and we hope we have answered them in this book.

In *Entertaining with Mary Berry* we give you all the advice you need to make cooking for a crowd easy and stress free. There are recipes for summer and winter, for formal occasions and informal occasions, inside the home and out. We give prepare-ahead and freezing information where appropriate.

We kick off with the basics—how to plan your feast and how to guarantee there's enough for everyone to eat. We advise on ways to get the most from your kitchen and let you in on a few cheats and shortcuts to make life easier. We also give you ideas on setting the scene and on how to keep your cool on the day itself. Then it's on to the recipes.

Whether you are cooking for the family or entertaining for a larger number, the recipes in this book are perfect for a range of styles. There are hors d'oeuvres for a cocktail party, impressive entrees for a sit-down dinner party, and bowl food for a more casual feast. The choice is yours—and we have included all the tips you'll need.

To take the effort out of estimating quantities, for the vast majority of recipes we give a list of ingredients to serve 6 and a list of ingredients to serve 12, with notes on any special equipment.

So here it is—the much-requested book to answer all your party needs and put your mind at rest when cooking for a crowd. We hope each and every one of you enjoys it and finds the inspiration and confidence you're looking for as you plan your special day.

Remember—no feast is worth stressing over. Whatever happens, fun will be had by everyone—including you!

Mary Berry   *Lucy Young*

THE RIGHT EQUIPMENT

If you haven't cooked for a crowd before, there's a chance your kitchen might not be set up for it. Help is at hand—in various guises. Here are our tips for assembling the equipment you'll need for success.

Once you've fine-tuned your menu, check you have all the pots, pans, and dishes you'll need. If you don't have absolutely everything, don't worry—there are often ways round it. In this book we've aimed to keep fancy equipment to a minimum and to use standard-size pieces whenever possible. For cooking some dishes for larger numbers, you'll need to invest in a big 10 quart (11 liter) pan. Buy a long-handled spatula, too.

CHOOSING DISHES

The majority of recipes for 12 in this book can be cooked in two standard dishes for 6 rather than in a single huge one. There's even an advantage to doing this—smaller dishes are a lot less heavy to handle. If you don't have a second dish, borrow one from a friend or buy a foil dish. The cooking times for two dishes should be the same as for one large dish, but keep an eye on the food toward the end of cooking—the important thing is that it's cooked all the way through.

Foil dishes are not as sturdy as porcelain cookware, so always sit them on a cookie sheet, particularly when you're taking them in and out of the oven, and take care not to puncture them. Because they are made of metal, cooking times are slightly less. Again, check toward the end of cooking to see if the food is done.

IMPROVISING

Take a look around your kitchen to see if there are any pieces of equipment you can improvise with. A roasting pan, for example, can stand in as an ovenproof dish, and we find no end of uses for our jam pan. To check the capacity of a dish, fill it with water from a measuring jug. Slightly too big is better than too small—for obvious reasons.

PERFECT TIMING

With so much going on in the kitchen when you're cooking for a crowd, it's worth putting your mind at rest by investing in a good digital kitchen timer. They are relatively inexpensive, extremely simple to use, and the best models can time up to four dishes at once.

FRIDGE KNOW-HOW

If you are preparing food in advance, your fridge will be working hard in the run-up to your feast. The average domestic fridge isn't that big, and when it's full to capacity, it has to work overtime to cope. As a result, the temperature inside can rise, even if the weather outside isn't that warm. A fridge that's full to capacity doesn't allow the cold air to circulate freely either, which can sometimes mean foods are inadequately chilled.

Check frequently that yours is working at the correct temperature—39–41°F (4–5°C)—and adjust the controls to lower the temperature, if necessary. If your fridge doesn't have a temperature display, invest in a fridge thermometer—it's an inexpensive piece of equipment.

STORING AND WRAPPING

Be mindful of not using single-use plastics. Beeswax sheets are a great product to use instead of plastic wrap for storing and keeping food. Use recyclable materials whenever possible and reuse as much as you can.

GLASSES

Provide all the right glasses for the drinks you have to offer—wine glasses (both red and white), beer glasses, and glasses for water or soft drinks—and make sure there are plenty of them. Some nonbreakable glasses or plastic cups are a good idea if there are going to be children present. You might want to supply an ice bucket and some recyclable paper straws, too. A corkscrew and a bottle opener are essential items, as is a container for corks and caps.

• Red wine can be swirled easily in a large-bowled glass to release aromas.

• White wine will keep cooler in a narrow glass with a stem to hold it by.
• Beer tastes better from a chalice glass, which also maintains the head.
• Soft drinks or water are best served in tall highball glasses.

"Keep an eye on food cooked in one large dish toward the end of cooking—the important thing is that it's cooked all the way through."

SERVING THE RIGHT AMOUNT

From experience, we know it's better to serve too much food than not enough. That said, you don't want so much left over that you do not know what to do with it. Here's how to get the quantities right.

Almost every recipe in this book is designed to serve 6 or 12. These quantities depend to some extent, of course, on who your guests are. In general, though, we tend to err on the generous side. And to make doubly sure that there will be enough food, we always provide a plentiful supply of bread or potatoes, so that guests can tuck in and help themselves. How much food we serve also depends on the time of day.

SUGGESTED SERVING QUANTITIES
HORS D'OEUVRES
• 8–10 per person at an occasion such as a cocktail party where you're serving no other food. Serve up to five different types—cold and/or hot—depending on the number of people you've invited.
• 3 per person at a meal with no appetizer. Serve two different types of canapé—cold and/or hot.
• 1–2 per person at a meal with an appetizer. Serve just one kind of hors d'oeuvre, either cold or hot.

APPETIZERS
• **Soup:** around 10fl oz (300ml) per serving, depending on the vessels used. Soup bowls usually hold 10fl oz; mugs a little less. For 12, you will need 6 pints (3.5 liters) soup; for 20–25, 10½ pints (6 liters) soup.
• **Arugula** (as a garnish): 7oz (200g) for 12; 14oz (400g) for 20–25.

MAIN-COURSE SIDE DISHES
• **Baby new potatoes:** 3lb 3oz (1.5kg) for 12; 5½lb (2.5kg) for 20–25.
• **Baked potatoes:** 1 medium potato per person.
• **Mashed potatoes:** 8oz (225g) (unpeeled weight of potatoes) per serving. So 6lb (2.7kg) for 12; 10lb (4.5kg) for 20–25.
• **Roast potatoes:** Three small potatoes per serving.
• **Green salad/mixed leaf salad:** 11oz (300g) for 12; 1lb 2oz (500g) for 20–25.
• **Tomato salad:** 1 small or ½ large tomato per serving.
• **Rice/bulgur wheat/couscous:** 1lb 5oz (600g) for 12; 2¾lb (1.25kg) for 20–25.
• **Noodles:** 1 nest per person.
• **Bread:** 1 large baguette cuts into 10–12 slices.
• **Green vegetables:** About 2½oz (75g) per serving. So 2lb (900g) for 12; 3lb 3oz (1.5kg) for 20–25.
• **Gravy:** 2 pints (1.2 liters) for 12; 2½–3 pints (1.4–1.7 liters) for 20. If your guests are helping themselves from the gravy boat, you might wish to make a little more, as they may serve themselves rather generously.

FOR A BUFFET
• **Poached salmon:** 6–6½lb (2.7–3kg) salmon (head on, gutted) for 12; 13lb (6kg) salmon for 20–25.
• **Ham:** 2 slices per serving (if accompanied by

another meat or fish); 3 slices per serving (if served on its own).
- **Roast fillet of beef:** 5–6oz (140–175g) per serving when hot; 3½oz (100g) per serving when cold (cold beef is easier to carve thinly).

DESSERTS
- **Light cream:** 1 pint (600ml) for 12; 2 pints (1.2 liters) for 20–25.
- **Crème fraîche/yogurt:** 14oz (400ml) tub for 12; 2 x 14oz (400ml) tubs for 20–25.
- **Custard:** 2 pints (1.2 liters) for 12; 4 pints (2.4 liters) for 20–25.
- **Ice cream:** 1 scoop per person served as an accompaniment; 2 scoops per person on its own.
- For a cheese board, serve 3–5 cheeses, about 1lb 10oz (750g) in total for 12; 2¼lb (1kg) for 20–25. Accompany with your favorite savory crackers, a good chutney, and some fresh figs or grapes.

TEA
- For a tea with cakes, serve one round of sandwiches (two slices of bread) per person.
- Most people will drink a couple of cups of tea. For 20 cups, you'll need about 15 tea bags (although it depends of course on how strong you make it) and 1 pint (600ml) milk.

COOKING FOR DIFFERENT NUMBERS
When cooking for 10 or 11 people, just cook for 12 (using the quantities in the book) and freeze any leftovers. When cooking for 8 or 9 people, use the quantities for 6 people and make one and a half portions where possible—this will work for some things, but not for all, as liquid quantities can be erratic. Recipes this will work for include Tiger Shrimp Balti (page 210), Hot Mustard Spiced Beef (page 150), Boneless Winter Lamb Shanks (page 160), and 21st-Century Coronation Chicken (page 96). When this won't work, just cook for six and then add another element or dish—this helps with the "feast" idea, too:
- **Serve soup** with a salad or salads from the book, or bread and oil on a platter.
- **Add extra vegetables** to bulk out sauces such as bolognese.
- **For casseroles and curries**, cook more rice; add breads.
- **For desserts** (such as cheesecakes) don't mess around with the quantities—just make two!

CHEATS AND SHORTCUTS

If you're cooking last minute, you might appreciate a helping hand. Luckily, cutting the odd corner won't affect the final quality of the dish—as long as you choose the right corners to cut. These cheats will take the pressure off.

There are many ways you can cheat and make cooking for a party easier. A quick visit to your local supermarket or delicatessen will provide you with all the ready-prepared ingredients you need to rustle up a speedy dish like the Express Mediterranean Platter (page 90), for instance. What could be more delicious and trouble-free to serve as your appetizer? Think simple and in season—if you don't have the time to make an elaborate dessert in the summer, simply serve fresh strawberries or raspberries with cream, or make our Magenta Fruit Compote with White Chocolate Sauce (page 298). Simplicity itself.

SALADS AND VEGETABLES

Bags of prepared salads are an excellent time saver. Buy the different varieties of leaves in separate packages, then you don't end up getting enormous amounts of shredded iceberg lettuce (not our favorite), and mix them together just before serving. A bottle of good-quality vinaigrette won't go amiss, either.

Due to over-use of plastics we are not so keen on ready-prepared vegetables, but they are available in bags should you need them. You could also pair frozen vegetables with fresh vegetables—frozen peas go well with softened leeks or zucchini, for instance, and frozen baby fava beans can be mixed with any variety of fresh bean.

EQUIPMENT

Certain pieces of equipment can save you time and effort as well. Cake-pan liners take the headache out of lining cake pans. They are also guaranteed to be a perfect fit. Recyclable foil containers, such as tart pans, casserole dishes, roasting pans, and platters are not only convenient, they don't need washing either. You might appreciate that more than you think at the end of the day.

PREPARING AHEAD

Okay, so preparing food in advance isn't exactly cheating, but it is a simple way of making life easier for yourself on the day. Throughout this book we give you advice on preparing ahead, but there are plenty of other little shortcuts you can take, too. When you're making the gravy for the Mini Pork en Croûtes (page 164), for instance, you can mix all the ingredients together, ready to add the juices from the meat at the last minute. We do this all the time.

We also keep fresh white bread crumbs, grated Cheddar, grated Parmesan, and nuts in separate plastic containers in the freezer. They thaw in minutes, ready to cook with, and taste as fresh as they were the moment you put them in there.

MAKING SERVING EASIER

Serving food to large numbers might seem daunting, but there are many ways of simplifying the task. When serving pies and lasagna, we often lightly mark portion sizes on the surface with a knife so guests (or you) know where to cut. This works well with whole fish, too.

Cheesecakes, tarts, and quiches can be cut into slices or wedges, so you know they'll be enough to go round. Place them on a flat platter to serve, and reassemble them so they look whole. To make serving ice cream speedier, once it is frozen, scoop out the number of balls of ice cream you need and arrange on a tray. Cover with plastic wrap and place in the freezer. Then all you need to do is arrange the balls in bowls when you are ready to serve, or pile them into a mound and let guests serve themselves.

"Preparing food in advance isn't exactly cheating, but it is a simple way of making life easier for yourself on the day."

PLANNING THE OCCASION

No matter the occasion, when you're having a party the first thing to do is to make a plan. Careful planning and meticulous organization are key to success. Here's our advice on the things to consider ahead of your feast.

Take a look at your menu. What's sitting in the fridge waiting to be transferred to a dish or platter? What needs to be reheated or have the finishing touches put on it? And what has to be put together from scratch? Even if it's only the potatoes you're serving with your entrée or a salad you have to dress, make sure they're on your list.

CALCULATE THE WORKLOAD

With your proposed menu at hand, jot down what you can prepare ahead and what you can freeze in readiness for your big day. Will you be comfortable putting the finishing touches on dishes while your guests are there? Or would you rather it was just a simple matter of popping them in the oven? Dishes you can reheat and serve are ideal if you want to spend as much time as you can with your guests or if you think you might get flustered. Even better are cold dishes that will be sitting there ready for you to bring out and serve.

Remember to make a note if a dish can't be served right away—roasted meats, for instance, need 15–20 minutes to rest before you carve them, and some tarts are tricky to cut when hot. Check, too, that you'll have enough room in your oven or on your stove top and that you won't be trying to finish off too many dishes at once.

CHOOSING WHAT TO SERVE

When choosing an appetizer, look at your menu as a whole. If you're serving fish as an entrée, offer a meat or vegetarian dish as your appetizer, and vice versa. A simple appetizer is good before a more elaborate entrée—you don't want to spoil people's appetites or fill them up when the meal has barely begun. But a rich or elaborate appetizer is fine before a simple entrée.

A platter of tasty ingredients passed around the table makes a sociable appetizer. If you're serving 12, prepare two individual platters. If your guests are going to be standing up to eat, dot several platters around the room so they can help themselves.

A buffet usually consists of one or two entrées, with a selection of side dishes and a choice of desserts. Take care what dishes you serve together— most guests will want to sample everything, and poached salmon might not be the perfect partner for chicken tikka masala.

HOT OR COLD?

A cold appetizer makes life easy when you're serving large numbers of people and is ideal in summer. Hot soup is perfect in winter, but bear in mind that if you're working single-handedly it can be trickier than you think to serve soup to a crowd—it has to be piping hot, as do the bowls you pour it into. Again, look at your menu as a whole. You might feel more relaxed if you know one course is made, ready to take out of the fridge and serve.

Cold buffets are easier because almost everything can be prepared ahead. However, we always serve warm new potatoes or baked potatoes, even at a cold buffet.

FIGURE OUT THE SCHEDULE

Although you don't want to keep your guests hanging around, you don't want to hurry proceedings either. If you're not serving an appetizer, seat people before you bring out your entrée. If you are serving an appetizer and your entrée needs reheating, do it while you're eating the appetizer. Remember to allow 15–20 minutes for roast meats to rest before you carve them. Reheat your dessert, if necessary, while you're eating the entrée.

ASK FOR HELP IF YOU NEED IT

If you think you'll need help at some point during the party, make sure you line up volunteers in plenty of time. You might need someone to take people's coats and bags, for instance, or someone to go around with a plate of canapés or a bottle of wine. If you have any last-minute cooking to do, you might appreciate a helping hand in the kitchen, too, even if it's only asking someone to toss the salad. But beware of enlisting too much help—people could end up getting in your way.

TABLE TALK

Since you're pulling out the stops with the food, it makes sense to go to a little extra effort with the table decorations. Use your most impressive china, arrange fresh flowers in a vase, and light the candles before your guests come to the table to sit down. Easy-to-use LED string lights also give a lovely mood.

IT'S ALL IN THE DETAILS

One of the lovely things about entertaining is sitting down after your guests have gone home and looking back at the day, thinking of all the little things that went well. It could be how succulent the lamb was, how pretty the flowers looked on the table, and how happy people looked as they stood around and chatted. That's why we think that setting the scene is so important—joyful memories for you and joyful memories for them.

PREPARING TO ENTERTAIN

The best way to stop last-minute panic is to prepare as much as you can, and do so well ahead of time. Follow these tips and you'll be able to relax and enjoy the company of your guests, knowing everything is under control.

Before you start any of the cooking, clear a space next to your oven and lay out all the equipment you'll need—knives, utensils, oven mitts, a kitchen timer. Try to think of everything. Make space on a counter and pile the serving platters on it. Don't forget dishes for sauces and a basket for bread. Sort out all the plates, bowls, cutlery, napkins, and serving utensils you'll require and place them on your dining table or buffet table. If you're serving food hot, have the plates or bowls ready to pop in the oven to heat through.

DEFROSTING FOOD

If you've frozen food ahead of time, it's important to defrost (thaw) it completely before cooking. We always advise defrosting in the fridge because it's the safest method of doing it. Overnight should be fine for small dishes, but a large, deep dish can take up to two days. If time is against you, however, you can defrost non-meat and non-fish dishes at room temperature for a maximum of six hours. Once thawed, transfer to the fridge until needed. Never defrost in a warm oven or warm cupboard—the risk of attracting bacteria is high.

Transfer food into plastic bags or plastic containers to keep it in the fridge or freezer—they make better use of the limited space available.

WHEN TO BRING OUT THE HORS D'OEUVRES

• Don't bring out your canapés until most of your guests have arrived. You don't want them all to have been gobbled up by the time everyone gets there.

• Start with your most stunning hors d'oeuvre—just like the curtain going up at the theater, this is your signal that the action is about to commence.

• To begin with, serve one kind of canapé per plate or platter, so you can keep track of which guests have had what.

• Once the hors d'oeuvres have started to disappear, pass around mixed plates or platters instead of half-empty ones—these can look rather sad and uninviting.

• Allow 45 minutes to an hour for guests to enjoy their canapés before you serve your appetizer or entrée. Don't rush things—you want to keep the atmosphere relaxed.

• At a cocktail party you expect to last for 2–3 hours, serve the hors d'oeuvres for a couple of hours and then wind down.

• As a sign that it's closing time and the curtain's about to come back down, we serve something sweet—brownies or cupcakes presented in paper truffle cases.

BUFFETS

- Prepare all the dishes to serve the number of people you have coming. If you make them any smaller, there's the risk that some will run out. People will go back for second helpings, and any leftovers can be kept in the fridge for a few days or frozen.
- Make portions attractive and small. With guests tucking into more than one dish, you don't want to overwhelm them. We score suggested serving portions on the top of large dishes such as pies and lasagna.
- If you're serving a whole ham, carve a few slices to get people going.
- If you're offering an appetizer at a formal meal, serve it at the tables where guests will sit.

DRINKS

At a buffet, set the drink and glasses out on a separate table. Site it well away from the door— the first thing guests generally do at a party is pour themselves a drink and you don't want them blocking the entrance to the room.

TEA

- Bake scones on the day. If you do have to prepare them in advance, freeze them and then gently reheat in the oven at low heat once defrosted.

At a buffet, serve them with bowls of jam and cream (there's no need for butter) for guests to help themselves. Otherwise top them before you serve them.
- Although you can ice cakes ahead, the icing will be at its shiniest if you do it on the day itself. Provide forks with iced cakes as they can be messy to eat with your hands.
- Depending on the filling you're using, most sandwiches can be prepared up to a day ahead. Kept correctly, they will taste as fresh as the moment you made them. Other sandwiches, such as cucumber and tomato, are best made no more than 10 hours ahead. For more on this, turn to page 314.
- Offer fresh herb teas, mint from the garden, or infused herbal.

ON THE DAY

It's the day of your feast and the countdown's on. If you've prepared ahead and kept well organized, the pressure shouldn't be too intense. It's now time to make the final preparations. Here's what to keep in mind right before—and during—the party.

No matter how much you are able to prepare in advance, there will still be plenty to do on the day itself. Before your guests arrive, lay the table, set out the drinks, arrange flowers in vases, and light candles.

LAY THE TABLE

If you're having a buffet, arrange a stack of plates or bowls at one end of the table, with the cutlery and napkins at the other end. The flow of traffic can go from right to left or from left to right, depending on the layout of your room.

For a large sit-down meal, it's a good idea to have a seating plan. For special occasions, you might want to have name cards. If it's a family affair and you have young children, get them to decorate the cards for you. If you're having flowers in the center of the table, arrange them in low vases so that people can still see each other and chat.

Think about the lighting, perhaps using lamps or candles to create a warm, relaxing atmosphere. Music can help to set the scene, too.

WARM THE PLATES AND PLATTERS

Plates must be piping hot for food you're serving hot. Platters may need heating, too. The easiest way to do this is in the oven at low heat. If your oven's already in use, you could either run them through a quick wash in the dishwasher (there's no need for any detergent) or stack them over a pan of simmering water. Swap them around every so often so they all get hot. Hot plates and hostess trolleys may not be high fashion any more, but they will certainly come in handy if you have one.

TASTE THE FOOD

In the same way that you taste food as you're making it, it's important to taste it again before you serve it. Adjust the seasoning, if need be—that way, you can present it with confidence.

SERVING HORS D'OEUVRES

If you've kept the canapés in the fridge, take them out about an hour before you want to serve them so they have a chance to come up to room temperature. The flavors will improve as a result. When serving hot canapés, work out timings carefully in advance—you don't want to keep people waiting. Nor do you want everything in the oven at once. Allow a little time for them to cool down before you take them out to serve.

SERVING COLD FOOD

If you've prepared food ahead and kept it in the fridge ready to serve cold, transfer it to platters just before serving. If you want to cover the platters with plastic wrap, make sure it's only lightly secured under the rim—when too tightly wrapped, it can be time-consuming to remove and there's always the risk of damaging the arrangement as you do so.

PORTION CONTROL

Whether you're serving individual plates of food or letting guests help themselves, it's important to keep an eye on the size of the portions. If you're serving guests, make sure the portions are a sensible size—you don't want to overwhelm people by putting too much on their plate to begin with. They can always have more. If you're serving food on platters for guests to help themselves, don't provide oversize utensils—they may seem practical, but guests will make full use of them and the food will be gone in no time.

KEEPING FOOD HOT

It is essential to keep hot food hot. Use the top of your stove to keep pans on a gentle simmer or pop things into the oven at low heat, but only after they have come to a boil on the stove top.

REHEATING FOOD

If you're going to reheat food, it needs to be done thoroughly. There can be serious health risks if you don't. We've indicated in the recipes when you can prepare a dish ahead and reheat it. If it doesn't say you can do this, don't do it—you'll spoil the dish.

If you've kept food you've prepared ahead in the fridge, allow time for it to come to room temperature before you reheat it. This can take much longer than you think—up to a few hours for a big dish. It depends to some extent on the temperature in your kitchen.

Whenever possible, reheat food in a wide, shallow pan or dish—it will heat up more quickly than in a small deep one. On the stove, use a large pan that covers the whole of the burner. When reheating a casserole, bring it up to a boil, then cover with a lid and leave it to simmer gently, stirring occasionally.

Before you preheat the oven, arrange the shelves so that the dishes will all fit in. Preheat it well ahead of time and, halfway through cooking, switch the dishes around in case your oven has hotter parts to it.

Remember that the more dishes you're reheating in the oven at the same time, the longer they'll take. Check toward the end of cooking to see if they're done—they must be piping hot in the middle.

GENTLY DOES IT

Don't rush to clear people's plates as soon as they've finished. Keep the atmosphere leisurely and relaxed. You might even encourage guests to swap places around the table before you serve the next course.

HORS D'OEUVRES

These tiny dishes will get your feast started with a flourish. We like to offer a selection of meat, fish, and vegetarian canapés to guarantee all tastes are catered to. At a cocktail party, offer no more than five different types, but lots of them—people are much more likely to remember them.

SMOKED SALMON ON RYE WITH CUCUMBER PICKLE

MAKES 60

4 tbsp light mayonnaise

2 tsp coarse mustard

1 tsp lemon juice

1 tbsp freshly chopped dill, plus extra to garnish

4 rectangular slices of rye bread, pumpernickel, or pumpkin seed bread

7oz (200g) smoked salmon slices

4 whole dill pickles, drained and very finely chopped

These are always a hit. As a twist on the traditional recipe, we use rye bread, pumpernickel, or pumpkin-seed bread.

1. Mix the mayonnaise, mustard, lemon juice, and dill in a small bowl.

2. Lay the bread on a cutting board and spread evenly with the mixture.

3. Cover the mayonnaise with smoked salmon, then cut each piece of bread into 15 squares. Top each one with chopped pickle, arrange on a serving plate, then garnish with dill and serve.

PREPARE AHEAD

The bites can be made up to 6 hours ahead. Not suitable for freezing.

MINI CHICKEN SATAYS

MAKES 24

Special equipment
24 skewers (we prefer wooden over metal)

4 large boneless skinless chicken breasts

4 tsp white wine vinegar or rice vinegar

4 tsp superfine sugar

2 tbsp sunflower oil or sesame oil

a little olive oil, to fry

For the satay sauce
1½ tbsp olive oil

1 large onion, finely chopped

1 large red chile, seeded and finely chopped

3 garlic cloves, crushed

1 tbsp medium curry powder

6 heaped tbsp crunchy peanut butter

1½ cups (350ml) water

1 heaped tsp superfine sugar

juice of ½ large lime

salt and freshly ground black pepper

a sprig of cilantro, to garnish

These warm canapés are always enthusiastically received and are a cinch to make. If you'd like to serve them as a starter, you'll need three to four per person. Soak wooden skewers in water for about 8 hours before use so they don't burn during cooking. Serve with a little ramekin of satay sauce.

1. Slice each chicken breast into six thin strips, then place them in a mixing bowl. Add the vinegar, sugar, and sunflower oil and toss together well. Leave to marinate in the fridge for about an hour.

2. To make the sauce, heat the oil in a frying pan over high heat, add the onion, chile, and garlic and saute for 1 minute. Cover with a lid, lower the heat, and cook for 5 minutes or until the onion is starting to soften.

3. Stir in the curry powder and saute for 1 minute. Add the peanut butter, water, sugar, and lime juice and stir over high heat until the sauce is quite thick and shiny, then season with salt and pepper. Spoon into a serving bowl and leave to cool completely.

4. Thread each strip of chicken onto a skewer—they should be fairly flat so they will cook evenly, with room at one end so they can be held comfortably.

5. Heat a little olive oil in a large frying pan and fry the chicken skewers for 1–2 minutes on each side or until golden all over and cooked through. You may need to do this in batches. Garnish the sauce with the cilantro sprig and serve with the warm chicken skewers.

PREPARE AHEAD
*The sauce can be made up to 3 days ahead.
The skewers can be threaded up to 2 days ahead. Not suitable for freezing.*

DUCK AND HOISIN SPRING ROLLS

MAKES 18

1 boneless duck breast, skin removed

a little olive oil

salt and freshly ground black pepper

6 sheets phyllo pastry

¼ cup (50g) butter, melted

3 tbsp hoisin sauce, plus a little extra for dipping

¼ cucumber, sliced in half lengthwise, seeds removed, then cut into 2½in (6cm) long matchsticks

3 scallions, cut into 2½in (6cm) long matchsticks

These are our take on the crispy duck pancakes you get in Chinese restaurants. And very good they are, too. We use phyllo pastry because it is much easier to roll than store-bought pancakes.

1. Preheat the oven to 400°F (200°C). Meanwhile, rub both sides of the duck breasts with a little olive oil, season with salt and pepper, then fry over high heat for 2 minutes on each side or until golden brown on the outside and still pink on the inside. Allow to cool slightly, then cut into very thin slices.

2. Lay a sheet of phyllo on the work surface and cut it into three 4 x 5in (10 x 12cm) strips (the dimensions of the phyllo will depend on the type, but cut strips that are roughly this size). Brush the edges of each strip with melted butter.

3. Spoon a little hoisin sauce near the bottom of each strip (leaving a gap around the edges), then sit a couple of slices of duck on top, followed by a few of the cucumber and scallion matchsticks.

4. Fold the sides of each strip in, then, starting at the bottom, roll them up into neatly shaped spring rolls. Make 15 more in the same way.

5. Brush the spring rolls with a little more melted butter, arrange on a cookie sheet, and bake, turning them halfway through cooking, for 10 minutes or until golden. Serve warm with extra hoisin sauce to dip into.

PREPARE AHEAD

The spring rolls can be made up to the end of step 4 up to 8 hours ahead. Not suitable for freezing.

BEEF REMOULADE ROLLS

MAKES 24

2 large fat fillet steaks
(weighing about 6oz/175g
each)

1 tbsp olive oil

salt and freshly ground
black pepper

1 small celeriac

4 tbsp good-quality
mayonnaise

1 tbsp Dijon mustard

large handful of arugula

Matchsticks of celeriac coated in mustardy mayonnaise, remoulade is a classic recipe—if you are short on time, cheat by buying 8oz (225g) ready-made remoulade from the deli counter of the supermarket. Here, the mixture is teamed with arugula and wrapped in wafer-thin slices of rare fillet steak.

1. Rub the steaks with the oil and season with salt and freshly ground black pepper. Heat any remaining oil in a nonstick frying pan, add the steaks, and fry for 3 minutes on each side or until still rare (this will depend on the thickness). Set aside to cool completely.

2. Peel the celeriac with a sharp knife, chop into pieces, then cut into very thin matchsticks with the matchstick attachment of a food processor. Immerse in boiling salted water for 3 minutes or until soft. Drain and dry on paper towel.

3. Put the mayonnaise and mustard into a bowl, season with salt and freshly ground black pepper, and mix well. Stir in the celeriac.

4. Slice each cold steak into 12 thin slices (you may get more depending on the size of the steak). Spoon a little remoulade on one end of each slice, put a few arugula leaves on top, then roll them up and arrange on a platter. Serve with cocktail sticks, if you wish.

PREPARE AHEAD

The remoulade can be made up to 3 days ahead. The rolls can be made up to 8 hours ahead. Not suitable for freezing.

PORK MEATBALLS WITH ASIAN DIPPING SAUCE

MAKES ABOUT 50

1lb (450g) lean ground pork

1 red chile, halved, seeded, and finely diced

1 tsp freshly grated ginger

½ onion, coarsely grated

¾ cup (50g) saltine crackers, finely crushed

1 tsp five-spice powder

1 egg yolk

small bunch of cilantro, coarsely chopped

zest and juice of ½ lime

salt and freshly ground black pepper

a little sunflower oil, to fry

For the dipping sauce

juice of ½ lime

2 tbsp light brown sugar

½ cup (100ml) plum sauce

1 tbsp soy sauce

4 tbsp cold water

Asian food always goes down well at a party. The consistency of the sauce is thin, as is traditional.

1. Put the pork, chile, ginger, onion, crackers, five-spice powder, egg yolk, cilantro, and lime zest and juice into a bowl and mix together with your hands. Season well with salt and pepper, then shape into about 50 small meatballs.

2. Heat a little oil in a large frying pan, add the meatballs, and fry slowly for 10–15 minutes or until lightly golden and cooked through. You might need to do this in batches. Keep the meatballs warm while you make the dipping sauce.

3. Put all the ingredients for the sauce into a small saucepan and heat until the sugar dissolves. Pour into a bowl and serve with the meatballs.

PREPARE AHEAD AND FREEZE

The meatballs can be made and fried up to 2 days ahead. The sauce can be made up to 3 days ahead. Freeze the uncooked meatballs for up to 2 months.

SAUSAGE AND APPLE PHYLLO ROLLS

MAKES 80

1lb (450g) pork sausage

1 small Granny Smith apple, peeled, cored, and coarsely grated

1 tbsp coarse mustard

1 tbsp freshly chopped sage

salt and freshly ground black pepper

10 sheets phyllo pastry (each about 7 x 10in/ 18 x 25cm in size)

½ cup (100g) butter, melted

These are divine. They are also very tiny, but you could make them larger if you prefer. Just remember to bake them for a few minutes longer—and keep your eye on them. In spring we like to make a variation with asparagus—see below left.

1. Put the sausage, apple, mustard, and sage into a mixing bowl, season with salt and pepper, and mix well.

2. Divide the mixture into 10, then roll each one into a sausage about the diameter of a breakfast sausage and as long as a sheet of phyllo.

3. Brush one sheet of phyllo with melted butter. Arrange a sausage down one side and roll it up. Repeat with the remaining phyllo and sausages, then chill in the fridge for 30 minutes.

4. To serve, preheat the oven to 400°F (200°C). Slice each roll into eight diagonally and arrange on two cookie sheets lined with parchment paper. Brush with melted butter.

5. Bake for 10–12 minutes or until golden and crisp. Serve hot or warm.

ASPARAGUS, GOAT CHEESE, AND PROSCIUTTO PHYLLO ROLLS

Cook 18 trimmed asparagus spears in boiling salted water for 2–3 minutes or until just tender. Drain and refresh in cold water, then dry on paper towel. Lay pairs of slices of prosciutto next to each other lengthwise on a board, and spread with soft goat cheese (you will need 12 slices prosciutto and 6 tablespoons cheese in total). Arrange the asparagus spears along the long edges of the prosciutto, then roll them up tightly. Then follow steps 4–5 as above, but using only 6 sheets of phyllo pastry, and cutting them into 48–60 pieces. Not suitable for freezing.

PREPARE AHEAD AND FREEZE

The sausage and apple rolls can be made up to the end of step 4 up to 12 hours ahead. Alternatively, you can bake them and reheat to serve. Freeze the uncooked rolls for up to 2 months.

SAUSAGES AND MUSTARD MASHED POTATOES

MAKES 20

20 cocktail sausages

½ cup (100g) mashed potatoes

a little milk (optional)

a little butter (optional)

salt and freshly ground black pepper

coarse mustard

a little freshly grated Parmesan cheese

paprika, to dust

We've been serving a version of this canapé for years and it is still one of our most popular. Our assistant, Lucinda, often cooks for parties and she says these are always the first to go.

1. Grill the sausages, turning them halfway through, until cooked and evenly brown. Set aside to cool completely.

2. Heat the mashed potatoes in a pan (if it is a bit stiff, stir in a little milk and butter—the mixture should be smooth and fairly loose). Season with salt and pepper and add coarse mustard to taste. Transfer to a piping bag fitted with a plain narrow nozzle (don't worry if you don't have one—you can use a teaspoon).

3. Slice each sausage open lengthwise. Squeezing the ends of each sausage together gently to create a pocket, pipe or spoon the mashed potatoes into the opening.

4. Arrange on a baking tray, sprinkle with the Parmesan, and lightly dust with paprika.

5. To serve, preheat the oven to 400°F (200°C). Reheat the sausages for 10 minutes or until hot all the way through. Transfer to a platter and serve. Do warn your guests they may be hot!

PREPARE AHEAD AND FREEZE

The sausages and mashed potatoes can be prepared up to the end of step 3 up to 1 day ahead. Freeze at the end of step 3 for up to 1 month.

MINI SAUSAGES WITH MUSTARD AND BACON

MAKES 18

6 thin rashers dry-cured, unsmoked bacon

1 tbsp coarse mustard

18 cocktail sausages

These little sausages make a great canapé for a festive gathering. They are also perfect for a holiday dinner to go with your main meat dish.

1. Preheat the oven to 400°F (200°C).

2. Lay the bacon in rows on a board. Spread a little coarse mustard on each rasher of bacon. Cut each piece into three.

3. Wrap a piece of bacon (with the mustard on the inside) tightly around each sausage and put onto a cookie sheet ready for cooking. Cook in the preheated oven for about 25–30 minutes or until cooked and crisp.

PREPARE AHEAD AND FREEZE

The sausages can be wrapped up to 1 day ahead. Cook up to 1 day ahead and reheat to serve. Freeze well raw and wrapped.

BACON AND WATER CHESTNUT BITES WITH MANGO CHUTNEY

MAKES ABOUT 21

7 rashers unsmoked bacon

4 tbsp mango chutney

8oz (220g) can whole water chestnuts, drained and dried

Every can of water chestnuts we open seems to contain 21, but you may end up with one more or one less. It doesn't matter in the slightest for these, our version of the traditional devils on horseback.

1. Preheat the oven to 425°F (220°C). Lay a rasher of bacon on a cutting board. Hold on to one end of the rasher and drag the blade of a large knife along the surface of the rasher to stretch it out. This will help you wrap it easily around the water chestnut. Cut across into three equal pieces. Repeat with the other rashers.

2. Lay all the rashers on the board. Spoon ½ teaspoon of the chutney on one end, sit a water chestnut on top, then roll the rashers up and arrange them on a cookie sheet lined with parchment paper.

3. Spoon a little more chutney on top of each bite, then bake, turning them halfway through, for 15–20 minutes or until crisp and golden. Serve hot with a cocktail stick.

PREPARE AHEAD

The bites can be made up to the end of step 2 up to 1 day ahead. Not suitable for freezing.

CRISPY BACON AND QUAIL EGG TARTLETS

MAKES 24

2 large eggs

12 quail eggs

2 tbsp mayonnaise

dash of Tabasco

2 tbsp freshly snipped chives

salt and freshly ground black pepper

4 rashers bacon

24 store-bought pastry canapé cases

celery salt, for sprinkling

These are utterly delicious—crispy bacon and egg mayonnaise tartlets, each topped with half a quail egg. To make the eggs easier to peel, do it when they are just cool enough to handle. For speed, we use store-bought pastry cases, but you can make them yourself if you prefer.

1. Put the large eggs in a saucepan. Cover with cold water, bring to a boil, and boil for 5 minutes. Add the quail eggs and boil for a further 3 minutes. Drain and cover with cold water. Peel as soon as they are cool enough to handle.

2. Put the mayonnaise, Tabasco, and half the chives into a bowl with some salt and pepper and mix together. Quarter the large eggs, add to the mayonnaise, and mash well with a fork. Cut the quail eggs in half and set aside.

3. Fry the bacon in a nonstick frying pan until crisp, then drain on paper towel and set aside.

4. Spoon the egg mayonnaise mixture into the pastry cases and sit half a quail egg cut side up on top of each one. Snip the bacon into pieces and arrange a piece next to the quail eggs.

5. Sprinkle with a pinch of celery salt, garnish with the remaining chives, and serve at once.

PREPARE AHEAD

The tartlets can be prepared up to 3 hours ahead. Not suitable for freezing.

DIP PLATTER

Dips are so easy to serve at a party. Here are two of our favorites. Vegetables such as peppers, carrots, and cucumbers are the classic dippers and always popular. If you're serving chips, tortillas, or bread, choose plain varieties so they don't overpower the flavor of the dip.

SERVES 6–12
(DEPENDING ON
WHAT YOU SERVE
IT WITH)

1 green chile, halved, seeded, and cut into three

3 small scallions, finely chopped

3 garlic cloves, halved

small handful of flat-leaf parsley

small bunch of chives

6oz (200ml) full-fat crème fraîche

1 tsp Dijon mustard

1 tbsp lemon juice

salt and freshly ground black pepper

GARLICKY HERB DIP

1. Put the chile, scallions, garlic, and parsley into a food processor and process until very finely chopped. Add the remaining ingredients, season with salt and pepper, and process again until smooth.

2. Spoon the dip into a bowl or ramekin and chill. To serve, place in the center of a large plate, with your choice of dippers around the edge. The dip also goes well with potato wedges or dolloped on a baked potato.

SERVES 6–12
(DEPENDING ON
WHAT YOU SERVE
IT WITH)

10 Peppadew peppers, drained, rinsed, and cut in half

1 red chile, cut in half

2 tsp freshly grated ginger

6 tbsp mayonnaise

2 tbsp mango chutney

3½oz (100g) full-fat cream cheese

a few drops of Tabasco

salt and freshly ground black pepper

SCORCHING CHILI DIP

1. Put all the ingredients into a food processor and process until smooth. Season with salt and pepper.

2. Spoon the dip into a bowl or ramekin and place in the center of a large plate. Arrange your choice of dippers around the edge.

PREPARE AHEAD

The dips can be made up to 4 days ahead. The flavors will get stronger the longer they keep. Not suitable for freezing.

GOLDEN ROLLS WITH CHEESE AND CHUTNEY

MAKES 32

16 ready-to-bake rolls

scant 2 tbsp (25g) butter

¾ cup (100g) sharp Cheddar cheese, grated

1 tbsp milk

salt and freshly ground black pepper

1 egg yolk

2 tbsp freshly snipped chives

3 tbsp mango chutney

Ready-to-bake rolls are available in most supermarkets. They often come in a box with garlic butter, but you can also buy them in bags without the butter. They make an excellent base for hot canapés.

1. Slice each roll in half horizontally, then cut a small piece off the rounded base so they'll sit flat on the cookie sheet without toppling over.

2. Melt the butter in a saucepan, add the cheese, and stir to melt. Add the milk and stir until smooth. Leave to cool slightly, then season with salt and pepper and stir in the egg yolk and chives. Transfer to the fridge to firm up—when the mixture looks like soft butter, it will be easier to spread.

3. Preheat the oven to 400°F (200°C). Line a cookie sheet with parchment paper or foil. Spread the cheese mixture over the flat side of each roll, spreading right to the edges. Spoon a small blob of the chutney on top.

4. Bake for 10–12 minutes or until golden brown and hot. Arrange on a platter and serve immediately.

RED PEPPER ROLLS

As a variation on this scrummy recipe, cut small slices of chargrilled red peppers from a jar and arrange them in a cross on the top of each roll when they come out of the oven.

PREPARE AHEAD AND FREEZE

The rolls can be made up to the end of step 3 up to 12 hours ahead. Freeze without the chutney for up to 1 month.

SWEET CORN AND FETA FRITTERS

MAKES 40

4 rashers unsmoked back bacon

¾ cup (100g) self-raising flour

2 eggs

½ cup (100ml) milk

salt and freshly ground black pepper

4 tbsp freshly snipped chives

5oz (150g) canned corn, drained

⅓ cup (50g) feta cheese, finely crumbled

a little sunflower oil, to fry

7oz (200g) low-fat cream cheese

These fritters are delicious and quick to make. Made a little larger, they are also great for brunch.

1. Fry the bacon over high heat until crisp. Set aside to cool, then snip into 40 pieces.

2. Put the flour into a mixing bowl, make a well in the center, and add the eggs. Whisk by hand, gradually adding the milk, until you have a smooth batter. Season with salt and pepper, then stir in half the chives along with the corn and feta.

3. Heat the oil in a nonstick frying pan, add the batter to the pan half a teaspoon at a time, then fry for 2–3 minutes on each side or until golden and cooked through. You may need to do this in batches. Set aside to cool.

4. Put the cream cheese into a bowl, add the remaining chives, and season with salt and pepper.

5. Using a teaspoon, spoon the cream cheese mixture on top of the fritters, then top with a piece of crispy bacon. Arrange on a platter and serve.

PREPARE AHEAD

The fritters can be made up to 1 day ahead and assembled up to 6 hours ahead. Not suitable for freezing.

CROSTINI WITH SLOW-ROASTED TOMATOES AND HERBS

MAKES 30

1 very thin baguette

a little olive oil

15 small cherry tomatoes

salt and freshly ground black pepper

dash of superfine sugar

2 tbsp full-fat cream cheese

2 heaped tsp freshly chopped mint

2 heaped tsp freshly chopped basil

The time spent roasting the tomatoes is worth every moment—the depth of flavor they acquire is wonderful. Paired with an herby cream cheese, they make a wonderful cold canapé.

1. Preheat the oven to 275°F (140°C). Meanwhile, cut the bread into 30 thin slices and brush both sides with a little of the oil.

2. Slice the tomatoes in half and arrange cut side up on a cookie sheet. Sprinkle with a little salt, some pepper, and a dash of sugar. Cook in the oven for 30 minutes or until just softened and beginning to shrivel. Set aside to cool.

3. Heat a little olive oil in a frying pan and fry the slices of bread over high heat until golden brown on both sides. Set aside to cool.

4. Mix the cream cheese and herbs together in a bowl and season with salt and pepper. Spoon onto the cold crostini and top each one with a cold tomato half.

PREPARE AHEAD AND FREEZE

The crostini can be made up to 1 week ahead. Freeze without the topping for up to 4 months.

CROSTINI WITH PROSCIUTTO AND PEPPERED CREAM CHEESE

MAKES 30

For the onion marmalade

1 tbsp olive oil

1 red onion, thinly sliced

½ tsp balsamic vinegar

1 tsp brown sugar

salt and freshly ground black pepper

1 thin white baguette

a little olive oil

2½ oz (75g) full-fat cream cheese

freshly ground black pepper

1 tbsp freshly snipped chives

6 slices prosciutto

These are so popular whenever we serve them. If you are short on time, use onion marmalade from a jar.

1. Preheat the oven to 325°F (160°C). Meanwhile, make the onion marmalade. Heat the oil in a saucepan, add the onion, and saute over high heat, stirring, for 5 minutes or until lightly colored. Cover with a lid and cook slowly for 20 minutes or until soft. Add the vinegar and sugar and stir over high heat for a few minutes until combined and glossy. Season with salt and pepper, then set aside to cool.

2. Cut the bread into 30 slices. Brush each side with a little olive oil, then arrange on a cookie sheet. Bake for 30–45 minutes or until crisp. Leave to cool.

3. Spoon the cream cheese into a bowl, add the black pepper and the chives, and stir to combine.

4. To serve, spread a little of the cream cheese mixture on top of each of the crostini. Snip each slice of prosciutto into 5 pieces and arrange on top of the cream cheese. Top with a little onion marmalade, arrange on a platter, and serve.

PREPARE AHEAD AND FREEZE

The marmalade and crostini can be made up to 1 week ahead. The topping can be added to the crostini up to 6 hours ahead. Freeze the crostini without the topping for up to 4 months.

HOMEMADE BLINIS WITH SALMON AND CRÈME FRAÎCHE

MAKES 30

¾ cup (100g) all-purpose flour

½ tsp baking powder

2 eggs

4 tbsp milk

2 tbsp freshly snipped chives

1 tbsp sunflower oil

For the topping

3½oz (100g) full-fat cream cheese

3 tbsp crème fraîche

2 tbsp freshly chopped dill, plus a few sprigs to garnish

1 tsp lemon juice

7oz (200g) smoked salmon

We like our blinis quite thin, but the thickness is entirely up to you. If you make them too thick by mistake, simply slice them in half horizontally and you'll have twice the number.

1. Put the flour, baking powder, eggs, milk, and chives into a bowl and mix to make a smooth batter. Heat the oil in a frying pan, add the batter half a teaspoon at a time, and fry for 1–2 minutes or until little bubbles form and the blinis start to curl at the edges. Turn over and lightly brown the other side, then transfer to a wire rack to cool. You may need to do this in batches.

2. To make the topping, mix the cream cheese, crème fraîche, chopped dill, and lemon juice in a small bowl, then spoon a little onto each blini.

3. Top the blinis with a small swirl of smoked salmon and a tiny sprig of dill. Arrange on a platter and serve.

PREPARE AHEAD AND FREEZE

The blinis can be made up to the end of step 1 up to 2 days ahead. They can be assembled up to 6 hours ahead. Freeze at the end of step 1 for up to 3 months.

TOPPINGS FOR BLINIS AND CROSTINI

Four delicious toppings for blinis or crostini. Each is enough to top 30. Prepare the blinis according to the method on page 48 and the crostini according to the method on page 47.

MOZZARELLA, PESTO, AND CHERRY TOMATO

6 heaped tbsp pesto

5½oz (150g) mozzarella, broken into pieces

8 cherry tomatoes, quartered

Spoon a little pesto onto each blini or crostini, top with a piece of mozzarella and then a quartered tomato. You should have two quarters left over.

PROSCIUTTO, PEPPADEW PEPPER, AND CREAM CHEESE

8 tbsp cream cheese

10 slices prosciutto, each cut into three

6 Peppadew peppers, drained and each cut into five slices

Spread a little of the cream cheese onto each of the blinis or crostini, then arrange a swirl of prosciutto and a slice of pepper on top.

QUAIL EGG, HOLLANDAISE, AND ASPARAGUS

15 quail eggs

30 asparagus tips

salt and freshly ground black pepper

6oz (170ml) hollandaise sauce

Put the quail eggs into a pan, cover with cold water, and bring to a boil. Boil for 3 minutes, then plunge into cold water. When cool, peel and cut in half. Cook the asparagus tips in boiling salted water for 2–3 minutes or until tender. Drain and refresh in cold water. Spoon a blob of hollandaise onto each blini or crostini, sit half a quail egg and an asparagus tip on top, then sprinkle with freshly ground black pepper. Serve cold or reheat in an oven preheated to 325°F (160°C) for 10 minutes or until warmed through.

CRAB, CREAM CHEESE, AND CHILI DIPPING SAUCE

6oz (170g) can white crabmeat, drained

3 heaped tbsp cream cheese

3 tsp chili sauce

salt and freshly ground black pepper

Mix the ingredients together in a bowl, season with salt and pepper, then spoon onto the blinis or crostini.

CROSTINI, BLINIS, AND TARTLETS
Recipes on pages 49 and 53

HUMMUS AND FETA TARTLETS

The addition of Parmesan cheese and pesto makes the pastry for these tartlet cases out of this world!

MAKES 48

Special equipment *12-cup mini muffin pan; 2in (5cm) round pastry cutter*

For the tartlet cases

1½ cups (175g) all-purpose flour, plus a little extra to dust

¾ cup (75g) freshly grated Parmesan cheese

⅓ cup (75g) cold butter, cubed

2 tbsp pesto

2 tbsp cold water

For the filling

¾ cup (200g) hummus

4 small carrots, grated

juice of ½ lemon

salt and freshly ground black pepper

1⅓ cup (200g) feta cheese, crumbled

7oz (200g) mixed pitted olives, sliced in half

1. Preheat the oven to 350°F (180°C). Meanwhile, put the flour, cheese, and butter into a food processor and process until the mixture resembles fine bread crumbs. Add the pesto and water and process until the dough just comes together. Turn out on to a floured work surface and knead lightly into a ball. Roll out very thinly and then cut 48 rounds with a 2in (5cm) round cutter (don't worry if you don't get exactly 48). Use 12 of these to line the muffin pan.

2. Bake for 12–15 minutes or until golden brown. Turn out onto a wire rack to cool and bake the remaining tartlet cases in the same way.

3. When the tartlet cases are completely cooled, spoon a little hummus into the base of each one. Mix the carrots and lemon juice together in a bowl and season with salt and pepper. Pile a little carrot on top of the hummus, then arrange some feta and half an olive on top. Serve cold.

PREPARE AHEAD AND FREEZE

The tartlet cases can be made up to 10 days ahead and kept in the fridge. The tartlets can be filled up to 4 hours ahead. Freeze the empty tartlet cases for up to 2 months.

FILLINGS FOR TARTLETS

Four excellent fillings for tartlets. Each recipe makes enough to fill 48 cases. Prepare the tartlets according to the recipe on page 52, but leave out the pesto.

RARE BEEF, BEET, AND HORSERADISH

½ tbsp olive oil

8oz (225g) fillet steak

1 large cooked beet, coarsely grated

6 heaped tbsp creamed horseradish sauce

Heat the oil in a frying pan, add the steak, and fry for 3 minutes on each side or until cooked on the outside and rare on the inside. Leave to cool, then cut into 48 thin slices and arrange in the tartlet cases. Sprinkle with grated beets and a blob of horseradish sauce.

GOAT CHEESE AND MEDITERRANEAN VEGETABLES

2 medium zucchini, cut in half lengthwise and thinly sliced

2 red peppers, halved, seeded, and cut into tiny dice

olive oil, to roast

salt and freshly ground black pepper

3½oz (100g) firm goat cheese, cut into cubes

Preheat the oven to 400°F (200°C). Toss the zucchini and peppers with a little olive oil and season with salt and pepper. Roast in the oven for 15 minutes or until golden and tender. Spoon into the tartlet cases and top with the goat cheese. Serve cold or reheat in an oven preheated to 325°F (160°C) for 10 minutes or until warmed through.

DOLCELATTE, WATERCRESS, AND PEAR

2½ oz (70g) watercress

1lb (450g) dolcelatte (or gorgonzola) cheese, cut into 48 small cubes

1 ripe pear, peeled, cored, and cut into 48 small cubes

To serve cold, divide the watercress among the tartlets, then top with a cube of cheese and a cube of pear. To serve warm, top tartlets with the cheese and pear, then reheat in an oven preheated to 325°F (160°C) for 10 minutes or until the cheese has melted. Add the watercress before serving.

SHRIMP COCKTAIL WITH MANGO

12oz (350g) cooked shrimp

8 tbsp mayonnaise

1 tbsp tomato ketchup

2 tsp creamed horseradish sauce

1 tbsp lemon juice

salt and freshly ground black pepper

1 small mango, halved, stoned, and the flesh cut into 48 cubes

Mix the shrimp with the mayonnaise, ketchup, horseradish sauce, and lemon juice. Season with salt and pepper and spoon into the tartlet cases. Top each with a cube of mango.

CHESTNUT, CRANBERRY, AND BRIE CHRISTMAS PARCELS

MAKES 24

1 tbsp olive oil

2 onions, chopped

4½ oz (125g) chestnuts, finely chopped

salt and freshly ground black pepper

1 tbsp cranberry sauce

3 sheets phyllo pastry

½ cup (100g) butter, melted

3½oz (100g) firm brie, chopped into 24 small cubes

A festive, crisp, delicious canapé for any special party. With the taste of Christmas in each bite, we call them parcels or moneybags. Use frozen or vacuum-packed chestnuts.

1. Preheat the oven to 400°F (200°C).

2. To make the filling, heat the oil in a frying pan. Add the onions and saute over high heat for a few minutes. Cover, lower the heat, and cook for about 10 minutes until soft. Add the chestnuts, then increase the heat and saute for 2 minutes until toasted. Spoon into a bowl and leave to cool. Season with salt and pepper and add the cranberry sauce.

3. Cut the pastry into 9 x 4in (24 x 10cm) squares. Brush each square with melted butter. Put a small tablespoon of the filling into the center of the square. Place one cube of cheese on top. Pinch the ends to seal in the middle so it looks like a money bag. Repeat with the remaining squares.

4. Place the canapés on a cookie sheet lined with parchment paper. Bake for about 15 minutes until golden and crisp. Serve warm.

PREPARE AHEAD AND FREEZE

The parcels can be made and assembled up to 6 hours ahead. Freeze well uncooked for up to 1 month.

OUR BEST APPETIZERS

The appetizer is an opportunity to wow your guests.
If you are sitting down to eat, put the appetizer on the
table before guests come into the room. At a more
informal occasion, go around with the appetizer on
a platter—this is a very sociable way to entertain.

FENNEL AND SMOKED SALMON TARTLETS

These are perfect as an appetizer, but you could equally serve them as a light lunch. Serve warm with dressed salad leaves. If you don't have time to make pastry, use store bought— 8oz (225g) piecrust for eight tartlets and 12oz (350g) for 12 tartlets.

MAKES 8

Special equipment
2 x 4-cup Yorkshire pudding pans or 4in (8 x 10cm) tart pans

For the pastry

1½ cups (175g) all-purpose flour, plus a little extra to dust

⅓ cup (85g) butter

1 egg

1 tbsp water

a pat of butter

1 large fennel bulb, coarsely chopped

1 small red chile, seeded and chopped

5½oz (150g) smoked salmon, chopped

large handful of freshly chopped parsley

¾ cup (200ml) heavy cream

2 eggs

salt and freshly ground black pepper

½ cup (50g) sharp Cheddar cheese, grated

MAKES 12

Special equipment
3 x 4-cup Yorkshire pudding pans or 4in (12 x 10cm) tart pans

For the pastry

2¾ cups (350g) all-purpose flour, plus a little extra to dust

¾ cup (175g) butter

1 egg

1–2 tbsp water

a pat of butter

2 medium fennel bulbs, coarsely chopped

1 large red chile, seeded and chopped

7oz (200g) smoked salmon, chopped

large handful of freshly chopped parsley

1¼ cup (300ml) heavy cream

3 eggs

salt and freshly ground black pepper

⅔ cup (75g) sharp Cheddar cheese, grated

1. To make the pastry, put the flour and butter into a food processor and process until the mixture resembles bread crumbs. Add the egg and water and process until it forms a ball. Roll the pastry out thinly on a lightly floured work surface, then cut circles with a 5in (12cm) cutter or the bottom of a saucer. Place in the pans and chill for 20 minutes.

2. Heat the pat of butter in a frying pan, add the fennel and chile, and saute for 1 minute. Cover with a lid and cook over low heat for 15 minutes or until soft. Set aside to cool.

3. Preheat the oven to 400°F (200°C) and put a cookie sheet in to get hot (two sheets for 12). Meanwhile, divide the cooled fennel mixture among the pastry cases, then sprinkle over the smoked salmon and parsley. Whisk the cream and eggs together in a measuring jug, season with salt and pepper, and stir in half the cheese. Pour into the cases, then sprinkle over the remaining cheese.

4. Bake for 20 minutes (25 minutes for 12) or until golden brown and the pastry is crisp.

PREPARE AHEAD AND FREEZE
You can make the tartlets up to 2 days ahead. Freeze for up to 2 months.

DOUBLE SALMON AND EGG TERRINE

This is ideal for any occasion—buffet, picnic, even a fancy dinner party. Serve it with toast or on individual plates with dressed arugula leaves.

SERVES 6

Special equipment *1lb (450g) loaf pan lined with plastic wrap*

3½oz (100g) fresh salmon fillet, skinned

a pat of butter, plus scant 2 tbsp (25g), at room temperature

salt and freshly ground black pepper

3½oz (100g) smoked salmon trimmings

3½oz (100g) full-fat cream cheese

3 tbsp light mayonnaise

1 tbsp freshly chopped chives

2 tbsp lemon juice

4 large hard-boiled eggs, chopped fairly finely

cress, to garnish

SERVES 12

Special equipment *2lb (900g) loaf pan lined with plastic wrap*

8oz (225g) fresh salmon fillet, skinned

a large pat of butter, plus ¼ cup (50g), at room temperature

salt and freshly ground black pepper

6oz (170g) smoked salmon trimmings

7oz (200g) full-fat cream cheese

6 tbsp light mayonnaise

2 tbsp freshly chopped chives

juice of ½ lemon

8 large hard-boiled eggs, chopped fairly finely

cress, to garnish

1. Preheat the oven to 350°F (180°C). Place the salmon on some foil, spoon the pat of butter on top, and season with salt and pepper. Scrunch the sides of the foil together at the top to make a parcel, place on a cookie sheet, and bake for 12–15 minutes (15–20 minutes for 12) or until just cooked. Set aside to cool in the foil.

2. Pick out the nicest pieces of smoked salmon (around half) and put the rest into a food processor with the cream cheese, the remaining butter, mayonnaise, chives, and lemon juice. Break up the cold salmon in the foil and add to the processor with the juices. Season with salt and pepper, then process until smooth. Spoon into a mixing bowl.

3. Add the eggs and stir until combined. Scatter the remaining smoked salmon trimmings (chopped, if necessary) on top of the plastic wrap in the base of the loaf pan.

4. Spoon the mousse mixture on top and level the surface. Cover with plastic wrap and chill in the fridge for at least 6 hours to firm up.

5. To serve, pop the terrine in the freezer for about 30 minutes to make slicing easier, then turn it out of the pan and cut into slices. Scatter with cress and serve.

PREPARE AHEAD

The terrine can be made up to the end of step 4 up to 2 days ahead. Not suitable for freezing.

SHRIMP AND CRAYFISH COCKTAIL

SERVES 6

8 tbsp mayonnaise

juice of ½ lemon

2 tbsp tomato ketchup

2 tsp creamed horseradish sauce

3 tbsp capers, drained, rinsed, dried, and coarsely chopped

salt and freshly ground black pepper

11oz (300g) small cooked shelled North Atlantic shrimp

6oz (175g) cooked crayfish tails, drained

4 Baby Gem lettuces

2 tbsp freshly chopped parsley

SERVES 12

1 cup (240ml) mayonnaise

juice of 1 lemon

4 tbsp tomato ketchup

1 heaped tbsp creamed horseradish sauce

6 tbsp capers, drained, rinsed, dried, and coarsely chopped

salt and freshly ground black pepper

1lb 5oz (600g) small cooked shelled North Atlantic shrimp

12oz (250g) cooked crayfish tails, drained

8 Baby Gem lettuces

4 tbsp freshly chopped parsley

You can prepare this attractive appetizer ahead and have it ready and waiting in the fridge. Serve with lightly buttered brown bread.

1. Mix the first five ingredients together in a bowl and season with salt and pepper.

2. Dry the shrimp and crayfish tails on paper towel and stir into the sauce.

3. Peel the lettuce leaves from the heart and arrange 18 leaves (36 for 12) on a platter or on individual plates, allowing three leaves per person. Spoon the shrimp mixture into the leaves and sprinkle with a little of the parsley.

PREPARE AHEAD

The sauce can be made up to 4 days ahead. The dish can be assembled up to 6 hours ahead. Not suitable for freezing.

QUICK SALMON AND
SHRIMP DILL SALAD

An appetizer with wow factor, yet it is surprisingly easy to make. These are perfect for a crowd because they are individual servings, so you'll always know you have the right number. For very special occasions, arrange a fresh king prawn in the shell on the top of each portion. Serve cold with warm brown rolls or some good brown bread.

SERVES 6

7oz (200g) shelled cooked North Atlantic shrimp

7oz (200g) sliced smoked salmon

small bunch of fresh dill

6oz (170ml) full-fat sour cream

finely grated zest of 1 lemon

juice of ½ lemon

pinch of ground cayenne pepper

freshly ground black pepper

lamb's lettuce, a little vinaigrette, and 6 lemon wedges, to serve

SERVES 12

14oz (400g) shelled cooked North Atlantic shrimp

14oz (400g) sliced smoked salmon

large bunch of fresh dill

12oz (170ml) full-fat sour cream

finely grated zest of 2 lemons

juice of 1 lemon

big pinch of ground cayenne pepper

freshly ground black pepper

lamb's lettuce, a little vinaigrette, and 12 lemon wedges, to serve

1. Lay the shrimp on paper towel and squeeze out any excess liquid.

2. Cut one long strip, about ½ x 2in (1 x 5cm), per serving from the salmon slices and put to one side. Cut the remaining smoked salmon into small pieces about ½in (1cm) in size.

3. Set aside a sprig of dill per serving, then finely chop the rest of the bunch and tip into a mixing bowl. Add the sour cream, lemon zest, lemon juice, cayenne pepper, and some pepper and stir to combine.

4. Add the shrimp and chopped salmon pieces.

5. Arrange the lamb's lettuce on individual plates, drizzle with vinaigrette, then pile the shrimp mixture in the center.

6. Arrange the reserved salmon strips on top of the shrimp. Garnish with a sprig of dill and a wedge of lemon.

PREPARE AHEAD

The shrimp and salmon mixture can be made up to the end of step 4 up to 8 hours ahead—the flavors will actually improve. The plates can be arranged up to 3 hours ahead. Not suitable for freezing.

CRAB, AVOCADO, AND SMOKED SALMON TIANS

A delicious and impressive appetizer, which looks stunning at a dinner party, wedding, or other celebration. If you don't have metal cooking rings to shape the tians, don't worry—you can use ramekins lined with plastic wrap. Serve with dressed salad leaves, lemon wedges, and buttered brown bread.

SERVES 6

Special equipment *6 x 2¾in (7cm) metal cooking rings arranged on a cookie sheet lined with plastic wrap*

11oz (300g) fresh crabmeat

3½oz (100g) full-fat cream cheese

bunch of dill, finely chopped

juice of 1 lemon

dash of Tabasco

½ tsp Dijon mustard

salt and freshly ground black pepper

3 small ripe avocados, halved, stoned, and peeled

6 handfuls of salad leaves such as watercress, arugula, or lamb's lettuce, to garnish

6 slices smoked salmon

SERVES 12

Special equipment *12 x 2¾in (7cm) metal cooking rings arranged on a cookie sheet lined with plastic wrap*

1lb 5oz (600g) fresh crabmeat

7oz (200g) full-fat cream cheese

large bunch of dill, finely chopped

juice of 2 lemons

generous dash of Tabasco

1 tsp Dijon mustard

salt and freshly ground black pepper

6 small ripe avocados, halved, stoned, and peeled

12 handfuls of salad leaves such as watercress, arugula, or lamb's lettuce, to garnish

12 slices smoked salmon

1. Mix the crabmeat, cream cheese, dill, half the lemon juice, the Tabasco, and mustard in a bowl and season with salt and pepper.

2. Mash one avocado with a fork until smooth (two avocados for 12) and cut the remaining avocados into small pieces. Mix the mashed and chopped avocados together, stir in the remaining lemon juice, and season with salt and pepper.

3. Spoon the avocado mixture into the base of each cooking ring and press down with the back of a spoon.

4. Divide the crab mixture among the rings and spread to the edges to cover the avocado entirely. Cover with plastic wrap and chill in the fridge for a few hours.

5. When ready to serve, arrange a handful of salad leaves on each plate, place a ring on top, then carefully remove the plastic wrap and ring. Top each tian with a swirl of smoked salmon.

PREPARE AHEAD

The tians can be made up to 6 hours ahead.
Not suitable for freezing.

SMOKED MACKEREL
AND WATERCRESS PÂTÉ

A quick-to-prepare appetizer served with smoked trout. You'll find it in the refrigerated section at the supermarket. Serve with warm rolls or toast.

SERVES 6

Special equipment
7½in (19cm) square cake pan, lined with plastic wrap

½ cup (100g) butter, at room temperature

6oz (175g) full-fat cream cheese

1 tbsp creamed horseradish

juice of ½ lemon

11oz (300g) smoked mackerel, skin removed

a few drops of Tabasco

1oz (25g) fresh watercress, plus a little extra to garnish

freshly ground black pepper

6 small slices smoked trout

6 lemon wedges, to garnish

SERVES 12

Special equipment
9 x 12in (23 x 30cm) baking pan or roasting pan, lined with plastic wrap

1 cup (225g) butter, at room temperature

12oz (350g) full-fat cream cheese

2 tbsp creamed horseradish

juice of 1 lemon

1lb 5oz (600g) smoked mackerel, skin removed

a few drops of Tabasco

1¾oz (50g) fresh watercress, plus a little extra to garnish

freshly ground black pepper

12 small slices smoked trout

12 lemon wedges, to garnish

1. Put the butter, cream cheese, horseradish, and lemon juice into a food processor and process until completely smooth.

2. Remove any tiny bones from the mackerel, then break the flesh into pieces and add to the processor. Add the Tabasco and watercress, season with pepper, and process again until just blended.

3. Spoon into the tin and level the top. Cover with plastic wrap and chill overnight.

4. To serve, pop the pâté in the freezer for about 30 minutes to make slicing easier, then turn it out and cut into squares, triangles, slices, or rounds. Arrange a piece on each plate, top with a slice of smoked trout in a swirl, then garnish with watercress and a lemon wedge, and serve with toast or brown bread.

PREPARE AHEAD

The pâté can be made up to the end of step 3 up to 2 days ahead. Not suitable for freezing.

RUSTIC MUSHROOM LIVER PÂTÉ

SERVES 6

Special equipment 1lb (450g) loaf pan, lined with plastic wrap

½oz (15g) dried porcini mushrooms

2 tbsp olive oil

1 onion, coarsely chopped

1¾oz (50g) smoked bacon, snipped into small pieces and rind removed

1 garlic clove, crushed

¾ cup (50g) button mushrooms, thinly sliced

1 tsp each freshly chopped parsley and thyme leaves

7oz (200g) fresh chicken livers

½ cup (25g) fresh white bread crumbs

¼ cup (50g) butter, at room temperature

3½oz (100g) full-fat cream cheese

2 tsp Worcestershire sauce

salt and freshly ground black pepper

a little freshly chopped parsley, to garnish

SERVES 12

Special equipment 2lb (900g) loaf pan, lined with plastic wrap

scant 1oz (25g) dried porcini mushrooms

4 tbsp olive oil

1 large onion, coarsely chopped

3½oz (100g) smoked bacon, snipped into small pieces and rind removed

2 garlic cloves, crushed

1½ cups (100g) button mushrooms, thinly sliced

2 tsp each freshly chopped parsley and thyme leaves

14oz (400g) fresh chicken livers

1 cup (50g) fresh white bread crumbs

½ cup (100g) butter, at room temperature

7oz (200g) full-fat cream cheese

1 tbsp Worcestershire sauce

salt and freshly ground black pepper

a little freshly chopped parsley, to garnish

This is so easy to make in a food processor. What's more, it requires no oven-baking. Serve with toast and slices of gherkin, if liked.

1. Put the porcini into a bowl and pour over just enough boiling water to cover. Set aside to soften for about 30 minutes, then drain and dry well with paper towel.

2. Heat half the oil in a frying pan, add the onion, bacon, and porcini, and fry for 1 minute. Cover with a lid and cook over low heat for 10 minutes or until the bacon is cooked. Add the garlic, button mushrooms, parsley, and thyme and saute for 5 minutes or until the mushrooms are just cooked. Transfer to a mixing bowl.

3. Heat the remaining oil in the unwashed pan and fry the chicken livers for 1–2 minutes on each side or until brown on the outside and still pink in the center. Add to the bowl with the porcini mixture and leave to cool.

4. Spoon half the cold chicken liver mixture into a food processor, add the bread crumbs, butter, cream cheese, and Worcestershire sauce, and process until smooth. Season with salt and pepper and process again until smooth and combined. Transfer into a bowl.

5. Chop the remaining cold chicken liver mixture coarsely, then add to the bowl with the smooth pâté and stir to combine. Spoon into the prepared pan and level the top. Cover with plastic wrap and chill for a minimum of 6 hours or overnight.

6. To serve, turn the pan upside down onto a serving plate and remove the plastic wrap. Press some chopped parsley on top, cut the pâté in fairly thick slices, and serve.

PREPARE AHEAD

The pâté can be made up to 3 days ahead.
Not suitable for freezing.

CELEBRATORY FISH PLATTER

Mary made this as part of a New Year's Eve pot luck supper party. The tray was quick to prepare and easy to bundle into the car with a plate of brown bread and butter.

SERVES 6

For the gravlax

1lb 2oz (500g) piece salmon fillet, from the thick end, skin on

2 tbsp dried dill

2 tbsp coarse sea salt

2 tbsp superfine sugar

salt and freshly ground black pepper

6 tbsp mayonnaise

1 tsp Dijon mustard

2 tsp freshly chopped dill

For the shrimp cocktail

11oz (300g) small cooked shelled North Atlantic shrimp

6 tbsp light mayonnaise

juice of ½ lemon

2 tbsp tomato ketchup

2 tbsp creamed horseradish sauce

To serve

2½oz (75g) lamb's lettuce or arugula

6 large Little Gem lettuce leaves

6 large cooked king prawns, shells removed but heads on

lemon wedges

SERVES 12

For the gravlax

2¼lb (1kg) piece salmon fillet, from the thick end, skin on

4 tbsp dried dill

4 tbsp coarse sea salt

4 tbsp superfine sugar

salt and freshly ground black pepper

12 tbsp mayonnaise

1 tbsp Dijon mustard

1 tbsp freshly chopped dill

For the shrimp cocktail

1lb 5oz (600g) small cooked shelled North Atlantic shrimp

12 tbsp light mayonnaise

juice of 1 small lemon

4 tbsp tomato ketchup

4 tbsp creamed horseradish sauce

To serve

6oz (175g) lamb's lettuce or arugula

12 large Little Gem lettuce leaves

12 large cooked king prawns, shells removed but heads on

lemon wedges

1. To make the gravlax, place the salmon skin side down on a large piece of foil, then pull out any bones with tweezers or a small knife. Sprinkle over the dried dill, salt, sugar, and some pepper, making sure all the salmon is covered. Wrap in the foil and place on a cookie sheet or cookie sheet. Place another cookie sheet on top and put some heavy weights or canned food on it to weigh the fish down. Transfer to the fridge for 12 hours or overnight.

2. Take the salmon from the fridge and pour away any juices. Place in the freezer for 30 minutes to make slicing easier. Then, using a sharp knife, cut into thin slices. Keep the knife angled at about 45 degrees so the slices are wide. Discard the skin.

3. To make the shrimp cocktail, dry the shrimp thoroughly with paper towel. Mix the mayonnaise, lemon juice, ketchup, and horseradish in a bowl, add the shrimp, and season with salt and pepper.

4. To serve, scatter the lamb's lettuce or arugula over the base of a platter. Spoon the shrimp cocktail into the Little Gem lettuce leaves, then arrange on one area of the platter. Arrange the gravlax and the king prawns alongside, then add the lemon wedges. Mix the mayonnaise for the gravlax with the mustard and fresh dill, season with salt and pepper, and serve in a bowl.

PREPARE AHEAD AND FREEZE

The gravlax can be made up to 2 days ahead. Freeze for up to 1 month. The cocktail sauce can be made up to 12 hours ahead. Not suitable for freezing. The platter can be assembled up to 4 hours ahead.

FILLET OF BEEF WITH BEETS AND HORSERADISH DRESSING

SERVES 6

11oz (300g) middle-cut fillet steak, trimmed

1 tbsp olive oil, plus a little extra to serve

salt and freshly ground black pepper

4 medium-sized cooked beets, thinly sliced

2½ cups (50g) arugula

1¾oz (50g) piece Parmesan cheese

For the horseradish dressing

2 tbsp creamed horseradish sauce

3 tbsp light mayonnaise

2 tbsp lemon juice

SERVES 12

2 x 11oz (300g) middle-cut fillet steaks, trimmed

2 tbsp olive oil, plus a little extra to serve

salt and freshly ground black pepper

8 medium-sized cooked beets, thinly sliced

5 cups (100g) arugula

3½oz (100g) piece Parmesan cheese

For the horseradish dressing

4 tbsp creamed horseradish sauce

6 tbsp light mayonnaise

4 tbsp lemon juice

When you're serving numbers at a fancy dinner party, it's always a good feeling to know the first course is made and waiting in the fridge. This recipe is perfect for that. When you carve the fillet, you want the slices to be long and thin rather than round—middle-cut fillets give you the correct shape. Serve with brown bread rolls.

1. Rub the steak with the oil and season with salt and pepper.

2. Heat a frying pan until very hot, then fry the fillet for 2½ minutes on each side (fry each fillet separately for 12). This will give you a rare steak. If you prefer medium, cook for another minute on each side. Remove from the pan and leave to cool.

3. To make the dressing, put the ingredients into a small bowl and whisk with a hand whisk until smooth and combined. Season with salt and pepper.

4. When the steak is cold, carve it into very thin slices—you're aiming to get 30 slices per fillet. Arrange five thin slices in a star shape on each plate. Arrange five slices of beet in the middle of the plate in a spiral shape, then drizzle with the horseradish dressing.

5. Gather together a little bundle of arugula for each plate and place on top of the beets. Using a potato peeler, shave little shavings of Parmesan over the top.

6. Drizzle with a little olive oil and serve immediately.

PREPARE AHEAD

The plates can be prepared up to the end of step 5 up to 6 hours ahead. Drizzle with oil just before serving. Not suitable for freezing.

ROASTED FIGS WITH PROSCIUTTO AND GOAT CHEESE

SERVES 6

7oz (200g) firm goat cheese, such as Capricorn

6 fresh figs

12 slices prosciutto

arugula or salad leaves, to serve

balsamic vinegar, to serve

olive oil, to serve

SERVES 12

14oz (400g) firm goat cheese, such as Capricorn

12 fresh figs

24 slices prosciutto

arugula or salad leaves, to serve

balsamic vinegar, to serve

olive oil, to serve

Mary was given this recipe by a friend in Portugal who makes full use of fruits in season. We use vacuum-packed dry-cured ham, as it comes in convenient even-sized slices. Swap the figs for tomatoes, if you like—see below left.

1. Pop the goat cheese in the freezer for about an hour or until firm.

2. Preheat the oven to 425°F (220°C). Cut off the pointed stem at the top of each fig, then stand the figs upright on a board. Cut a cross in the top of each one, but don't cut right down to the base.

3. Trim the ends off the cheese and discard, then cut into slices of just over 1oz. Cut each slice in half to give semi-circles. Cut half the semi-circles in half again to give quarters.

4. Lie each slice of ham out flat and trim off any excess fat.

5. Put a semi-circle of cheese into each fig where you've made the cross. Use the quarters to fit in either side, so the complete cross is filled with goat cheese.

6. Wrap each fig in a piece of ham, then wrap it in another piece, working in the other direction. Squeeze the ham together at the top.

7. Roast for 8 minutes (10 minutes for 12) or until the cheese has melted and the ham is crisp.

8. Arrange the figs on serving plates with some arugula or salad leaves, drizzle with a little balsamic vinegar and olive oil, and serve at once.

ROASTED TOMATOES WITH PESTO

When figs are not in season, we use skinned, medium-sized, slightly under-ripe tomatoes prepared in the same way. Spoon a teaspoon of pesto over the cheese and tomato before wrapping it in the prosciutto.

PREPARE AHEAD

You can prepare the figs up to the end of step 6 up to 12 hours ahead. Not suitable for freezing.

ASPARAGUS WITH PARMESAN AND MUSTARD SAUCE

This is such an easy appetizer for when asparagus is plentiful and at its best in the months of May and June. We like to cook the asparagus on a cookie sheet and serve them in individual portions, but you can bake them in a large ovenproof dish and take it to the table if you prefer.

SERVES 6

1lb 10oz (750g) asparagus spears, woody ends removed

salt and freshly ground black pepper

½ cup (50g) freshly grated Parmesan cheese

For the mustard sauce

4 tsp Dijon mustard

2 tsp white wine vinegar

4 tbsp sunflower oil

2 tbsp mayonnaise

juice of ½ lemon

1 tsp superfine sugar

SERVES 12

3lb 3oz (1.5kg) asparagus spears, woody ends removed

salt and freshly ground black pepper

1 cup (100g) freshly grated Parmesan cheese

For the mustard sauce

2 heaped tbsp Dijon mustard

1½ tbsp white wine vinegar

8 tbsp sunflower oil

4 tbsp mayonnaise

juice of 1 lemon

2 tsp superfine sugar

1. Preheat the oven to 425°F (220°C). Meanwhile, put the asparagus spears into a shallow pan of boiling salted water and bring back up to a boil. Boil for 3 minutes, then drain, refresh in cold water, and dry on paper towel.

2. Arrange six bundles of asparagus on a large cookie sheet lined with parchment paper (12 bundles on two cookie sheets for 12), season with salt and pepper, and sprinkle with the cheese.

3. Bake for 8 minutes (12 minutes for 12) or until the cheese has melted and browned and the asparagus is piping hot.

4. Meanwhile, make the sauce: put all the ingredients into a bowl and whisk with a hand whisk until well combined, then season with salt and pepper.

5. Carefully transfer the bundles onto hot plates and serve with the mustard sauce.

PREPARE AHEAD

The asparagus can be prepared up to the end of step 2 up to 1 day ahead. The sauce can be made up to 4 days ahead. Not suitable for freezing.

ROQUEFORT AND PARSLEY MOUSSELINE CREAMS

These make a delicious creamy appetizer. Serve them in ramekins with crusty bread alongside.

SERVES 6

Special equipment *6 x 5fl oz (150ml) ramekins, greased*

¼ cup (45g) butter

⅓ cup (45g) all-purpose flour

1¼ cup (300ml) hot milk

3 large eggs, separated

3½oz (100g) Roquefort, coarsely grated

1 tbsp freshly chopped parsley

salt and freshly ground black pepper

dash of Tabasco

SERVES 12

Special equipment *12 x 5fl oz (150ml) ramekins, greased*

⅓ cup (75g) butter

⅔ cup (75g) all-purpose flour

2½ cups (600ml) hot milk

6 large eggs, separated

8oz (225g) Roquefort, coarsely grated

2 tbsp freshly chopped parsley

salt and freshly ground black pepper

dash of Tabasco

1. Preheat the oven to 375°F (190°C). Meanwhile, melt the butter in a large saucepan, add the flour and then the milk, and whisk until the mixture thickens to a smooth white sauce. Remove from the heat and allow to cool slightly.

2. Meanwhile, whisk the egg whites in a bowl with an electric hand whisk until stiff.

3. Stir the cheese and parsley into the warm sauce and season with salt and pepper (not too much salt, as the cheese is salty). Add the egg yolks and Tabasco and stir to combine.

4. Mix a spoonful of the egg whites into the sauce until smooth, then fold in the rest so the mixture is light and combined. Spoon evenly into the ramekins and sit on a cookie sheet.

5. Bake for 15–20 minutes (20–25 minutes for 12) or until risen and golden.

6. Serve hot in the ramekins with a dressed salad alongside.

PREPARE AHEAD

The creams can be made up to the end of step 4 up to 6 hours ahead. Not suitable for freezing.

SWEET POTATO SOUP
WITH CUMIN AND GINGER

SERVES 6

1 tbsp olive oil

2lb (900g) sweet potatoes, peeled and cut into ½in (1cm) cubes

1lb (450g) carrots, cut into ½in (1cm) cubes

¾in (2cm) piece fresh ginger, peeled and finely grated

1 tsp ground cumin

5 cups (1.4 liters) vegetable stock

salt and freshly ground black pepper

heavy cream, to garnish

chopped chives, to garnish

SERVES 12

2 tbsp olive oil

4lb (1.8kg) sweet potatoes, peeled and cut into ½in (1cm) cubes

2lb (900g) carrots, cut into ½in (1cm) cubes

2in (5cm) piece fresh ginger, peeled and finely grated

2 tsp ground cumin

10½ cups (3 liters) vegetable stock

salt and freshly ground black pepper

heavy cream, to garnish

chopped chives, to garnish

Vibrant in color and quick to make, this soup is ideal for any winter party. Serve with croutons or crispy bread, if liked.

1. Heat the oil in a deep saucepan, add the sweet potatoes, carrots, ginger, and cumin and saute over high heat, stirring, for 10 minutes or until starting to brown.

2. Add the stock, bring to a boil, then season with salt and pepper. Cover with a lid and simmer over low heat for 20–30 minutes (35–40 minutes for 12) or until the sweet potatoes and carrots are tender.

3. Carefully scoop out half the vegetables into a bowl using a slotted spoon. Process the remainder in a food processor or blender until smooth, then return to the pan.

4. Add the reserved vegetables, bring to a boil again, and check the seasoning.

5. To serve, garnish with a swirl of heavy cream and some chopped chives.

PREPARE AHEAD AND FREEZE

The soup can be made up to 3 days ahead. Freeze for up to 3 months.

HONEY-GLAZED PARSNIP SOUP

SERVES 6

1 tbsp olive oil

2lb (900g) parsnips, coarsely chopped

2 large onions, coarsely chopped

4 celery sticks, sliced

1 leek, coarsely chopped

1½ tbsp honey

5 cups (1.4 liters) vegetable stock

salt and freshly ground black pepper

⅓ cup (150ml) heavy cream

SERVES 12

2 tbsp olive oil

3lb 3oz (1.5kg) parsnips, coarsely chopped

4 large onions, coarsely chopped

8 celery sticks, sliced

2 leeks, coarsely chopped

3 tbsp honey

10 cups (2.8 liters) vegetable stock

salt and freshly ground black pepper

1¼ cup (300ml) heavy cream

Our lovely friend Jane gave us the idea for this recipe. It's creamy and luxurious—ideal before a light meal. Garnish with croutons and cracked black pepper, and a drizzle of cream if you like.

1. Heat the oil in a deep saucepan, add the vegetables, and saute over high heat for a few minutes. Stir in the honey and saute for 4–5 minutes or until the vegetables are becoming golden brown and caramelized.

2. Add the stock and season with salt and pepper. Cover with a lid, lower the heat, and simmer for 20–30 minutes (35–40 minutes for 12) or until the parsnips are completely tender.

3. Transfer to a food processor or blender and process until completely smooth.

4. Return to the pan to reheat, stir in the cream, and check the seasoning. Serve piping hot.

PREPARE AHEAD AND FREEZE

The soup can be made up to the end of step 3 up to 2 days ahead. Freeze at the end of step 3 for up to 1 month.

FRENCH ONION SOUP WITH MUSTARD GRUYÈRE CROUTONS

SERVES 6

scant 2 tbsp (25g) butter

4 large onions (about 1½lb/675g), thinly sliced

2 tsp light brown sugar

6 cups (1.7 liters) chicken stock

1 tbsp cornstarch

salt and freshly ground black pepper

1½ tbsp balsamic vinegar

For the croutons

1 small thin soft bread stick

scant 2 tbsp (25g) butter, at room temperature

2 tbsp Dijon mustard

1¾oz (50g) Gruyère, finely grated

SERVES 12

¼ cup (50g) butter

8 large onions (about 3lb/1.35kg), thinly sliced

2 tbsp light brown sugar

12½ cups (3.6 liters) chicken stock

2 tbsp cornstarch

salt and freshly ground black pepper

4 tbsp balsamic vinegar

For the croutons

1 large thin soft bread stick

¼ cup (50g) butter, at room temperature

4 tbsp Dijon mustard

3½oz (100g) Gruyère, finely grated

The onions are caramelized in sugar in this traditional recipe. We toast the croutons to make a perfect winter appetizer or lunch dish.

1. Melt the butter in a deep saucepan, add the onions, and saute for 5 minutes, stirring. Lower the heat, cover with a lid, and cook for 20 minutes or until completely soft.

2. Remove the lid, stir in the brown sugar, and continue to saute the onions over high heat for 10 minutes or until lightly browned. Add the stock, bring to a boil, cover with a lid again, and simmer for 5–10 minutes.

3. Mix the cornstarch in a cup with a little cold water to make a thin paste, then stir into the soup. Season with salt and pepper, add the balsamic vinegar, and stir well. Bring to a boil, stirring continuously, until slightly thickened.

4. To make the croutons, preheat the broiler. Slice the bread into 18 thin slices (36 for 12), butter both sides, then toast on one side until golden. Turn the croutons over, spread a little mustard on the untoasted side and top with the cheese. Slide back under the broiler for 3–5 minutes or until the cheese is golden and melted.

5. Serve the soup in hot bowls with three croutons per person.

PREPARE AHEAD AND FREEZE

The soup can be made up to 3 days ahead. The croutons can be assembled up to 6 hours ahead and popped under the grill before serving. Freeze the soup without the croutons for up to 3 months.

PUY LENTIL AND PEARL BARLEY SOUP

SERVES 6

1 tbsp olive oil

1 large onion, finely chopped

2 carrots, finely diced

2 garlic cloves, crushed

½ cup (100g) dried Puy lentils

½ cup (100g) pearl barley

2¾ cups (680g) tomato puree

5½ cups (1.5 liters) chicken stock or vegetable stock

salt and freshly ground black pepper

2 tsp sugar

1 tbsp balsamic vinegar

SERVES 12

2 tbsp olive oil

2 onions, finely chopped

2 large carrots, finely diced

4 garlic cloves, crushed

1⅛ cup (225g) dried Puy lentils

1⅛ cup (225g) pearl barley

5½ cups (1.36kg) tomato puree

11 cups (3 liters) chicken stock or vegetable stock

salt and freshly ground black pepper

1 tbsp sugar

2 tbsp balsamic vinegar

This is a hearty, healthy soup full of flavor and goodness. Serve it piping hot with some crusty bread.

1. Heat the oil in a deep frying pan, add the onions and carrots, and saute over high heat, stirring, for 10 minutes or until lightly brown.

2. Add the garlic, lentils, and barley and saute for 1 minute. Blend in the tomato puree and stock and season with salt and pepper.

3. Bring to a boil, cover with a lid, and simmer for 40–45 minutes (50–55 minutes for 12) or until the lentils and barley are tender.

4. Add the sugar and balsamic vinegar, check the seasoning, and serve.

PREPARE AHEAD

The soup can be made up to 3 days ahead. Not suitable for freezing.

EXPRESS MEDITERRANEAN PLATTER

SERVES 6

8 Peppadew peppers, drained and sliced

1 tbsp freshly chopped parsley

7oz (200g) hummus

salt and freshly ground black pepper

6 stuffed grape leaves

7oz (200g) feta cheese, cut into bite-sized cubes

7oz (200g) marinated chargrilled artichokes in oil, drained and oil reserved

7oz (200g) Kalamata olives in oil, drained and oil reserved

6 pita breads

SERVES 12

16 Peppadew peppers, drained and sliced

2 tbsp freshly chopped parsley

14oz (400g) hummus

salt and freshly ground black pepper

12 stuffed grape leaves

14oz (400g) feta cheese, cut into bite-sized cubes

14oz (400g) marinated chargrilled artichokes in oil, drained and oil reserved

14oz (400g) Kalamata olives in oil, drained and oil reserved

12 pita breads

A very sociable appetizer that's also a bit of a cheat. For a variation on this platter, try the quick, flavorful tapenade recipe given below. If you are serving 12, arrange the food on two platters or a large wooden board.

1. Take a large flat platter or round tart plate and put a small bowl in the center. Mix the Peppadew pepper slices and parsley with the hummus, season with salt and pepper, and spoon into the bowl.

2. Arrange the grape leaves, feta, artichokes, and olives in piles around the platter.

3. Toast the pita and slice into fingers, then arrange in a pile alongside the artichokes.

4. Drizzle the feta with some of the oil from the olives or artichokes and serve chilled or at room temperature.

TAPENADE AND TOMATO PLATTER

Swap the olives for baby tomatoes on the vine, if you like. To make a green olive, basil, and tomato tapenade, mix a sliced clove of garlic, 2 tbsp sun-dried tomato paste, 3 tbsp drained capers, 2½oz (70g) pitted green olives, 2 tbsp olive oil, and a small bunch of basil, chopped, in a processor. Season with freshly ground black pepper and spoon into a bowl. Serve as a dip or to go with bread and cheeses.

PREPARE AHEAD

The hummus can be mixed with the parsley and peppers up to 4 days ahead. The platter can be assembled up to 8 hours ahead.

ANTIPASTI

You can use any variety of sliced meats you like for this appetizing selection of roasted vegetables with an eggplant and mint dip. Serve with chunky bread, flat bread, or toasted pita bread.

SERVES 6

For the eggplant and mint dip

2 large eggplants

2 tbsp olive oil

3 fat garlic cloves (unpeeled)

3½oz (100ml) full-fat Greek yogurt

juice of ½ lemon

3 tbsp freshly chopped mint, plus a sprig to garnish

salt and freshly ground black pepper

For the roasted vegetables

4 zucchini, thickly sliced

1 yellow pepper, halved, seeded, and sliced into large chunks

1 red pepper, halved, seeded, and sliced into large chunks

2 tbsp olive oil

2 tbsp balsamic vinegar

Sliced meats

6 slices prosciutto

6 slices salami

6 slices chorizo

SERVES 12

For the eggplant and mint dip

4 large eggplants

4 tbsp olive oil

6 fat garlic cloves (unpeeled)

7oz (200ml) full-fat Greek yogurt

juice of 1 lemon

6 tbsp freshly chopped mint, plus 2 sprigs to garnish

salt and freshly ground black pepper

For the roasted vegetables

8 zucchini, thickly sliced

2 yellow peppers, halved, seeded, and sliced into large chunks

2 red peppers, halved, seeded, and sliced into large chunks

4 tbsp olive oil

4 tbsp balsamic vinegar

Sliced meats

12 slices prosciutto

12 slices salami

12 slices chorizo

1. Preheat the oven to 425°F (220°C).

2. To make the eggplant and mint dip, slice the eggplants in half lengthwise, arrange cut side up in a roasting pan, and drizzle with the oil. Add the garlic to the pan and roast for 30–35 minutes or until the eggplant flesh is soft.

3. Scoop the flesh out of the eggplants and place in a food processor. Discard the skins. Squeeze the garlic from their skins and add to the eggplants, then process until smooth. Add the yogurt, lemon juice, and mint, season with salt and pepper, and process again until combined. Spoon into a serving bowl (two bowls for 12) and set aside to cool.

4. Meanwhile, make the roasted vegetables. Arrange the zucchini, yellow pepper, and red pepper in a roasting pan, drizzle over the oil, and roast in the preheated oven for 30–40 minutes or until just cooked. Drizzle over the balsamic vinegar, season with salt and pepper, and set aside to cool.

5. To assemble the dish, arrange the cold meats in piles on a platter (two platters for 12), garnish the dip with mint and place at one end, then arrange the roasted vegetables alongside the meats. Serve with bread of your choice.

PREPARE AHEAD

The dip can be made up to 3 days ahead. The vegetables can be roasted up to 1 day ahead. The platter can be assembled up to 8 hours ahead. Not suitable for freezing.

POULTRY AND GAME ENTRÉES

These recipes are low on effort, but high on impact—perfect for when you're cooking for a crowd. Chicken is always popular, and the duck and game dishes at the end of this chapter are even more special.

21ST-CENTURY CORONATION CHICKEN

SERVES 6

2 tbsp apricot jam

1 tbsp curry powder

1¼ cup (300ml) mayonnaise

5oz (150ml) half-fat crème fraîche

1 tbsp tomato paste

finely grated zest and juice of 1 lemon

1lb (450g) cooked chicken, cut into bite-size pieces

2 scallions, finely chopped

salt and freshly ground black pepper

6oz (175g) black and green seedless grapes, cut in half lengthwise

arugula, to garnish

SERVES 12

4 tbsp apricot jam

2 tbsp curry powder

2½ cups (600ml) mayonnaise

10oz (300ml) half-fat crème fraîche

2 tbsp tomato paste

finely grated zest and juice of 2 lemons

2lb (900g) cooked chicken, cut into bite-size pieces

4 scallions, finely chopped

salt and freshly ground black pepper

11oz (300g) black and green seedless grapes, cut in half lengthwise

arugula, to garnish

No buffet would be complete without coronation chicken. It's also delicious made with cooked turkey. Serve with baby new potatoes and dressed salad.

1. Put the jam and curry powder in a small saucepan and heat gently, stirring until the jam has melted. Set aside to cool a little.

2. Meanwhile, put the mayonnaise, crème fraîche, and tomato paste in a mixing bowl with the lemon zest and lemon juice and mix together until combined.

3. Stir in the jam mixture, then add the chicken and scallions. Season with salt and pepper, add half the grapes, and stir until combined.

4. Spoon onto a serving platter and garnish with the remaining grapes and the arugula.

PREPARE AHEAD

The dish can be made up to 1 day ahead.
The sauce can be made up to 3 days ahead.
Not suitable for freezing.

HERB CHICKEN WITH GARLIC SAUCE

SERVES 6

5oz (150g) full-fat cream cheese

2½oz (75g) sharp Cheddar cheese, grated

2 tsp chopped fresh basil

2 tsp chopped chives

1 small garlic clove, crushed

6 boneless skinless chicken breasts

salt and freshly ground black pepper

1 tbsp honey

a pinch of paprika

¾ cup (200ml) dry white wine

2 large garlic cloves, sliced in half

1¼ cup (300ml) heavy cream

2 tbsp sun-dried tomato paste

7oz (200g) haricot verts, trimmed and sliced into three

11oz (300g) frozen fava beans

11oz (300g) frozen petits pois

a pat of butter

2 tbsp freshly chopped basil

SERVES 12

10oz (300g) full-fat cream cheese

6oz (175g) sharp Cheddar cheese, grated

2 tbsp chopped fresh basil

2 tbsp chopped chives

2 garlic cloves, crushed

12 boneless skinless chicken breasts

salt and freshly ground black pepper

2 tbsp honey

a pinch of paprika

1⅔ cup (400ml) dry white wine

4 large garlic cloves, sliced in half

2½ cups (600ml) heavy cream

4 tbsp sun-dried tomato paste

14oz (400g) haricot verts, trimmed and sliced into three

1lb 5oz (600g) frozen fava beans

1lb 5oz (600g) frozen petits pois

a large pat of butter

4 tbsp freshly chopped basil

This is such a simple yet classy dish, easy to cook for a crowd on formal occasions. Serve with new potatoes.

1. Preheat the oven to 425°F (220°C). Mash the cream cheese, Cheddar, herbs, and crushed garlic together with a fork in a small bowl. Make three diagonal slashes in the top of each chicken breast, cutting about halfway through. Season with salt and pepper, then spoon the cheese into the gaps. Arrange in a flat ovenproof dish.

2. Drizzle with the honey and sprinkle with paprika. Roast in the oven for 20–25 minutes or until cooked, then remove from the oven and leave to rest for 5 minutes.

3. Meanwhile, put the wine and sliced garlic into a saucepan and boil until reduced by half. Add the cream and boil until reduced by one-third or until the sauce has thickened to a pouring consistency. Remove the garlic and season with salt and pepper, then stir in the sun-dried tomato paste.

4. Bring a pan of salted water to a boil. Add the haricot verts, fava beans, and petits pois and boil for 4 minutes or until just cooked. Drain and toss with the butter.

5. Reheat the sauce and add the basil. Spoon the vegetables onto plates. Slice a chicken breast into thick pieces and arrange on top of each one. Serve with a little of the sauce.

PREPARE AHEAD

The chicken breasts can be prepared up to the end of step 1 up to 1 day ahead. The sauce can be made up to 3 days ahead. Add the basil just before serving. Not suitable for freezing.

PAN-FRIED CHICKEN WITH MUSHROOMS AND TARRAGON

SERVES 6

1 tbsp olive oil

5 small boneless skinless chicken breasts, cut into thin strips

salt and freshly ground black pepper

1 large onion, finely chopped

2 medium zucchini, cut into thick matchsticks

12oz (350g) button mushrooms, quartered

2 large garlic cloves

¾ cup (200ml) dry white wine

¾ cup (200ml) heavy cream

juice of ½ lemon

1 heaped tbsp freshly chopped tarragon

SERVES 12

This dish is not suitable for more than six because the sauce would not reduce to a thick consistency and would be wet from the large quantity of vegetables.

This is one of Lucy's fail-safe recipes that can be rustled up quickly while everyone is enjoying a glass of wine. Serve with plain rice, or mashed potatoes.

1. Heat the oil in a deep frying pan, add half the chicken strips, season with salt and pepper, and brown over high heat until golden all over. Remove with a slotted spoon and set aside on a plate. Cook the rest of the chicken strips in the same way.

2. Add the onion and saute over high heat for a few minutes or until golden. Cover with a lid, lower the heat, and cook for 15 minutes or until tender. Turn up the heat, add the zucchini, mushrooms, and garlic, and saute for 3 minutes or until the vegetables start to soften. Remove from the pan and set aside with the chicken.

3. Add the wine to the pan and boil over high heat until it has reduced in volume to about 4 tablespoons. Stir in the cream and boil again for a few minutes until the sauce thickens. Stir in the lemon juice and season with salt and pepper. Return the chicken and vegetables to the pan for a couple of minutes to heat through.

4. Add the tarragon and serve immediately.

TRADITIONAL CHICKEN, LEEK, AND MUSHROOM PIE

This is an old-fashioned pie, perfect for a winter Sunday lunch. If you're cooking for 12, we think it is easier to make two pies rather than one really large one, but it's up to you.

SERVES 6

Special equipment *9in (2.4 liter) pie pan*

⅓ cup (75g) butter

3 large leeks, sliced

⅔ cup (75g) all-purpose flour, plus a little extra to dust

1¼ cup (300ml) apple juice

2 cups (450ml) chicken stock

9oz (250g) portobello mushrooms, sliced

1 tbsp Dijon mustard

1 tbsp freshly chopped thyme leaves

3 tbsp full-fat crème fraîche

1lb 10oz (750g) cooked chicken, sliced

salt and freshly ground black pepper

17oz (500g) package all-butter puff pastry

1 egg, beaten with a little milk

SERVES 12

Special equipment *2 x 9in (2.4 liter) pie pans or 1 x 12in (4 liter) pan*

¾ cup (175g) butter

6 leeks, sliced

1½ cup (175g) all-purpose flour, plus a little extra to dust

2½ cups (600ml) apple juice

4 cups (900ml) chicken stock

1lb (450g) portobello mushrooms, sliced

2 tbsp Dijon mustard

2 tbsp freshly chopped thyme leaves

6 tbsp full-fat crème fraîche

3lb 3oz (1.5kg) cooked chicken, sliced

salt and freshly ground black pepper

2 x 17oz (500g) package all-butter puff pastry

2 eggs, beaten with a little milk

1. Preheat the oven to 400°F (200°C). Meanwhile, melt the butter in a large frying pan, add the leeks, and saute over high heat for 2 minutes. Cover with a lid, lower the heat, and cook for 10 minutes or until tender.

2. Turn up the heat, stir in the flour, then blend in the apple juice and stock. Bring to a boil, stirring all the time, then add the mushrooms, mustard, thyme, and crème fraîche. Add the chicken, season with salt and pepper, and simmer for 5 minutes. Spoon into the pie pan and set aside to cool.

3. Meanwhile, make the pastry top. On a countertop lightly dusted with flour, roll out the pastry until it is a little bigger than the dish. Cut strips of pastry to the size of the lip of the pan, then wet the lip with water and attach the strips on top. Wet the top of the strips with water, then lay the pastry lid on them and press to seal the edges. Crimp the edges with your fingers.

4. Brush the pastry with the egg and bake in the oven for 35 minutes (1 hour for a large pie for 12—cover it with foil if it begins to get too brown) or until the pastry is crisp and golden and the filling is piping hot.

PREPARE AHEAD AND FREEZE

The pie can be made up to the end of step 3 up to 1 day ahead. Freeze at the end of step 3 for up to 2 months.

STICKY CHICKEN DRUMSTICKS

Drumsticks are always a favorite at a barbecue—with adults and children alike. Marinating aside, they are also quick to make. Serve hot or cold with salad and baked potatoes.

SERVES 6

6 tbsp ketchup

2 tbsp Worcestershire sauce

2 tbsp coarse mustard

2 tbsp honey

salt and freshly ground black pepper

6 chicken drumsticks (skin on)

SERVES 12

¾ cup (175ml) ketchup

4 tbsp Worcestershire sauce

4 tbsp coarse mustard

4 tbsp honey

salt and freshly ground black pepper

12 chicken drumsticks (skin on)

1. Put the ketchup, Worcestershire sauce, mustard, and honey into a bowl, mix together well, then season with salt and pepper.

2. Add the chicken and marinate for a minimum of 2 hours or overnight.

3. Preheat the oven to 425°F (220°C). Season the drumsticks with salt and pepper and cook for 30–40 minutes (45 minutes for 12) or until golden brown and sticky. Turn halfway through. Alternatively, cook on the grill.

PREPARE AHEAD AND FREEZE

The drumsticks can be marinated overnight. Freeze in the marinade for up to 2 months.

SPICY MARINATED CHICKEN WITH SUMMER SALSA

Fresh and healthy, this dish is great for garden parties. Marinate it overnight for maximum flavor. Serve with salad and new potatoes.

SERVES 6

2 red chiles, halved, seeded, and finely diced

4 garlic cloves, crushed

6 tbsp freshly chopped parsley

zest and juice of 1 large lemon

4 tbsp olive oil

2 tbsp honey

4 tsp paprika

6 boneless skinless chicken breasts

For the salsa

2 large tomatoes, cut in half, seeded, and diced

6 scallions, finely sliced

½ cucumber, peeled, halved, seeded, and diced

small bunch of cilantro, coarsely chopped

finely grated zest and juice of 1 lime

2 tsp balsamic vinegar

2 tbsp olive oil

1 tsp superfine sugar

salt and freshly ground black pepper

SERVES 12

4 red chiles, halved, seeded, and finely diced

8 garlic cloves, crushed

bunch of parsley, chopped

zest and juice of 2 lemons

8 tbsp olive oil

4 tbsp honey

2 heaped tbsp paprika

12 boneless skinless chicken breasts

For the salsa

4 large tomatoes, cut in half, seeded, and diced

12 scallions, finely sliced

1 cucumber, peeled, halved, seeded, and diced

large bunch of cilantro, coarsely chopped

finely grated zest and juice of 2 limes

1 tbsp balsamic vinegar

4 tbsp olive oil

2 tsp superfine sugar

salt and freshly ground black pepper

1. Mix the chiles, garlic, parsley, lemon zest and juice, olive oil, honey, and paprika together in a large bowl. Add the chicken breasts and turn to coat. Leave to marinate in the fridge for 1–2 hours or overnight.

2. Preheat the oven to 425°F (220°C). Heat a grill pan until hot, add the chicken, and brown for 20–30 seconds on each side or until grill marks are left. You may need to do this in batches. Arrange on a cookie sheet lined with parchment paper.

3. Roast for 25 minutes (35 minutes for 12) or until golden and cooked through. Remove from the oven and allow to rest for 5 minutes.

4. Meanwhile, make the salsa: mix all the ingredients in a large bowl and season with salt and pepper.

5. Carve the chicken into thick slices and serve with the salsa.

PREPARE AHEAD

The chicken can be prepared up to the end of step 2 up to 1 day ahead. The salsa ingredients can be prepared up to 1 day ahead and mixed together 1 hour ahead. Not suitable for freezing.

SUN-BLUSHED TOMATO AND HERB CHICKEN

SERVES 6

1 tbsp freshly chopped parsley

3 tbsp freshly snipped chives

1 tbsp freshly chopped basil

7oz (200g) full-fat cream cheese

1 egg yolk

2 tsp lemon juice

1¾oz (50g) sun-blushed or sun-ripened tomatoes, snipped into small pieces

salt and freshly ground black pepper

6 boneless chicken breasts, skin on

a little honey

For the sauce

⅔ cup (150ml) dry white wine

1¼ cup (300ml) heavy cream

1 tbsp freshly chopped parsley

SERVES 12

2 tbsp freshly chopped parsley

6 tbsp freshly snipped chives

2 tbsp freshly chopped basil

14oz (400g) full-fat cream cheese

2 egg yolks

1 tbsp lemon juice

3½oz (100g) sun-blushed or sun-ripened tomatoes, snipped into small pieces

salt and freshly ground black pepper

12 boneless chicken breasts, skin on

a little honey

For the sauce

1¼ cup (300ml) dry white wine

2½ cups (600ml) heavy cream

2 tbsp freshly chopped parsley

A quick recipe that you can either prepare ahead or at the last minute. Partly dried (rather than completely dried) tomatoes are sold under different names in different shops, but sun-blushed and sun-ripened tomatoes are the same thing. Serve with new potatoes and green vegetables or salad.

1. Preheat the oven to 400°F (200°C). Put the parsley, chives, basil, cream cheese, egg yolks, lemon juice, and tomatoes into a bowl, season with salt and pepper, and stir until combined.

2. Loosen the skin from the chicken breasts, but keep it attached at one side. Spoon the filling underneath and replace the skin.

3. Arrange the chicken breasts in a roasting pan, season with salt and pepper, then drizzle with a little honey.

4. Roast for 25–30 minutes (35–40 minutes for 12) or until golden and cooked through.

5. Meanwhile, make the sauce: put the wine into a pan (use a wide-based pan for 12, to make the reduction quicker) and boil over high heat until it has reduced to about 3 tablespoons (6 tablespoons for 12). Add the cream and boil for a couple of minutes to thicken. Season with salt and pepper.

6. Allow the chicken breasts to rest for a few minutes after roasting, then add any juices from the pan to the sauce. Carve each breast into three or serve whole. Add the parsley to the hot sauce and serve with the chicken.

PREPARE AHEAD

The chicken can be prepared up to the end of step 2 up to 1 day ahead. The sauce can be made up to 2 days ahead. Not suitable for freezing.

CHICKEN WITH PESTO, TALEGGIO, AND ROASTED TOMATOES

SERVES 6

6 boneless skinless chicken breasts

salt and freshly ground black pepper

6oz (175g) Taleggio cheese (straight from the fridge), cut into small cubes

3 tbsp pesto

2 tbsp freshly chopped basil

3 tbsp full-fat cream cheese

1 cup (50g) fresh bread crumbs

a pinch of paprika

14oz (400g) cherry tomatoes on the vine

2 tbsp olive oil

1 tbsp balsamic vinegar

SERVES 12

12 boneless skinless chicken breasts

salt and freshly ground black pepper

11oz (300g) Taleggio cheese (straight from the fridge), cut into cubes

5 tbsp pesto

4 tbsp freshly chopped basil

5 tbsp full-fat cream cheese

1⅔ cup (75g) fresh bread crumbs

a pinch of paprika

2lb (900g) cherry tomatoes on the vine

3 tbsp olive oil

2 tbsp balsamic vinegar

This is truly scrumptious. It's also quick to make. Homemade pesto is best, but you can use good-quality pesto from a jar if you're short on time. Serve with potatoes and salad.

1. Preheat the oven to 425°F (220°C). Arrange the chicken breasts in a single layer in an ovenproof dish or roasting pan and season with salt and pepper.

2. Mix the Taleggio, pesto, basil, and cream cheese in a bowl and season with salt and pepper. Spoon onto the chicken breasts, spreading the mixture out to cover them completely. Sprinkle with the bread crumbs and dust with a little paprika.

3. Bake for 20 minutes, then arrange the tomatoes around the chicken, pour the oil and balsamic vinegar over them, and return to the oven for a further 10 minutes (30 minutes for 12) or until the chicken is just cooked through. Be careful not to overcook it.

4. To serve, arrange a chicken breast on each plate with a few tomatoes, then spoon over some of the juices from the dish.

PREPARE AHEAD AND FREEZE

The chicken can be prepared up to the end of step 2 up to 12 hours ahead. Freeze at the end of step 2 for up to 2 months.

CHICKEN AND BACON CAESAR SALAD

SERVES 6

7oz (200g) smoked bacon lardons

4 thick slices white bread, crusts removed

3 tbsp olive oil

3 boneless skinless chicken breasts

2 romaine lettuces, cut into 2in (5cm) slices

½ cup (50g) coarsely grated Parmesan cheese

salt and freshly ground black pepper

For the dressing

¼ garlic clove, crushed

2 tbsp white wine vinegar

½ tsp Dijon mustard

2 tbsp olive oil

6 tbsp mayonnaise

3 tbsp water

¼ cup (25g) finely grated Parmesan cheese

1 tsp superfine sugar

SERVES 12

14oz (400g) smoked bacon lardons

8 thick slices white bread, crusts removed

6 tbsp olive oil

6 boneless skinless chicken breasts

4 romaine lettuces, cut into 2in (5cm) slices

1 cup (100g) coarsely grated Parmesan cheese

salt and freshly ground black pepper

For the dressing

½ garlic clove, crushed

4 tbsp white wine vinegar

1 tsp Dijon mustard

4 tbsp olive oil

¾ cup (175ml) mayonnaise

4 tbsp water

½ cup (50g) finely grated Parmesan cheese

2 tsp superfine sugar

A meal in itself. We serve it cold with crusty bread, but you can keep the bacon, croutons, and chicken warm and add just before serving.

1. Preheat the oven to 425°F (220°C). Meanwhile, scatter the lardons over the base of a roasting pan. Cut each slice of bread into 20 even-sized cubes and scatter next to the lardons. Drizzle over two-thirds of the oil and cook in the oven for 15–20 minutes (20 minutes for 12) or until golden and crisp. Shake the pan occasionally.

2. Lay the chicken breasts between two sheets of plastic wrap and flatten with a rolling pin until half as thick. Heat the remaining oil in a frying pan, add the chicken, and fry for 3 minutes on each side or until golden all over and cooked through. You may need to do this in batches. Allow to cool slightly, then cut into thin slices.

3. Put the lettuce and Parmesan into a large salad bowl and season with salt and pepper. Add the lardons and croutons and toss together.

4. To make the dressing, put the garlic, vinegar, mustard, and oil into a bowl and whisk by hand until smooth. Add the mayonnaise, water, Parmesan, and sugar and whisk again. Season with salt and pepper. Pour the dressing over the salad and toss to combine. Arrange the chicken on top and serve at once.

PREPARE AHEAD

The lettuce and Parmesan can be placed in a bowl up to 6 hours ahead. The dressing can be made up to 3 days ahead. Not suitable for freezing.

MEDITERRANEAN LEMON AND
HERB CHICKEN SALAD

This is a wonderfully fresh, light salad, perfect for a picnic or for eating al fresco. You can replace the chicken with turkey if you prefer. Serve with salad leaves and your favorite bread.

1. Put all the ingredients for the dressing into a large bowl and whisk by hand until well combined.

2. Add the chicken and toss well. Add the olives, half the peppers, the basil, parsley, and two-thirds of the feta. Season with salt and pepper and toss to combine.

3. Arrange on a platter and scatter the remaining peppers and feta attractively along the center. Chill in the fridge before serving.

SERVES 6

For the dressing

2 tbsp Dijon mustard

2 tbsp pesto

juice of 1 lemon

4 tbsp olive oil

1 tbsp superfine sugar

salt and freshly ground black pepper

1lb 10oz (750g) cooked boneless skinless chicken, cut into thin strips

5½oz (150g) pitted green olives, halved

10oz (290g) jarred roasted red peppers, drained and thinly sliced

2 tbsp freshly chopped basil

2 tbsp freshly chopped flat-leaf parsley

7oz (200g) feta cheese, broken into small pieces

SERVES 12

For the dressing

4 tbsp Dijon mustard

4 tbsp pesto

juice of 2 lemons

8 tbsp olive oil

2 tbsp superfine sugar

salt and freshly ground black pepper

3lb 3oz (1.5kg) cooked boneless skinless chicken, cut into thin strips

11oz (300g) pitted green olives, halved

20oz (580g) jarred roasted red peppers, drained and thinly sliced

4 tbsp freshly chopped basil

4 tbsp freshly chopped flat-leaf parsley

14oz (400g) feta cheese, broken into small pieces

PREPARE AHEAD

The salad can be made up to 8 hours ahead. Not suitable for freezing.

SARDINIAN CHICKEN

SERVES 6

2 tbsp olive oil

2½oz (75g) pancetta, cut into strips

6 large chicken thighs (bone in), skinned

1 large onion, chopped

1 small red pepper, halved, seeded, and diced

3 garlic cloves, crushed

8oz (225g) button mushrooms, quartered

½ cup (120ml) red wine

1 level tbsp all-purpose flour

14oz (400g) can diced tomatoes

5 tbsp tomato paste

salt and freshly ground black pepper

1 tsp freshly chopped thyme leaves

grated zest of 1 lemon

2 tbsp capers, drained and chopped

SERVES 12

4 tbsp olive oil

6oz (175g) pancetta, cut into strips

12 large chicken thighs (bone in), skinned

2 large onions, chopped

1 large red pepper, halved, seeded and diced

6 garlic cloves, crushed

1lb (450g) button mushrooms, quartered

1 cup (250ml) red wine

1 heaped tbsp all-purpose flour

2 x 14oz (400g) cans diced tomatoes

⅔ cup (150ml) tomato paste

salt and freshly ground black pepper

2 tsp freshly chopped thyme leaves

grated zest of 2 lemons

4 tbsp capers, drained and chopped

Mary's sister-in-law, Margaret, made this for 90 people for a charity lunch and it was a triumph. You can use boneless thighs if you prefer; they'll take about 30 minutes less to cook. Serve with new potatoes or mashed potatoes and green vegetables.

1. Preheat the oven to 350°F (180°C). Heat half the oil in a large, deep frying pan or casserole dish, add the pancetta and chicken, and cook over high heat for a few minutes or until the pancetta is crisp and the chicken golden all over. You may need to do this in batches. Remove with a slotted spoon and set aside.

2. Add the remaining oil to the pan, then add the onion, pepper, garlic, and mushrooms and saute for a few minutes or until starting to soften.

3. Put the wine and flour into a jug and blend to a smooth paste.

4. Add the tomatoes and tomato paste to the pan, then blend in the wine mixture, season with salt and pepper, and bring to a boil. Return the chicken and pancetta to the pan, add the thyme, lemon zest, and capers, and bring to a boil.

5. Cover with a lid and transfer to the oven for 1 hour (1¼ hours for 12) or until the chicken is tender. Serve piping hot.

PREPARE AHEAD AND FREEZE

The casserole can be made up to 2 days ahead. Freeze for up to 2 months.

ITALIAN FARMHOUSE CHICKEN

SERVES 6

1 tbsp olive oil

1 large onion, coarsely chopped

2 garlic cloves, crushed

2 x 14oz (400g) cans diced tomatoes

2 tbsp tomato paste

1 tsp superfine sugar

salt and freshly ground black pepper

3 red peppers, cut in half and seeded

For the stuffing

1lb (450g) pork sausage

finely grated zest of ½ lemon

small bunch of basil leaves, torn

1 tbsp Dijon mustard

12 boneless skinless chicken thighs

SERVES 12

2 tbsp olive oil

2 large onions, coarsely chopped

4 garlic cloves, crushed

4 x 14oz (400g) cans diced tomatoes

4 tbsp tomato paste

2 tsp superfine sugar

salt and freshly ground black pepper

6 red peppers, cut in half and seeded

For the stuffing

2lb (900g) pork sausage

finely grated zest of 1 lemon

large bunch of basil leaves, torn

2 tbsp Dijon mustard

24 boneless skinless chicken thighs

If time is short, you can use peppers from a jar for this. Serve with rice or mashed potatoes and a green vegetable.

1. Preheat the oven to 400°F (200°C). Heat the oil in a frying pan, add the onion and garlic, and saute over high heat for a few minutes or until starting to soften. Stir in the tomatoes, tomato paste, sugar, and ½ cup (100ml) water [¾ cup (200ml) for 12], season with salt and pepper, and bring to a boil. Cover with a lid and simmer for 15 minutes or until the onion is tender.

2. Meanwhile, arrange the peppers cut side down on a cookie sheet and bake for 20 minutes or until the skin has started to blacken. Transfer to a plastic bag, seal the top, and set aside (this makes it easier to remove the skin). Once cool, peel and cut each half in two.

3. To make the stuffing, put the sausage into a mixing bowl, add the lemon zest, basil, and mustard, season with salt and pepper, and mix well. Divide the mixture into 12 (24 for 12) and shape into little sausages.

4. Place the chicken thighs skinned side down on a board between sheets of plastic wrap, opened up flat, and bash with a rolling pin to make them a little thinner. Make sure each thigh is the same thickness. Season with salt and pepper.

5. Place a slice of pepper on each thigh, add one of the sausages, and roll the thigh up. Repeat with the other thighs. Arrange with ends down in a single layer in a large, shallow, ovenproof dish and pour over the tomato sauce.

6. Bake for 40–45 minutes (45–50 minutes for 12) or until bubbling and the chicken is cooked.

PREPARE AHEAD AND FREEZE

The chicken thighs can be prepared up to the end of step 5 up to 12 hours ahead. Freeze the uncooked stuffed rolled chicken thighs for up to 2 months.

CHICKEN TIKKA MASALA

Bright and full of flavor, this is a very popular curry. It is ideal for making in one large batch. Make sure you measure the spices accurately to get the right balance of flavors, and stir often. Serve with naan and Pilaf Rice (pages 246–247).

SERVES 6

12 boneless skinless chicken thighs, each cut into 6 pieces

1 tbsp medium curry powder

1 tsp paprika

1 tbsp olive oil

3 onions, coarsely chopped

2 garlic cloves, crushed

2½in (6cm) piece fresh ginger, peeled and finely grated

2 tbsp garam masala

½ tsp turmeric

¾ cup (200ml) water

2 cups (500ml) tomato puree

2 tbsp tomato paste

1 tbsp sugar

salt and freshly ground black pepper

juice of ½ lime

¾ cup (200ml) heavy cream

1 heaped tbsp freshly chopped cilantro, to garnish

SERVES 12

24 boneless skinless chicken thighs, each cut into 6 pieces

2 tbsp medium curry powder

2 tsp paprika

2 tbsp olive oil

5 onions, coarsely chopped

4 garlic cloves, crushed

3in (7.5cm) piece fresh ginger, peeled and finely grated

4 tbsp garam masala

1 tsp turmeric

1½ cup (400ml) water

4 cups (1 liter) tomato puree

4 tbsp tomato paste

2 tbsp sugar

salt and freshly ground black pepper

juice of 1 lime

1¼ cup (300ml) heavy cream

2 tbsp freshly chopped cilantro, to garnish

1. Put the chicken pieces into a bowl, sprinkle over the curry powder and paprika, cover, and chill for 15 minutes.

2. Heat the oil in a deep frying pan or casserole dish, add the chicken, and quickly brown all over. Remove with a slotted spoon and set aside. You may need to do this in batches.

3. Add the onions, garlic, and ginger and saute for 2 minutes or until starting to soften. Add the garam masala and turmeric and saute for 1 minute. Blend in the water, tomato puree, tomato paste, and sugar, return the chicken to the pan, and season with salt and pepper.

4. Bring to a boil, cover with a lid, and simmer, stirring occasionally, for 30–40 minutes (1 hour for 12) or until the chicken is tender.

5. Add the lime juice, check the seasoning, bring to a boil again, then add the cream. Serve garnished with the cilantro.

PREPARE AHEAD AND FREEZE

The curry can be made up to the end of step 4 up to 2 days ahead. Freeze without the lime juice and cream for up to 2 months.

MINI CHICKEN BURGERS

These chicken burgers are so easy to make and are perfect for a barbecue. Make them larger if you prefer, but cook them for a little longer.

SERVES 6

Special equipment 2½in (6cm) round cutter

2 slices white bread

1lb 2oz (500g) boneless skinless chicken breasts or thighs, coarsely chopped

zest and juice of ½ small lemon

½ cup (50g) freshly grated Parmesan cheese

small bunch of chives, snipped

1 egg yolk

salt and freshly ground black pepper

a little olive oil, to fry

To serve

6 sesame burger buns

coarse mustard

lettuce leaves

mayonnaise

2 tomatoes, sliced

SERVES 12

Special equipment 2½in (6cm) round cutter

4 slices white bread

2¼lb (1kg) boneless skinless chicken breasts or thighs, coarsely chopped

zest and juice of 1 small lemon

1 cup (100g) freshly grated Parmesan cheese

large bunch of chives, snipped

1 large egg

salt and freshly ground black pepper

a little olive oil, to fry

To serve

12 sesame burger buns

coarse mustard

lettuce leaves

mayonnaise

4 tomatoes, sliced

1. Put the bread into a food processor and process to fine bread crumbs. Transfer to a large mixing bowl. Put the chicken into the processor and process until coarsely minced. You may need to do this in batches. Add to the bowl with the bread crumbs.

2. Add the lemon zest, lemon juice, cheese, chives, and egg yolk (whole egg for 12) and mix together with your hands. Season with salt and pepper, then shape the mixture into 12 small burgers (24 for 12) and chill in the fridge for 30 minutes.

3. Heat a little oil in a frying pan and fry the burgers for 3–3½ minutes on each side or until lightly golden and cooked through. You may need to do this in batches. Alternatively, cook on a grill.

4. Slice the buns in half horizontally. Stamp out 12 rounds (24 for 12), using a 2½in (6cm) round cutter. Use the top and bottom of the buns. Spread each with a little mustard, then add a lettuce leaf. Place a burger on top, add a blob of mayonnaise, and garnish with a slice of tomato. Arrange the burgers on a platter and serve.

PREPARE AHEAD AND FREEZE

The burgers can be prepared up to the end of step 2 up to 1 day ahead. Freeze for up to 3 months.

DUCK BREASTS WITH A PIQUANT LIME AND GINGER SAUCE

SERVES 6	SERVES 12
6 duck breasts, skin on	12 duck breasts, skin on
salt and freshly ground black pepper	salt and freshly ground black pepper
1 tbsp olive oil	2 tbsp olive oil
2 tsp freshly grated ginger	4 tsp freshly grated ginger
10oz (300ml) full-fat crème fraîche	1 pint (600ml) full-fat crème fraîche
juice of 1 lime	juice of 2 limes
small pat of butter, at room temperature	large pat of butter, at room temperature
3 tbsp lime marmalade	6 tbsp lime marmalade
chives, to garnish	chives, to garnish

This is an easy way to cook duck breasts, as you brown them well ahead. You then cook them at the last minute, without the worry about whether they will be golden or not. Serve with green beans.

1. Season the duck breasts with salt and pepper, then heat the oil in a frying pan and brown each one on its skin side for a minute or so or until golden. Set aside. Add the ginger to the pan and heat over low heat for 1 minute. Whisk in the crème fraîche and lime juice until smooth and combined. Set aside until needed.

2. Mix the butter and marmalade together in a bowl, then spread over the browned side of the cold duck breasts. Arrange in a roasting pan, browned side up.

3. When ready to serve, preheat the oven to 425°F (220°C). Roast the duck for 12–15 minutes (15–20 minutes for 12) or until cooked but still pink. Set aside to rest.

4. Meanwhile, place the roasting pan on the stove top, add the lime and ginger sauce, and heat until hot, scraping up any sticky bits from the bottom of the pan.

5. Carve each duck breast diagonally into three and serve on the hot sauce with a garnish of chives.

PREPARE AHEAD

You can prepare the duck up to the end of step 2 up to 1 day ahead. Not suitable for freezing.

PHEASANT BREASTS WITH MUSHROOMS AND MADEIRA

SERVES 6

2 onions, sliced

3 thyme sprigs

3 young pheasants

2½ cups (600ml) hot game stock or chicken stock

¼ cup (50g) butter

9oz (250g) small button mushrooms, quartered

⅓ cup (45g) all-purpose flour

4 tbsp cold water

⅔ cup (150ml) Madeira

1 tbsp balsamic vinegar

1 tbsp freshly chopped thyme leaves

1 tbsp full-fat crème fraîche

salt and freshly ground black pepper

SERVES 12

4 onions, sliced

6 thyme sprigs

6 young pheasants

4 cups (1.2 liters) hot game stock or chicken stock

½ cup (100g) butter

1lb 2oz (500g) small button mushrooms, quartered

⅔ cup (85g) all-purpose flour

8 tbsp cold water

1¼ cup (300ml) Madeira

2 tbsp balsamic vinegar

2 tbsp freshly chopped thyme leaves

2 tbsp full-fat crème fraîche

salt and freshly ground black pepper

A warming dish that's perfect for sharing with friends when game is in season. Serve with mashed potatoes and red cabbage or green vegetables.

1. Preheat the oven to 400°F (200°C). Line a large roasting pan with foil and scatter the onions over the base.

2. Put a sprig of thyme in the cavity of each bird. Arrange them breast side down on top of the onions in the pan.

3. Pour over the hot stock, cover with foil, and roast for 1 hour and 10 minutes (1 hour and 20 minutes for 12) or until the breasts are tender. Remove the birds from the pan and allow to rest. Reserve the stock.

4. Melt the butter in a saucepan, add the mushrooms, and saute over high heat for a few minutes or until soft. Strain the stock from the roasting pan into a measuring jug until you have 2 cups/450ml (4 cups/900ml for 12), and discard the onions.

5. Mix the flour and cold water to a runny paste, then stir in with the mushrooms and saute for 1 minute. Gradually add the measured stock and Madeira, stirring until blended. Bring to a boil, add the balsamic vinegar, thyme, and crème fraîche, and season with salt and pepper.

6. Using a sharp knife, detach the pheasant breasts from the carcass and cut each into three diagonally. Arrange in a serving dish and pour over the hot sauce. If the thighs are tender, they can also be served. If tough, use to make game stock with the carcass.

PREPARE AHEAD

The dish can be prepared up to 1 day ahead and reheated. Not suitable for freezing.

GAME CASSEROLE WITH THYME AND MUSTARD DUMPLINGS

This is the perfect casserole for a winter buffet. Start it the day before so that the game has time to absorb the flavors of the Port. If you don't have quite enough game, make up the weight with stewing beef. Serve with creamy mashed potatoes.

SERVES 6

2lb (900g) mixed game, sliced into large pieces

⅔ cup (150ml) Port

2 tbsp sunflower oil

2 tbsp (30g) butter

2 large leeks, sliced

4 celery sticks, sliced

1 apple, peeled, cored, and chopped into small cubes

1 tbsp brown sugar

⅓ cup (45g) all-purpose flour

2 cups (450ml) chicken stock or game stock

1 tbsp Worcestershire sauce

2 tsp Dijon mustard

1 tbsp balsamic vinegar

salt and freshly ground black pepper

For the dumplings

1½ cup (175g) self-raising flour

3oz (85g) suet (or lard)

2 tbsp coarse mustard

1 tsp freshly chopped thyme leaves, plus extra to garnish

SERVES 12

4lb (1.8kg) mixed game, sliced into large pieces

1¼ cup (300ml) Port

4 tbsp sunflower oil

¼ cup (50g) butter

4 large leeks, sliced

8 celery sticks, sliced

2 apples, peeled, cored, and chopped into small cubes

2 tbsp brown sugar

⅔ cup (85g) all-purpose flour

4 cups (900ml) chicken stock or game stock

2 tbsp Worcestershire sauce

1 heaped tbsp Dijon mustard

2 tbsp balsamic vinegar

salt and freshly ground black pepper

For the dumplings

2¾ cups (350g) self-raising flour

6oz (175g) suet (or lard)

4 tbsp coarse mustard

2 tsp freshly chopped thyme leaves, plus extra to garnish

1. Put the game and Port into a bowl and leave to marinate for a few hours or overnight.

2. Preheat the oven to 325°F (160°C). Meanwhile, heat the oil in a large frying pan or casserole dish. Drain the meat from the marinade (reserving the marinade) and brown quickly over high heat. Remove with a slotted spoon and set aside. You may need to do this in batches.

3. Melt the butter in the frying pan, add the leeks, celery, and apple, and saute for 2 minutes. Add the brown sugar and saute for 2 minutes more or until the leeks are starting to soften.

4. Add the flour, then blend in the reserved marinade and stock. Return the meat to the pan and add the Worcestershire sauce, mustard, balsamic vinegar, and some salt and pepper.

5. Bring to a boil, cover with a lid, then transfer to the oven for 1–1½ hours (1½–2 hours for 12) or until the meat is tender.

6. Remove from the oven and increase the temperature to 400°F (200°C).

7. To make the dumplings, mix all the ingredients together in a large mixing bowl. Add about ⅔ cup (150ml) cold water (1¼ cup/300ml for 12) to make a sticky but manageable dough. Lightly knead the dough in the bowl, then shape into 12 small balls (24 for 12).

8. Put the dumplings on top of the casserole and bake without a lid near the top of the oven for 20 minutes or until the dumplings have risen and are golden brown on top. Garnish with chopped thyme.

PREPARE AHEAD AND FREEZE

The casserole can be made up to the end of step 5 up to 2 days ahead. The dumplings are best freshly made. Freeze without the dumplings for up to 2 months.

HIGHLAND GAME PIE

SERVES 10

Special equipment *3 pint (1.7 liter) ovenproof pie pan with a wide base, about 9 x 13in (23 x 33cm)*

2 tbsp olive oil

3lb 2oz (1.4kg) game meat, such as pheasant, guinea fowl, partridge, or venison, cut into 1½in (4cm) cubes

salt and freshly ground black pepper

3 large onions, chopped

½ cup (60g) all-purpose flour

1¼ cup (300ml) red wine

4 cups (1.2 liters) chicken or game stock

2 tbsp Worcestershire sauce

a little gravy browning, optional

10 pickled walnuts from a jar, quartered

For the suet pastry

1⅔ cup (200g) self-raising flour

3½oz (100g) shredded suet (or lard)

½ tsp salt

about ⅔ cup (150ml) water

1 egg, beaten

Full of flavor and perfect for feeding a crowd for that special occasion. You can buy game casserole meat from supermarkets, which comes diced and is perfect for this recipe.

1. Preheat the oven to 320°F (160°C).

2. Heat the oil in a large deep casserole dish or sauté pan. Season the game meat with salt and pepper. Saute in the hot oil until brown all over, stirring over high heat. Remove with a slotted spoon and set aside.

3. Add the onions to the pan and saute for a few minutes. Sprinkle in the flour and cook for 30 seconds. Gradually add the red wine and stock, then bring to a boil while stirring until smooth. Add the Worcestershire sauce and gravy browning, if using, and check the seasoning. Boil for a few minutes, then add the meat and stir. Cover and transfer to the oven for about 2 hours or until the meat is tender.

4. Stir in the walnuts and pour the mixture into the pie pan. Leave to cool before adding the pastry. Increase the oven to 400°F (200°C).

5. To make the pastry, measure the flour, suet, and salt into a bowl, and mix with your hand. Gradually add the water and mix with a fork or knife to combine. Bring together on a board and knead for 1 minute into a ball (there is no need to knead it like other pastries).

6. Roll out the pastry to the size of the dish. Brush the rim of the dish with beaten egg. Lay the pastry on top, press the edge of the pastry against the side of the dish firmly, and brush with beaten egg. Using a sharp knife, make a hole in the center of the pastry.

7. Bake in preheated oven for about 35 minutes or until golden brown and bubbling. Serve piping hot with vegetables.

PREPARE AHEAD AND FREEZE

The casserole can be made up to 2 days ahead. The assembled pie can be made up to 12 hours ahead. Freezes well uncooked with the pastry lid for up to 1 month. Defrost before cooking.

MEAT ENTRÉES

This chapter is full of classics, alongside some more unusual dishes. From hearty winter feasts to summer barbecues, these recipes will be enjoyed by your family and friends time and again.

FILLET STEAK WITH A CREAMY MUSHROOM SAUCE

SERVES 6

8oz (225g) button mushrooms, thinly sliced

2 tbsp brandy

1¼ cup (300ml) heavy cream

salt and freshly ground black pepper

6 x 5½oz (150g) middle-cut fillet steaks

1 tbsp olive oil

8oz (225g) baby spinach

1 cup (50g) fresh white bread crumbs

a little paprika, to dust

SERVES 12

1lb (450g) button mushrooms, thinly sliced

4 tbsp brandy

2½ cups (600ml) heavy cream

salt and freshly ground black pepper

12 x 5½oz (150g) middle-cut fillet steaks

2 tbsp olive oil

1lb (450g) baby spinach

1⅔ cup (75g) fresh white bread crumbs

a little paprika, to dust

This is a joy because it can be prepared ahead and reheated just before serving. Serve with new potatoes and a green vegetable.

1. Put the mushrooms and brandy into a wide-bottomed pan and toss over high heat for 2–3 minutes or until the liquid has reduced slightly. Scoop out the mushrooms with a slotted spoon, add the cream, and boil for 5 minutes or until it has reduced by half and reached a coating consistency. Return the mushrooms to the pan, season with salt and pepper, then set aside to cool completely.

2. Heat a large nonstick frying pan over high heat. Brush each steak with a little oil and season with salt and pepper. Pan-fry each steak for 1–2 minutes on each side or until golden and sealed. Transfer to a cookie sheet. You will need to do this in batches.

3. Add the spinach to the pan and cook for a few minutes or until just wilted. Place a mound on top of each steak. Spoon the cold mushroom sauce on top of the spinach (just enough to cover—you should have some sauce left over to reheat and serve with the steaks).

4. Preheat the oven to 425°F (220°C). Sprinkle the steaks with the bread crumbs and a dusting of paprika and bake for 8 minutes (11 minutes for 12) or until piping hot but just rare in the middle. Add 2 minutes for medium and 4 minutes for medium to well done. Rest for a couple of minutes before serving. Reheat the remaining mushroom sauce in a pan.

5. Serve the steaks piping hot with the sauce alongside.

PREPARE AHEAD

The steaks can be prepared up to the end of step 3 up to 12 hours ahead. Not suitable for freezing.

TERIYAKI STEAK

SERVES 6

½ cup (100ml) mirin

3 tbsp soy sauce

2 tbsp light brown sugar

1 garlic clove, crushed

6 x 5½oz (150g) sirloin steaks or rump steaks

2 tbsp olive oil

8oz (225g) mixed wild mushrooms, such as oyster, shiitake, and button, sliced

SERVES 12

We think this dish is not suitable for more than six people because you would have to cook it in two batches, which would mean some steaks would end up being overcooked.

Apart from the marinating—which is vital for the flavor of the sauce to come through—this is a very quick dish. You'll find mirin in a bottle in the world food section of the supermarket. It is a traditional Japanese rice seasoning, similar to rice wine or sake, but with a low alcohol content. Buy steaks of the same thickness, so they cook at the same rate. Serve with noodles.

1. Put the mirin, soy sauce, sugar, and garlic into a wide, shallow dish and stir together.

2. Add the steaks and turn to coat. Leave to marinate for a minimum of 30 minutes and up to 8 hours.

3. Heat half the oil in a nonstick frying pan. Remove the steaks from the marinade (reserving the marinade) and fry for 2½ minutes on each side—they should be medium rare. Transfer to a hot plate to rest. You may need to do this in batches.

4. Heat the remaining oil in the pan, add the mushrooms, and saute over high heat for a few minutes or until just cooked. Pour in the reserved marinade and bring to a boil.

5. Serve the steaks whole or in slices with the mushrooms and sauce spooned on top.

PREPARE AHEAD

The marinade can be made up to 4 days ahead. The steaks can be marinated for up to 8 hours. Not suitable for freezing.

THAI BEEF WITH LIME AND CHILE

The advantage of using center-cut beef fillet is that it's the same diameter all around, which means it roasts evenly and won't overcook at one end. This is delicious with our Thai green rice on page 248.

SERVES 6

2lb (900g) center-cut beef fillet

1 tbsp olive oil

1 large red chile, seeded and coarsely chopped

1in (2.5cm) fresh ginger, peeled and coarsely chopped

1 fat garlic clove, coarsely chopped

small bunch of mint, stalks removed

finely grated zest and juice of 1 lime

⅓ cup (100g) coconut cream

7oz (200ml) full-fat crème fraîche

1 tbsp sweet chili dipping sauce

1 tbsp sugar

½ tbsp fish sauce

3 heaped tbsp light mayonnaise

SERVES 12

4lb (1.8kg) center-cut beef fillet

2 tbsp olive oil

2 large red chiles, seeded and coarsely chopped

2in (5cm) fresh ginger, peeled and coarsely chopped

2 fat garlic cloves, coarsely chopped

large bunch of mint, stalks removed

finely grated zest and juice of 2 limes

⅔ cup (200g) coconut cream

14oz (400ml) full-fat crème fraîche

2 tbsp sweet chili dipping sauce

2 tbsp sugar

1 tbsp fish sauce

6 heaped tbsp light mayonnaise

1. Preheat the oven to 425°F (220°C). Rub the beef with the oil and brown quickly on all sides in a large pan.

2. Transfer to a roasting pan and roast for 20 minutes (30 minutes for 12)—it should be medium rare—then cover loosely with foil and leave to rest for 15–20 minutes.

3. Meanwhile, put the chile, ginger, garlic, mint, lime zest, and lime juice into a food processor and process until finely chopped. Add the coconut cream, crème fraîche, chili sauce, sugar, fish sauce, and mayonnaise and process again.

4. Carve the beef, allowing 2–3 slices per person, and arrange on a platter with the Thai green rice, if serving. Place the sauce alongside in a bowl.

PREPARE AHEAD

The sauce can be made up to 3 days ahead.
The beef can be browned up to 12 hours ahead.
Not suitable for freezing.

SIRLOIN STEAK AND VEGETABLE STIR-FRY

SERVES 6

12oz (350g) thin sirloin steak or fillet steak, sliced into very thin strips

1 tbsp honey

salt and freshly ground black pepper

2 tbsp olive oil

2 carrots, sliced into matchsticks

6 scallions, sliced

5½oz (150g) baby corn, cut into thick slices

5½oz (150g) sugar snap peas, sliced in half lengthwise

9oz (250g) bok choy, white and green separated and cut into thick slices

For the sauce

3 tbsp mirin

2 tbsp soy sauce

2 tbsp hoisin sauce

2 tbsp water

2 tsp cornstarch

SERVES 12

We think this dish is not suitable for more than six people because the vegetables would release too much water and make the stir-fry soggy.

Light and fresh, this stir-fry is the perfect dish to rustle up as a speedy supper for up to six people. Serve with noodles or rice.

1. Toss the steak in the honey and season well with salt and pepper.

2. Heat the oil in a large frying pan or wok over high heat, add the steak, and stir-fry for 1–2 minutes or until brown and just cooked. Transfer to a plate with a slotted spoon.

3. Add the carrots, scallions, and corn and stir-fry over high heat for 3 minutes. Add the sugar snap peas and the white part of the bok choy and stir-fry for 3 minutes.

4. To make the sauce, put the mirin, soy sauce, and hoisin sauce in a small bowl. Mix the water and cornstarch to a smooth paste in another bowl, then add to the sauce. Pour the sauce into the frying pan with the steak and the green leaves of the bok choy and saute for 1–2 minutes or until the green leaves have just wilted.

5. Season with salt and pepper and serve immediately.

PREPARE AHEAD

You can prepare all the ingredients up to 4 hours ahead. The sauce can be made up to 1 day ahead. Not suitable for freezing.

CLASSIC BEEF LASAGNA

Although there are many trendy new lasagnas out there, we are often asked for a classic lasagna. This is a recipe we've perfected over the years. Leave it to stand for six hours before cooking.

SERVES 6

Special equipment *4 pint (2.4 liter) shallow, wide-bottomed, ovenproof dish*

1 tbsp sunflower oil

2lb (900g) raw ground beef

2 onions, coarsely chopped

4 celery sticks, diced

2 garlic cloves, crushed

2 level tbsp all-purpose flour

2 x 14½oz (400g) cans diced tomatoes

⅔ cup (150ml) beef stock

3 tbsp tomato paste

1 tsp sugar

1 tbsp freshly chopped thyme leaves

For the white sauce

¼ cup (50g) butter

⅓ cup (50g) all-purpose flour

3 cups (750ml) hot milk

2 tsp Dijon mustard

1¾oz (50g) Parmesan cheese, freshly grated

salt and freshly ground black pepper

6–8 lasagna noodles

3oz (85g) sharp Cheddar cheese, grated

SERVES 12

Special equipment *2 x 4 pint (2.4 liter) shallow, wide-bottomed, ovenproof dishes or 1 x 7 pint (4 liter) dish*

1 tbsp sunflower oil

4lb (1.8kg) raw ground beef

4 onions, coarsely chopped

8 celery sticks, diced

4 garlic cloves, crushed

4 level tbsp all-purpose flour

4 x 14½oz (400g) cans diced tomatoes

1¼ cup (300ml) beef stock

6 tbsp tomato paste

2 tsp sugar

2 tbsp freshly chopped thyme leaves

For the white sauce

½ cup (100g) butter

¾ cup (100g) all-purpose flour

5½ cups (1.5 liters) hot milk

1 heaped tbsp Dijon mustard

3½oz (100g) Parmesan cheese, freshly grated

salt and freshly ground black pepper

12–16 lasagna noodles

6oz (175g) sharp Cheddar cheese, grated

1. Preheat the oven to 325°F (160°C). Heat the oil in a large frying pan until hot, then add the ground beef and cook until brown all over. Stir in the onions, celery, and garlic.

2. Add the flour and stir to coat the vegetables and beef, then stir in the tomatoes, stock, tomato paste, sugar, and thyme. Bring to a boil, cover with a lid, then transfer to the oven for 1–1½ hours or until the beef is tender.

3. Meanwhile, make the white sauce. Melt the butter in a saucepan, add the flour, and cook over the heat for 1 minute, stirring. Slowly add the hot milk, whisking until the sauce is thick and smooth. Add the mustard and Parmesan and season well with salt and pepper.

4. Remove the meat sauce from the oven and put one-third into the bottom of the ovenproof dish (two dishes for 12). Spoon one-third of the white sauce on top and arrange a layer of lasagna noodles on top of that. Season with salt and pepper.

5. Spoon half the remaining meat sauce on top, then half the remaining white sauce. Put another layer of lasagna noodles on top and season with salt and pepper. Add the rest of the meat sauce followed by the rest of the white sauce.

6. Sprinkle over the Cheddar, then transfer to the fridge for a minimum of 6 hours before cooking so the pasta has time to soften.

7. To serve, preheat the oven to 400°F (200°C), then cook the lasagna in the middle of the oven for 45 minutes (1 hour for 12) or until golden brown on top, bubbling around the edges, and the pasta is soft.

PREPARE AHEAD AND FREEZE

The lasagna can be made up to the end of step 6 up to 2 days ahead. Freeze the lasagna at the end of step 6 for up to 2 months.

CLASSIC SPAGHETTI BOLOGNESE

SERVES 6

2 tbsp sunflower oil

7oz (200g) fresh chicken livers, trimmed of any sinew and cut into small pieces

2lb (900g) raw lean ground beef

2 onions, finely chopped

2 garlic cloves, crushed

½ cup (100ml) Port

2 x 14½oz (400g) cans diced tomatoes

3 tbsp tomato paste

1 tsp superfine sugar

salt and freshly ground black pepper

1lb 2oz (500g) spaghetti

Parmesan cheese, grated

SERVES 12

4 tbsp sunflower oil

1lb (450g) fresh chicken livers, trimmed of any sinew and cut into small pieces

4lb (1.8kg) raw lean ground beef

4 onions, finely chopped

4 garlic cloves, crushed

¾ cup (200ml) Port

4 x 14½oz (400g) cans diced tomatoes

6 tbsp tomato paste

2 tsp superfine sugar

salt and freshly ground black pepper

2¼lb (1kg) spaghetti

Parmesan cheese, grated

This is a traditional bolognese sauce, with chicken livers for a lovely depth of flavor. It's well worth making double the quantity so you can freeze a batch for another day.

1. Preheat the oven to 325°F (160°C). Heat the oil in a large nonstick frying pan over high heat, add the chicken livers, and brown quickly all over. Remove with a slotted spoon and set aside.

2. Add the ground beef in batches and brown all over, adding a little more oil if the pan's getting dry. Return the chicken livers to the pan along with all the beef.

3. Add the onions and garlic and saute for 2 minutes. Stir in the Port, tomatoes, tomato paste, and sugar and bring to a boil. Season with salt and pepper, cover with a lid, and transfer to the oven for 1–1¼ hours or until tender.

4. To serve, cook the spaghetti in boiling salted water according to the package instructions. Drain well, transfer to a serving bowl, and top with the bolognese sauce. Sprinkle with the grated Parmesan to serve.

PREPARE AHEAD AND FREEZE

The sauce can be made up to 2 days ahead. Freeze for up to 3 months.

COLD FILLET OF BEEF
WITH MUSTARD SAUCE

SERVES 6

2¾lb (1.25kg) middle-cut fillet of beef

salt and freshly ground black pepper

1 tbsp olive oil

a small pat of butter

For the mustard sauce

7oz (200ml) full-fat crème fraîche

2 tbsp Dijon mustard

1 tsp white wine vinegar

1 tsp black mustard seeds

1 tsp superfine sugar

SERVES 12

4lb (1.8kg) whole middle-cut fillet of beef

salt and freshly ground black pepper

2 tbsp olive oil

a pat of butter

For the mustard sauce

17oz (500ml) full-fat crème fraîche

4 tbsp Dijon mustard

2 tsp white wine vinegar

2 tsp black mustard seeds

2 tsp superfine sugar

To avoid the meat turning gray once carved and exposed to the air, carve the cold beef up to 3 hours ahead, then reassemble into its original shape and wrap tightly in plastic wrap. Chill until needed and arrange on the plate just before serving. Serve with new potatoes and the salad on page 226.

1. Preheat the oven to 425°F (220°C). Meanwhile, season the beef with salt and pepper, then rub the oil over the meat.

2. Heat a wide-bottomed frying pan over high heat until very hot and brown the beef quickly on all sides.

3. Transfer to a small roasting pan, spread with the butter, and roast for 18–20 minutes (25 minutes for 12) or until medium rare. Set aside until cold.

4. To make the sauce, put all the ingredients into a bowl, season with salt and pepper, and stir to combine.

5. Thinly carve the beef and serve cold with the sauce.

PREPARE AHEAD

The fillet can be roasted up to 2 days ahead.
The sauce can be made up to 3 days ahead.
Not suitable for freezing.

GOOD OLD-FASHIONED BEEF STEW WITH RED WINE AND THYME

SERVES 6

2 tbsp sunflower oil

2lb (900g) stewing beef, cut into bite-size pieces

12 small shallots, peeled

2 medium carrots, diced

4 level tbsp all-purpose flour

1¼ cup (300ml) red wine

2 cups (450ml) beef stock

1 tbsp red currant jelly

1 tbsp Worcestershire sauce

5 thyme sprigs

salt and freshly ground black pepper

9oz (250g) button mushrooms

SERVES 12

2 tbsp sunflower oil

4lb (1.8kg) stewing beef, cut into bite-size pieces

24 small shallots, peeled

4 medium carrots, diced

¾ cup (100g) all-purpose flour

2½ cups (600ml) red wine

3¾ cups (900ml) beef stock

2 tbsp red currant jelly

2 tbsp Worcestershire sauce

small bunch of thyme sprigs

salt and freshly ground black pepper

1lb 2oz (500g) button mushrooms

This traditional stew has lots of flavor and is a favorite of Lucy's family, especially at holiday times when everyone is gathered together. Serve with creamy mashed potatoes and green vegetables.

1. Preheat the oven to 325°F (160°C). Meanwhile, heat the oil in a large frying pan or casserole dish and quickly brown the beef all over. Remove with a slotted spoon and set aside. You may need to do this in batches.

2. Add the shallots and carrots to the pan and brown over high heat. Add the flour and stir to coat the vegetables, then stir in the wine and stock. Add the red currant jelly, Worcestershire sauce, thyme, and some salt and pepper. Add the mushrooms and return the beef to the pan.

3. Bring to a boil, cover with a lid, and cook in the oven for 2–2½ hours (2½–3 hours for 12) or until the beef is tender. Serve piping hot.

PREPARE AHEAD AND FREEZE

The stew can be made up to 1 day ahead. Freeze for up to 2 months.

HOT MUSTARD SPICED BEEF

A wonderful untemperamental casserole—warming and spicy. Serve with cheese-topped dauphinois potatoes (page 253) and peas.

SERVES 6

1 tbsp sunflower oil

2lb (900g) chuck steak, cut into ¾in (2cm) cubes

2 large onions, chopped

3½oz (100g) button mushrooms, cut into quarters

1 tbsp Dijon mustard

2 tsp medium curry powder

1 tbsp muscovado sugar

2 tbsp Worcestershire sauce

¼ cup (25g) all-purpose flour

2½ cups (600ml) beef stock or 2 beef stock cubes dissolved in 2½ cups (600ml) water

salt and freshly ground black pepper

1lb (450g) Chantenay or baby carrots

freshly chopped parsley, to garnish (optional)

SERVES 12

2 tbsp sunflower oil

4lb (1.8kg) chuck steak, cut into ¾in (2cm) cubes

4 large onions, chopped

8oz (225g) button mushrooms, cut into quarters

2 tbsp Dijon mustard

4 tsp medium curry powder

2 tbsp muscovado sugar

4 tbsp Worcestershire sauce

½ cup (50g) all-purpose flour

4 cups (1.2 liters) beef stock or 4 beef stock cubes dissolved in 4 cups (1.2 liters) water

salt and freshly ground black pepper

2lb (900g) Chantenay or baby carrots

freshly chopped parsley, to garnish (optional)

1. Preheat the oven to 325°F (160°C). Meanwhile, heat the oil in a large nonstick frying pan or casserole dish, add the cubes of meat, and fry quickly until golden brown all over. Remove with a slotted spoon and drain on paper towel. You may need to do this in batches.

2. Add the onions and mushrooms to the pan and saute over high heat, stirring occasionally, for 3 minutes or until starting to soften.

3. Put the mustard, curry powder, sugar, Worcestershire sauce, and flour into a bowl and add ⅓ cup (75ml) of the stock (⅔ cup/150ml for 12). Whisk by hand until smooth.

4. Add the remaining stock to the pan and bring to a boil. Spoon about half the hot stock into the mustard mixture and whisk by hand to give a smooth paste. Pour the mixture back into the pan, whisking over high heat until thickened.

5. Season with salt and pepper, then return the meat to the pan. Bring to a boil, cover with a lid, and transfer to the oven for 2–2½ hours (2½–3 hours for 12) or until the meat is tender.

6. While the meat is cooking, cook the carrots—sliced in half lengthwise if they are a little on the large size—in boiling salted water for a few minutes or until just tender. Drain and refresh in cold water.

7. To serve, bring the casserole to a boil on the stove top. Add the carrots, check the seasoning, and boil for a few minutes or until the carrots are hot. Sprinkle with parsley, if using, and serve.

PREPARE AHEAD AND FREEZE

The dish can be made up to the end of step 5 up to 2 days ahead. Freeze without the carrots for up to 2 months.

AROMATIC BEEF CURRY WITH GINGER AND TOMATOES

SERVES 6

1 heaped tsp each ground cumin, ground coriander, and garam masala

½ tsp turmeric

10 cardamom pods, crushed, pods discarded, and seeds finely crushed

2 tbsp olive oil

2lb (900g) stewing beef, chopped into 1in (2.5cm) pieces

1 large onion, coarsely chopped

1 red chile, halved, seeded, and chopped

4 garlic cloves, crushed

¾in (2cm) piece fresh ginger, peeled and grated

14½oz (400g) can diced tomatoes

1¼ cup (300ml) beef stock

1 cinnamon stick

4 tbsp tomato paste

3 tbsp mango chutney

salt and freshly ground pepper

7oz (200g) okra or green beans, sliced into ¾in (2cm) pieces

SERVES 12

2 heaped tsp each ground cumin, ground coriander, and garam masala

1 tsp turmeric

20 cardamom pods, crushed, pods discarded, and seeds finely crushed

4 tbsp olive oil

4lb (1.8kg) stewing beef, chopped into 1in (2.5cm) pieces

2 large onions, coarsely chopped

2 red chiles, halved, seeded, and chopped

8 garlic cloves, crushed

2in (5cm) piece fresh ginger, peeled and grated

2 x 14½oz (400g) cans diced tomatoes

2½ cups (600ml) beef stock

2 cinnamon sticks

8 tbsp tomato paste

6 tbsp mango chutney

salt and freshly ground pepper

1lb (450g) okra or green beans, sliced into ¾in (2cm) pieces

A warming curry with lots of spice. Serve with popadams, naan, and Pilaf Rice (pages 246–247).

1. Preheat the oven to 325°F (160°C). Heat a large frying pan or casserole dish over high heat, add all the spices, and saute, stirring constantly, for 1 minute or until just toasted, then spoon into a small bowl.

2. Add the oil to the pan and quickly brown the beef until golden all over. Remove with a slotted spoon and set aside. You may need to do this in batches. Add the onion to the pan along with the toasted spices, the chile, garlic, and ginger and saute for 3–4 minutes.

3. Add the diced tomatoes, stock, cinnamon, tomato paste, and chutney. Return the beef to the pan, season with salt and pepper, cover with a lid, and transfer to the oven for about 2–2¼ hours (2½ hours for 12) or until the beef is tender.

4. Cook the okra or green beans in boiling salted water for 3 minutes, drain, and stir into the pan. Fish out the cinnamon and discard. Serve immediately.

PREPARE AHEAD AND FREEZE

The curry can be made up to 2 days ahead. Freeze without the okra or green beans for up to 2 months.

CHILI CON CARNE

The hotness of chili con carne is a personal choice. Taste it at the end and, if you like yours hot, add more chili powder, then bring to a boil to cook it through. The chutney adds a touch of sweetness. Serve with long-grain rice, grated Cheddar or Red Leicester cheese, and a dollop of sour cream.

SERVES 6

1 tbsp olive oil

2lb (900g) raw ground beef

2 medium onions, coarsely chopped

2 garlic cloves, crushed

2 red chiles, halved, seeded, and finely chopped

2 tbsp paprika

2 tsp cumin powder

½–1 tsp hot chili powder (depending on taste)

¾ cup (200ml) red wine

2 x 14½oz (400g) cans diced tomatoes

2 tbsp tomato paste

salt and freshly ground black pepper

2 x 14½oz (400g) cans kidney beans in water, drained and rinsed

1–2 tbsp mango chutney (depending on taste)

SERVES 12

2 tbsp olive oil

4lb (1.8kg) raw ground beef

3 large onions, coarsely chopped

4 garlic cloves, crushed

4 red chiles, halved, seeded, and finely chopped

4 tbsp paprika

1 heaped tbsp cumin powder

1–2 tsp hot chili powder (depending on taste)

1⅔ cup (400ml) red wine

4 x 14½oz (400g) cans diced tomatoes

4 tbsp tomato paste

salt and freshly ground black pepper

4 x 14½oz (400g) cans kidney beans in water, drained and rinsed

2–3 tbsp mango chutney (depending on taste)

1. Preheat the oven to 350°F (180°C). Meanwhile, heat the oil in a deep, nonstick frying pan or casserole dish, add the ground beef, and fry over high heat for 5 minutes or until brown all over. You may need to do this in batches.

2. Add the onions, garlic, and chiles and saute with the ground beef for a few minutes.

3. Sprinkle in the paprika, cumin, and chili powder and saute for a few minutes more. Blend in the wine, tomatoes, and tomato paste and stir as you bring to a boil. Season with salt and pepper, cover with a lid, and transfer to the oven for about an hour.

4. Add the kidney beans and chutney, return to the oven, and continue to cook for a further 30 minutes (1 hour for 12) or until the meat is completely tender. Serve immediately.

PREPARE AHEAD AND FREEZE

The chilli can be made up to 2 days ahead. Freeze for up to 2 months.

MARINATED MARMALADE AND WHISKEY LAMB FILLET

Lamb loin fillet is lean, tender, and very quick to cook. It's also quite expensive, so this recipe is for extra special occasions. Serve with creamy mashed potatoes and a green vegetable.

SERVES 6

3 large lamb loin fillets, trimmed

3 heaped tbsp thin-cut Seville orange marmalade

finely grated zest of ½ lemon

1 garlic clove, crushed

2 tbsp whiskey

2 tbsp olive oil

salt and freshly ground black pepper

For the sauce

1¼ cup (300ml) chicken stock

1½ tbsp soy sauce

2 tsp balsamic vinegar

2 level tsp cornstarch

1 tbsp cold water

SERVES 12

6 large lamb loin fillets, trimmed

6 heaped tbsp thin-cut Seville orange marmalade

finely grated zest of 1 lemon

2 garlic cloves, crushed

4 tbsp whiskey

4 tbsp olive oil

salt and freshly ground black pepper

For the sauce

2½ cups (600ml) chicken stock

3 tbsp soy sauce

4 tsp balsamic vinegar

4 level tsp cornstarch

2 tbsp cold water

1. Arrange the lamb fillets in a flat dish. Put the marmalade, lemon zest, garlic, and whiskey into a small bowl and mix together. Pour over the lamb, cover, and leave to marinate in the fridge for about an hour or up to 6 hours.

2. Preheat the oven to 425°F (220°C). Heat the oil in a large frying pan. Scrape the marinade off the fillets and reserve for the sauce. Season the lamb with salt and pepper, then fry quickly until brown on all sides. You may need to do this in batches. Arrange on a cookie sheet.

3. Roast for 8 minutes (12 minutes for 12) or until cooked but still pink in the middle. Set aside to rest.

4. Meanwhile, make the sauce. Rinse the frying pan, add the reserved marinade along with the stock, soy sauce, and balsamic vinegar, and bring to a boil. Put the cornstarch into a cup, add the cold water, and mix until smooth. Add a little of the hot sauce and mix again, then stir into the frying pan and bring to a boil to thicken it slightly.

5. Carve the lamb into slices, strain the sauce, and serve alongside.

PREPARE AHEAD AND FREEZE

The lamb can be marinated for up to 6 hours.
The sauce can be made up to 3 days ahead.
Freeze the sauce for up to 3 months.

SLOW-ROASTED LEG OF LAMB

SERVES 6

3lb 3oz (1.5kg) half-boned leg of lamb

8 garlic cloves, thinly sliced

bunch of fresh thyme

2 red onions, coarsely chopped

1 tbsp olive oil

salt and freshly ground black pepper

3 cups (750ml) water mixed with 1 beef stock cube

1 heaped tbsp all-purpose flour

3 tbsp water

1 heaped tbsp red currant jelly

a little gravy browning (optional)

SERVES 12

2 x 3lb 3oz (1.5kg) half-boned legs of lamb

16 garlic cloves, thinly sliced

large bunch of fresh thyme

4 red onions, coarsely chopped

2 tbsp olive oil

salt and freshly ground black pepper

5½ cups (1.5 liters) water mixed with 2 beef stock cubes

2 heaped tbsp all-purpose flour

6 tbsp water

2 heaped tbsp red currant jelly

a little gravy browning (optional)

Slow-roasted lamb is ideal for a crowd—it looks after itself in the oven, it's tender, and easy to carve. No wonder it's Mary's family lunch most Sundays. Serve with mint sauce and red currant jelly.

1. Preheat the oven to 425°F (220°C). Lay the lamb on a board and use a small sharp knife to make holes in the flesh. Push the garlic and thyme into the holes.

2. Arrange the onions in the base of a large roasting pan. Sit a grill rack over the onions and place the lamb on top. Drizzle over the oil and season with salt and pepper.

3. Roast for 30–40 minutes or until brown. Remove the pan from the oven and reduce the oven temperature to 325°F (160°C).

4. Pour the stock around the lamb, cover the pan with foil, and return to the oven for 5 hours (5½ hours for 12) or until the meat is tender and just falling off the bone.

5. Transfer the lamb to a board, cover with foil, and leave to rest while you make the gravy.

6. Put the flour and water into a cup and mix to a smooth runny paste. Heat the roasting pan on the stove top, whisk in the flour mixture and the red currant jelly, and bring to a boil, stirring all the time until smooth. Check the seasoning and add a little gravy browning if you'd like the gravy to be a rich brown color. Strain through a sieve for a smooth gravy.

7. Carve the lamb and serve with the hot gravy.

PREPARE AHEAD

The lamb can be prepared up to the end of step 2 up to 1 day ahead. Not suitable for freezing.

BONELESS WINTER LAMB SHANKS

A whole lamb shank can look too filling. Our recipe gives guests the option of having half. It tastes even better when made the day before. Serve with mashed potatoes and cabbage.

SERVES 6

Special equipment *4 pint (2.4 liter) shallow, ovenproof dish*

2 tbsp olive oil

6 lamb shanks, trimmed of any excess fat

2 medium onions, thinly sliced

3 garlic cloves, crushed

½ cup (50g) all-purpose flour

2½ cups (600ml) cold chicken stock

3 tbsp sun-dried tomato paste

⅔ cup (150ml) red wine or Port

3 tbsp soy sauce

1 tbsp freshly chopped thyme leaves

salt and freshly ground black pepper

1½ tbsp balsamic vinegar

SERVES 12

Special equipment *2 x 4 pint (2.4 liter) shallow, ovenproof dishes*

4 tbsp olive oil

12 lamb shanks, trimmed of any excess fat

4 medium onions, thinly sliced

6 garlic cloves, crushed

¾ cup (100g) all-purpose flour

4 cups (1.2 liters) cold chicken stock

6 tbsp sun-dried tomato paste

1¼ cup (300ml) red wine or Port

6 tbsp soy sauce

2 tbsp freshly chopped thyme leaves

salt and freshly ground black pepper

3 tbsp balsamic vinegar

1. Preheat the oven to 325°F (160°C). Heat half the oil in a large deep saucepan or casserole dish. Brown the shanks all over until golden. Remove and set aside. You may need to do this in batches.

2. Add the remaining oil to the pan, add the onions and garlic, and cook over high heat for 5 minutes or until starting to soften. Put the flour into a jug and slowly whisk in the cold stock until smooth. Add to the pan with the sun-dried tomato paste and red wine or Port and bring to a boil.

3. Return the lamb to the pan, add the soy sauce and thyme, and season with salt and pepper. Stir well, cover with a lid, and transfer to the oven for 3–4 hours (4 hours for 12) or until the meat is tender and starting to fall off the bone. Stir in the balsamic vinegar.

4. Remove the shanks from the sauce, wrap in foil, and set aside to cool. Pour the sauce into a 4 pint (2.4 liter) shallow, ovenproof dish (two dishes for 12), cool, and cover with foil. When the sauce and shanks are completely cold, transfer to the fridge overnight, if time allows.

5. To serve, preheat the oven to 350°F (180°C). Using a spoon, remove the fat from the surface of the sauce and discard. Remove the meat from the bone in one piece, then cut each piece in half. Add to the sauce and cover with foil.

6. Reheat in the oven for 45–50 minutes (1 hour for 12) or until piping hot.

PREPARE AHEAD AND FREEZE

This is best made the day before and reheated. Freeze for up to 6 weeks.

SHEPHERD'S PIE DAUPHINOIS

This variation on the classic shepherd's pie has a layered topping of potato and cream instead of mashed potatoes. Liquid gravy browning can be hard to track down these days, but it's well worth the hunt. Not only does it make a sauce or gravy an appetizing rich brown, it saves you time, too, as you don't have to brown the onions for so long. Serve with a green vegetable.

SERVES 6

Special equipment *4 pint (2.4 liter) shallow, wide-bottomed ovenproof dish*

2lb (900g) raw ground lamb

2 onions, chopped

2 large carrots, finely diced

⅓ cup (45g) all-purpose flour

1¼ cup (300ml) red wine

1¼ cup (300ml) beef stock

1 tbsp Worcestershire sauce

1 tbsp tomato paste

dash of gravy browning (optional)

salt and freshly ground black pepper

For the topping

2lb (900g) Russet potatoes or other starchy potatoes, cut into ⅛in (3mm) slices

⅔ cup (150ml) heavy cream

2½oz (75g) sharp Cheddar cheese, grated

SERVES 12

Special equipment *2 x 4 pint (2.4 liter) shallow, wide-bottomed ovenproof dishes*

4lb (1.8kg) raw ground lamb

4 onions, chopped

4 large carrots, finely diced

⅔ cup (75g) all-purpose flour

2½ cups (600ml) red wine

2½ cups (600ml) beef stock

2 tbsp Worcestershire sauce

2 tbsp tomato paste

dash of gravy browning (optional)

salt and freshly ground black pepper

For the topping

4lb (1.8kg) Russet potatoes or other starchy potatoes, cut into ⅛in (3mm) slices

1¼ cup (300ml) heavy cream

6oz (175g) sharp Cheddar cheese, grated

1. Preheat the oven to 325°F (160°C). Meanwhile, put the ground lamb, onions, and carrots into a deep frying pan or casserole dish and fry over high heat, stirring frequently, for 5 minutes or until the meat is brown. Drain away any fat.

2. Stir in the flour and, over high heat, add the wine, stock, Worcestershire sauce, and tomato paste (add the gravy browning, too, if you want the sauce to be a rich dark color). Stir until blended, then bring to a boil. Season with salt and pepper, cover with a lid, and transfer to the oven for 1–1½ hours or until the meat is tender.

3. Check the seasoning, then pour the meat into the ovenproof dish(es) and set aside to cool. Increase the oven temperature to 425°F (220°C).

4. Put the potatoes in a pan of boiling salted water for 4–5 minutes to blanch them. Drain, refresh in cold water, and dry well with paper towel.

5. Arrange a layer of potato on top of the cold lamb, then pour over half the cream and season with salt and pepper. Arrange the remaining potatoes on top, pour over the remaining cream, and sprinkle over the cheese.

6. Bake for 30 minutes (45–50 minutes for 12) or until golden and bubbling.

PREPARE AHEAD AND FREEZE

The pie can be prepared up to the end of step 5 up to 1 day ahead. Freeze for up to 2 months.

MINI PORK EN CROÛTES

As a team, we like to go to the pub occasionally, to chat and have a moment off from cooking. One evening we had a recipe similar to this—delicious and beautifully presented. Serve with spinach.

SERVES 6

2½oz (75g) sharp Cheddar cheese, grated

1 cup (50g) fresh white bread crumbs

2 tbsp freshly chopped parsley

1 tsp freshly chopped thyme

1 egg

salt and freshly ground black pepper

dash of Tabasco

2 x 12oz (350g) pork fillets, trimmed

8 slices prosciutto

a little all-purpose flour, to dust

13oz (375g) ready-to-bake puff pastry

1 egg, beaten with a little milk

For the apple gravy

a pat of butter

1 large onion, finely chopped

½ cup (50g) all-purpose flour

1⅔ cup (400ml) chicken stock

1⅔ cup (400ml) unsweetened apple juice

salt and freshly ground pepper

2 tbsp Worcestershire sauce

a little gravy browning, optional

SERVES 12

5oz (150g) sharp Cheddar cheese, grated

2¼ cups (100g) fresh white bread crumbs

4 tbsp freshly chopped parsley

2 tsp freshly chopped thyme

2 eggs

salt and freshly ground black pepper

generous dash of Tabasco

4 x 12oz (350g) pork fillets, trimmed

16 slices prosciutto

a little all-purpose flour, to dust

26oz (750g) ready-to-bake puff pastry

1 egg, beaten with a little milk

For the apple gravy

a large pat of butter

2 large onions, finely chopped

¾ cup (100g) all-purpose flour

3 cups (750ml) chicken stock

3 cups (750ml) unsweetened apple juice

salt and freshly ground pepper

4 tbsp Worcestershire sauce

a little gravy browning, optional

PREPARE AHEAD AND FREEZE

The pork can be prepared up to the end of step 3 up to 12 hours ahead. Not suitable for freezing. The gravy can be made up to 2 days ahead. Freeze for up to 1 month.

1. Put the cheese, bread crumbs, herbs, and egg into a small bowl. Season with salt and pepper, add the Tabasco, and mix well.

2. Slice each pork fillet in half horizontally, then cover with plastic wrap and bash with a rolling pin until they are slightly thinner. Spread the cheese mixture on top of the halved fillets, then put the fillet halves together again, with the cheese mixture in the middle.

3. Arrange four slices of the prosciutto side by side on a board. With the edges overlapping slightly, they should be about as wide as one of the pork fillets. Sit a fillet across the prosciutto at one end and roll it up so the pork is encased in the prosciutto. Do the same with the other fillet(s).

4. On a lightly floured work surface, roll the pastry into a 13 x 16in (33 x 40cm) rectangle (two rectangles for 12). Slice in half widthwise and brush with egg. Wrap each fillet in pastry and place seam side down on a cookie sheet. Brush with egg and chill for an hour.

5. Preheat the oven to 425°F (220°C). Bake the parcels for 25–30 minutes (45 minutes for 12) or until golden and crisp. Allow to rest for 5–10 minutes before carving.

6. Meanwhile, make the apple gravy. Heat the butter in a saucepan, add the onion, and saute for 2 minutes. Cover with a lid and cook over low heat for 15 minutes or until soft. Sprinkle in the flour, stir in the stock and apple juice, and bring to a boil, stirring. Season and add the Worcestershire sauce and a little gravy browning, if you'd like the gravy to be a rich brown. Push through a sieve and discard the onion.

7. Slice each en croûte in three, then slice each piece in half diagonally and stand them on a dinner plate. Serve hot with the apple gravy. Serve any extra gravy separately.

PAPRIKA PORK FILLET

A variation on one of Mary's best-loved pork recipes. Lucy's family adores it and always puts in a request for it on special occasions. Serve with mashed potatoes and green vegetables.

SERVES 6

2 tbsp olive oil

2lb (900g) pork fillet, trimmed and cut into ½in (1cm) slices

scant 2 tbsp (25g) butter

1 large onion, coarsely chopped

1 level tbsp paprika

2 level tbsp all-purpose flour

1¼ cup (300ml) chicken stock

5 tbsp sherry

1 tsp tomato paste

6oz (175g) button mushrooms, halved

salt and freshly ground black pepper

7oz (200g) full-fat crème fraîche

freshly chopped parsley (optional)

SERVES 12

4 tbsp olive oil

4lb (1.8kg) pork fillet, trimmed and sliced into ½in (1cm) slices

¼ cup (50g) butter

2 large onions, coarsely chopped

2 level tbsp paprika

4 level tbsp all-purpose flour

2½ cups (600ml) chicken stock

⅔ cup (150ml) sherry

2 tsp tomato paste

12oz (350g) button mushrooms, halved

salt and freshly ground black pepper

14oz (400g) full-fat crème fraîche

freshly chopped parsley (optional)

1. Heat the oil in a large nonstick frying pan or casserole dish. Add the pork and brown quickly on all sides. Remove with a slotted spoon and set aside. You may need to do this in batches.

2. Add the butter and onion to the pan, cover with a lid, and leave to soften over low heat for 15 minutes or until tender.

3. Stir in the paprika and flour and saute over high heat for 1 minute. Add the stock and sherry and bring to a boil, stirring constantly, to thicken slightly. Add the tomato paste and mushrooms.

4. Return the pork to the pan, season with salt and pepper, cover with a lid, and simmer over low heat for 15 minutes (25–30 minutes for 12) or until the pork is tender.

5. Stir in the crème fraîche and serve piping hot, with some chopped parsley scattered over if you like.

PREPARE AHEAD AND FREEZE

The dish can be prepared up to the end of step 4 up to 1 day ahead. Freeze at the end of step 4 for up to 1 month.

PASTA AND MEATBALL BAKE WITH TOMATO AND BASIL SAUCE

SERVES 6

Special equipment 3½ pint (2 liter) shallow, wide-bottomed ovenproof dish

For the sauce

1 tbsp olive oil

1 large onion, finely chopped

1 red chile, halved, seeded, and finely chopped

2 garlic cloves, crushed

2 x 14½oz (400g) cans diced tomatoes

2 tbsp tomato paste

salt and freshly ground black pepper

2 tbsp coarsely chopped fresh basil

a dash of superfine sugar (optional)

For the meatballs

1lb (450g) good-quality sausage

½ cup (25g) fresh fine bread crumbs

1 cup (100g) freshly grated Parmesan cheese

2 tbsp finely chopped fresh basil

1¾oz (50g) mozzarella, cut into about 30 cubes

1 tbsp olive oil

8oz (225g) elicoidali pasta

1¾oz (50g) mozzarella, chopped into small pieces

SERVES 12

Special equipment 2 x 3½ pint (2 liter) shallow, wide-bottomed ovenproof dishes or 1 x 7 pint (4 liter) dish

For the sauce

2 tbsp olive oil

2 large onions, finely chopped

2 red chiles, halved, seeded, and finely chopped

4 garlic cloves, crushed

4 x 14½oz (400g) cans diced tomatoes

3 tbsp tomato paste

salt and freshly ground black pepper

3 tbsp coarsely chopped fresh basil

a dash of superfine sugar (optional)

For the meatballs

2lb (900g) good-quality sausage

1 cup (50g) fresh fine bread crumbs

2 cups (200g) freshly grated Parmesan cheese

4 tbsp finely chopped fresh basil

3½oz (100g) mozzarella, cut into about 60 cubes

1 tbsp olive oil

1lb (450g) elicoidali pasta

3½oz (100g) mozzarella, chopped into small pieces

This is a perfect all-in-one dish. You can use rigatoni or penne if you can't get hold of elicoidali. Serve with dressed salad.

1. Preheat the oven to 400°F (200°C). Meanwhile, put the oil for the sauce into a deep saucepan, add the onion, and saute over high heat for a few minutes or until softened slightly but not colored.

2. Add the chile and garlic and saute over high heat for a few minutes. Add the tomatoes and tomato paste, then season with salt and pepper. Bring to a boil, cover with a lid, then lower the heat and simmer for 15 minutes. Add the basil and taste—if it is a little sharp, add a dash of superfine sugar.

3. Meanwhile, make the meatballs. Put the sausage, bread crumbs, half the Parmesan, and basil into a mixing bowl. Mix together with your hands, season with salt and pepper, and shape into 30 balls (60 for 12). Using your finger, make a hole in the middle of each meatball, then push a cube of mozzarella into the center and reshape so the mozzarella is hidden inside.

4. Heat the oil in a large frying pan and fry the meatballs for 4 minutes or until they are golden brown all over and just cooked through. You may need to do this in batches.

5. Meanwhile, cook the pasta in boiling salted water according to the package instructions until just tender. Drain, refresh in cold water, and dry well with paper towel.

6. Stir the pasta into the sauce and season with salt and pepper. Stir in the meatballs, then spoon into the ovenproof dish and sprinkle the remaining Parmesan and the mozzarella on top.

7. Bake for 20–25 minutes (45 minutes for 12) or until golden brown on top and piping hot in the center.

PREPARE AHEAD

You can make the bake up to the end of step 6 up to 8 hours ahead. Not suitable for freezing.

SMOKY SAUSAGE CASSOULET

SERVES 6

3 tbsp olive oil

12 sausages

4 large onions, sliced

2 tsp paprika

1¾oz (50g) chorizo, very finely chopped

2 x 14½oz (400g) cans diced tomatoes

2 tbsp tomato paste

2 tbsp Worcestershire sauce

2 tsp balsamic vinegar

salt and freshly ground black pepper

15oz (400g) can lima beans, drained and rinsed

SERVES 12

5 tbsp olive oil

24 sausages

7 large onions, sliced

4 tsp paprika

3½oz (100g) chorizo, very finely chopped

4 x 14½oz (400g) cans diced tomatoes

4 tbsp tomato paste

4 tbsp Worcestershire sauce

1 tbsp balsamic vinegar

salt and freshly ground black pepper

2 x 15oz (400g) cans lima beans, drained and rinsed

Use your favorite sausages for this smoky casserole. We like Cumberland or pork and leek. This dish is especially popular with the young. If they are not fond of chorizo, replace it with smoked bacon, cut into small pieces. Serve with a green vegetable.

1. Heat 1 tablespoon of the oil in a large nonstick frying pan or casserole dish over high heat, then brown the sausages until golden on all sides. Remove with a slotted spoon and set aside. You may need to do this in batches.

2. Add the remaining oil to the pan and saute the onions for a few minutes or until lightly golden. Add the paprika, chorizo, tomatoes, tomato paste, Worcestershire sauce, and balsamic vinegar and season with salt and pepper.

3. Simmer over a gentle heat for 20–25 minutes or until the onions are nearly soft. Add the lima beans and stir.

4. Arrange the sausages on top, cover with a lid, and cook for 20 minutes (35–40 minutes for 12) or until the sausages are completely cooked.

PREPARE AHEAD

The cassoulet can be made up to the end of step 3 up to 1 day ahead. Alternatively, cook it completely and reheat to serve. Not suitable for freezing.

GLAZED HAM WITH CUMBERLAND SAUCE

SERVES 6–12

3lb (1.35kg) cured ham

½ onion, cut in half

1 small celery stick, cut into three

1 small bay leaf

⅓ cup (50g) light or dark muscovado sugar

2 tbsp red currant jelly

2 tsp coarse mustard

SERVES 12–20

6½lb (3kg) cured ham

1 onion, quartered

1 celery stick, cut into four

1 bay leaf

⅔ cup (100g) light or dark muscovado sugar

4 tbsp red currant jelly

1 tbsp coarse mustard

FOR THE CUMBERLAND SAUCE

This sauce is wonderfully rich and vibrantly colored. To serve 6, use a potato peeler to remove thin strips of peel from an orange. Scrape off any white pith, then cut into needle-thin strips and place in a pan. Cover with water, bring to a boil, and simmer over low heat for 3–4 minutes or until soft. Drain, refresh in cold water, then dry well with paper towel and set aside. Put 1 cup (340g) red currant jelly and ⅓ cup (75ml) Port into a saucepan. Add the juice of the orange to the pan with 1 tsp Dijon mustard and a dash of Worcestershire sauce. Whisk over high heat until the jelly has melted, then boil rapidly for 4–5 minutes or until reduced by half. Season with salt and freshly ground black pepper, add the juice of ½ lemon to taste, then spoon into a serving dish and sprinkle with the orange strips. Serve warm or cold. To serve 12, double all quantities. The sauce can be made up to 1 week ahead. To serve warm, reheat gently in a pan. Not suitable for freezing.

PREPARE AHEAD

The ham can be prepared up to 5 days ahead. To serve warm, it can be boiled up to 5 days ahead and then glazed on the day. Not suitable for freezing.

Hot or cold, ham is irresistible and perfect for any buffet table. It feeds twice the number when cold because it's easier to slice thinly. When you're buying the ham, ask the butcher if it needs soaking to remove any excess saltiness. If you get it from supermarkets, it is usually presoaked, but always check the label. The Cumberland sauce is also very good with cold meats, turkey, and game pie.

1. Weigh the ham and calculate the cooking time based on 20 minutes per 1lb (450g). A 3lb (1.35kg) ham will take 1 hour. A 6½lb (3kg) ham will take 2 hours 10 minutes.

2. Place it skin side down in a large deep saucepan. Add the vegetables, bay leaf, and sugar, then cover with cold water and a lid.

3. Bring to a boil (this takes longer than you may imagine) and, once boiling, start the timing. Simmer very gently until cooked. Check from time to time and top up with boiling water, if needed, to ensure the ham is covered.

4. Once the ham is cooked through, carefully lift it out of the pan and, using a small sharp knife, remove the skin, leaving a very thin layer of fat on the ham. Preheat the oven to 400°F (200°C).

5. Meanwhile, put the red currant jelly and mustard into a bowl and stir until combined. Score the layer of fat on the ham in a lattice pattern with a knife, then spread the mixture over it.

6. Line a large roasting pan with foil and sit the ham in the center with the glaze at the top. Bring the foil up so the flesh is completely covered and only the glaze is exposed—this prevents the ham drying out.

7. Bake for 15–20 minutes or until the glaze has melted and started to caramelize. If serving hot, rest for a good 10 minutes before carving. If serving cold, set aside until needed.

QUICHE LORRAINE

Some classic recipes are unbeatable, but our quiche Lorraine—with added parsley—has the edge, we think. Serve warm with salad.

SERVES 6

Special equipment *8in (20cm) round 2in (5cm) deep loose-bottomed tart pan or quiche dish*

1½ cup (175g) all-purpose flour, plus a little extra to dust

⅓ cup (85g) cold butter, cubed

1 egg

For the filling

a pat of butter

1 large onion, coarsely chopped

8oz (225g) unsmoked bacon, cut into small pieces

1 heaped tbsp freshly chopped flat-leaf parsley

2½oz (75g) sharp Cheddar cheese, grated

3 eggs

7oz (200ml) full-fat crème fraîche

⅔ cup (150ml) heavy cream

salt and freshly ground black pepper

SERVES 12

Special equipment *11in (28cm) round 2in (5cm) deep loose-bottomed tart pan or quiche dish*

1¾ cup (225g) all-purpose flour, plus a little extra to dust

½ cup (115g) cold butter, cubed

1 egg

1–2 tbsp water

For the filling

a pat of butter

2 large onions, coarsely chopped

12oz (350g) unsmoked bacon, cut into small pieces

2 heaped tbsp freshly chopped flat-leaf parsley

6oz (175g) sharp Cheddar cheese, grated

6 eggs

10oz (300ml) full-fat crème fraîche

1¼ cup (300ml) heavy cream

salt and freshly ground black pepper

1. Put the flour and butter into a food processor and process until the mixture resembles bread crumbs. Add the egg (and the water if you're making the larger one) and process again until you have a smooth dough. Dust a work surface with flour and knead the dough lightly. Roll the dough out and use to line the pan (see page 267). Prick the base all over with a fork and chill for 15 minutes.

2. Preheat the oven to 400°F (200°C). Pop a cookie sheet in to get hot. Line the pastry case with parchment paper, fill with pie weights, and bake for 15–20 minutes (see page 311). Remove the pie weights and paper, lower the temperature to 325°F (160°C), and return the pastry case to the oven to dry out for 5–10 minutes. Set aside to cool. Turn the oven up to 375°F (190°C).

3. To make the filling, melt the butter in a frying pan, add the onion and bacon, and saute over high heat for 2 minutes or until starting to crisp. Cover with a lid, lower the heat, and cook slowly for 15–20 minutes or until the onion is tender and the bacon cooked. Spoon into the pastry case and spread out evenly. Scatter with half the parsley and half the cheese.

4. Put the eggs, crème fraîche, and heavy cream into a mixing bowl and whisk by hand until combined. Add the remaining parsley and season with salt and pepper. Pour into the pastry case and sprinkle over the remaining cheese.

5. Bake in the oven for 25 minutes (30–35 minutes for 12) or until golden brown and the egg mixture is just set.

PREPARE AHEAD AND FREEZE

The quiche can be made up to 2 days ahead. Freeze for up to 2 months.

SUMMER FRITTATA

SERVES 6

Special equipment *8in (20cm) round springform pan, greased and base-lined*

12oz (350g) potatoes, cut into 1¼in (3cm) cubes

1 small onion, coarsely chopped

salt and freshly ground black pepper

8 large eggs

1 tsp freshly chopped thyme leaves

3½oz (100g) goat cheese, cut into small cubes

1¾oz (50g) prosciutto or Black Forest ham, cut into thin strips

SERVES 12

Special equipment *2 x 8in (20cm) round springform pans, greased and base-lined*

1lb 9oz (700g) potatoes, cut into 1¼in (3cm) cubes

2 small onions, coarsely chopped

salt and freshly ground black pepper

16 large eggs

2 tsp freshly chopped thyme leaves

7oz (200g) goat cheese, cut into small cubes

3½oz (100g) prosciutto or Black Forest ham, cut into thin strips

A frittata is a baked omelette and this one—cooked in the oven rather than in a frying pan—is ideal for picnics. Black Forest ham is one of the most reasonably priced cured hams. If you can't get hold of it, use Serrano ham or prosciutto. Cut the frittata into wedges and serve warm or cold with a dressed salad and bread.

1. Preheat the oven to 400°F (200°C). Cook the potatoes and onion in boiling salted water for 5–8 minutes or until tender. Drain and refresh in cold water.

2. Crack the eggs into a large mixing bowl, add the thyme, and season with salt and pepper. Whisk by hand until combined. Add the potatoes and onion and stir in the cheese.

3. Pour into the pan and scatter over the strips of ham.

4. Bake for 12–15 minutes (15–20 minutes for 12) or until slightly risen and just firm. To make slicing easier, leave to cool slightly before serving.

PREPARE AHEAD

The frittata can be made up to 8 hours ahead. Not suitable for freezing.

PAPRIKA PORK GOULASH

Served with rice, this Hungarian classic is perfect bowl food. We like it made with pork shoulder, but you could also use pork fillet if you prefer. Reduce the cooking time by half if using fillet of pork.

SERVES 6

2 tbsp olive oil

2lb (900g) boneless pork shoulder, cut into 1½in (4cm) pieces

2 medium onions, sliced

2 garlic cloves, crushed

2 tbsp paprika

3 tbsp tomato paste

1¼ cup (300ml) chicken stock or beef stock

salt and freshly ground black pepper

2 red peppers

1 tbsp balsamic vinegar

1 tsp brown sugar

2–3 tbsp sour cream or crème fraîche (depending on taste)

2 tbsp freshly chopped flat-leaf parsley

SERVES 12

4 tbsp olive oil

4lb (1.8kg) boneless pork shoulder, cut into 1½in (4cm) pieces

3 large onions, sliced

4 garlic cloves, crushed

3 heaped tbsp paprika

5 heaped tbsp tomato paste

2½ cups (600ml) chicken stock or beef stock

salt and freshly ground black pepper

4 red peppers

2 tbsp balsamic vinegar

2 tsp brown sugar

6 tbsp sour cream or crème fraîche

4 tbsp freshly chopped flat-leaf parsley

1. Preheat the oven to 325°F (160°C). Meanwhile, heat the oil in a deep frying pan or casserole dish. Add the pork and brown quickly on all sides. You may need to do this in batches. Remove with a slotted spoon and set aside.

2. Add the onions to the pan and saute for 3 minutes or until starting to soften. Stir in the garlic and paprika and saute for 1 minute. Add the tomato paste and stock and return the meat to the pan. Bring to a boil, season with salt and pepper, cover with a lid, and transfer to the oven for 1¼–1½ hours (2 hours for 12) or until the pork is tender.

3. Meanwhile, blacken the skin of the peppers under the broiler, then pop them into a plastic bag and seal. When cold, peel off the charred skin with your fingers, then pull out the core and seeds, and slice the peppers.

4. Add the peppers, balsamic vinegar, and sugar to the pan and bring to a boil, then check the seasoning. Stir in the sour cream or crème fraîche to taste and serve garnished with the parsley.

PREPARE AHEAD AND FREEZE

You can make the goulash up to 1 day ahead. The flavor will improve, in fact. Freeze without the cream for up to 2 months.

PASTA WITH PANCETTA, FAVA BEANS, AND MASCARPONE

A delicious creamy pasta dish that's also quick to cook—it takes barely 15 minutes once you've prepared the ingredients. You can use bacon instead of pancetta if you prefer. Serve with salad.

SERVES 6

11oz (300g) shell pasta

salt and freshly ground black pepper

5½oz (150g) frozen small fava beans

7oz (200g) haricot verts, trimmed and sliced into three

5oz (140g) pancetta cubes

8oz (250g) full-fat mascarpone cheese

¾ cup (75g) freshly grated Parmesan cheese

juice of 1 small lemon

small bunch of basil, coarsely chopped

SERVES 12

1lb 5oz (600g) shell pasta

salt and freshly ground black pepper

11oz (300g) frozen small fava beans

14oz (400g) haricot verts, trimmed and sliced into three

10oz (280g) pancetta cubes

16oz (500g) full-fat mascarpone cheese

1¾ cup (175g) freshly grated Parmesan cheese

juice of 1 large lemon

large bunch of basil, coarsely chopped

1. Cook the pasta in boiling salted water according to the package instructions. Add the fava beans and haricot verts 5 minutes before the end of cooking.

2. Meanwhile, heat a large frying pan, add the pancetta, and fry until crisp. Stir in the mascarpone and two-thirds of the Parmesan and stir until melted.

3. Drain the pasta and beans, leaving a little of the cooking water in the saucepan. Add the pasta and beans to the frying pan along with 6 tablespoons of the cooking water (10 tablespoons for 12). Add the lemon juice and basil, toss together well, and season with salt and pepper.

4. Sprinkle with the remaining Parmesan and serve immediately.

PREPARE AHEAD

The pasta and beans can be cooked, drained, and refreshed in cold water up to 6 hours ahead. Remember to reserve a little of the cooking water. Not suitable for freezing.

FISH ENTRÉES

*Fish is a favorite for entertaining year round.
A whole fillet of salmon, poached, baked, or en croûte,
is a classic buffet centerpiece, which guests can't fail
to be impressed by. We find that cooking fish with the
skin on helps keep it from drying out.*

DOUBLE SALMON FISH CAKES WITH HORSERADISH SAUCE

So many people love fish cakes, which is why we always invent a new recipe for them for each of our books.

SERVES 6

12oz (350g) cooked salmon, skin and bones removed

3½oz (100g) hot-smoked salmon

1lb (450g) mashed potatoes

3 tbsp mayonnaise

2 tbsp creamed horseradish

2 heaped tbsp freshly snipped chives

2 heaped tbsp freshly chopped parsley

salt and freshly ground black pepper

1 egg, beaten

1 cup (50g) fresh bread crumbs

1 tbsp olive oil

1 lemon, cut into 6 wedges, to garnish

For the horseradish sauce

5oz (150ml) sour cream or full-fat crème fraîche

3 tbsp creamed horseradish

2 tbsp mayonnaise

2 tbsp freshly snipped chives

SERVES 12

1lb 9oz (700g) cooked salmon, skin and bones removed

7oz (200g) hot-smoked salmon

2lb (900g) mashed potatoes

6 tbsp mayonnaise

4 tbsp creamed horseradish

4 heaped tbsp freshly snipped chives

4 heaped tbsp freshly chopped parsley

salt and freshly ground black pepper

1 egg, beaten

2 cups (100g) fresh bread crumbs

2 tbsp olive oil

2 lemons, each cut into 6 wedges, to garnish

For the horseradish sauce

10oz (300ml) sour cream or full-fat crème fraîche

6 tbsp creamed horseradish

4 tbsp mayonnaise

4 tbsp freshly snipped chives

1. Put both kinds of salmon, the mashed potatoes, mayonnaise, horseradish, and herbs into a mixing bowl, season with salt and pepper, and stir well to combine.

2. Divide the mixture into 12 (24 for 12) and shape into fish cakes. They shouldn't be too thick. Brush with beaten egg, coat with bread crumbs, and chill for a minimum of 1 hour.

3. Meanwhile, make the sauce: put all the ingredients into a bowl, season with salt and pepper, and mix together well. Set aside.

4. Heat the oil in a nonstick frying pan and fry the fish cakes for 3–4 minutes on each side or until golden on the outside and hot in the middle. You may need to do this in batches and keep them warm in the oven.

5. Serve the fish cakes hot with a spoonful of the cold sauce and a lemon wedge.

PREPARE AHEAD AND FREEZE

The fish cakes can be made up to the end of step 2 up to 1 day ahead. Alternatively, fry them the day before and reheat. The sauce can be made up to 3 days ahead. Freeze the fish cakes at the end of step 2 for up to 2 months.

SALMON AND CRAYFISH PIE

This recipe is ideal for preparing the day before. Shelled crayfish tails can be bought in all good supermarkets or fishmongers. They come in tubs of brine. Serve the pie with steamed broccoli or salad.

SERVES 6

Special equipment 4 pint (2.4 liter) shallow, wide-bottomed, ovenproof dish

1lb 10oz (750g) Russet potatoes or other starchy potatoes, cut into 2in (5cm) pieces

a pat of butter

⅔ cup (150ml) milk

salt and freshly ground black pepper

For the pie

⅓ cup (75g) butter

1 onion, finely chopped

2 leeks, finely sliced

½ cup (50g) all-purpose flour

2½ cups (600ml) hot milk

juice of ½ lemon

2 tbsp freshly chopped dill

2 tbsp freshly chopped parsley

2 tbsp capers, drained

1lb 2oz (500g) skinned salmon fillet, cut into 2in (5cm) cubes

9oz (250g) cooked crayfish tails in brine, drained

2½oz (75g) Cheddar cheese, grated

lemon wedges, to serve

SERVES 12

Special equipment 2 x 4 pint (2.4 liter) shallow, wide-bottomed, ovenproof dishes or 1 x 7 pint (4 liter) dish

3lb 3oz (1.5kg) Russet potatoes or other starchy potatoes, cut into 2in (5cm) pieces

a large pat of butter

1¼ cup (300ml) milk

salt and freshly ground black pepper

For the pie

¾ cup (175g) butter

2 onions, finely chopped

4 leeks, finely sliced

1 cup (100g) all-purpose flour

4 cups (1.2 liters) hot milk

juice of 1 lemon

4 tbsp freshly chopped dill

4 tbsp freshly chopped parsley

4 tbsp capers, drained

2¼lb (1kg) skinned salmon fillet, cut into 2in (5cm) cubes

1lb 2oz (500g) cooked crayfish tails in brine, drained

6oz (175g) Cheddar cheese, grated

lemon wedges, to serve

1. Preheat the oven to 425°F (220°C). Put the potatoes in a pan of cold salted water, cover with a lid, bring to a boil, and cook for 15 minutes or until tender. Drain, add the butter and milk, season with salt and pepper, and mash until smooth. You may need a little more milk to get the right consistency.

2. Meanwhile, melt the butter for the pie in a large saucepan. Stir in the onion and leeks, cover with a lid, and cook over low heat for 15 minutes or until the onion is soft. Stir in the flour and, over high heat, gradually add the milk, stirring all the time until the sauce is smooth and thick.

3. Remove from the heat, add lemon juice, dill, parsley, capers, salmon, and crayfish, and season with salt and pepper. Spoon into the ovenproof dish and level the top. Cover with the mashed potatoes and fluff up the surface with a fork. Sprinkle over the cheese.

4. Bake for 35 minutes (50 minutes for 12) or until golden brown and piping hot. Serve at once with wedges of lemon.

PREPARE AHEAD

The pie can be made up to the end of step 3 up to 1 day ahead. Not suitable for freezing.

CLASSIC POACHED SALMON WITH HERB SAUCE

We find this the best way to poach salmon, and over the years we have perfected the method so it's foolproof. If you are cooking a very large salmon and it is too big for the fish poacher, cut off the head before poaching. The timing will be the same. If cooking for a very large crowd, buy extra salmon and poach separately.

SERVES 12

Special equipment *fish poacher*

6–6½lb (2.7–3kg) salmon (head on), gutted

small handful of salt

12 black peppercorns

cucumber, sliced into thin ribbons, to garnish

24 cooked North Atlantic shrimp, shelled but heads left on, to garnish

sprigs of parsley or dill, to garnish

For the sauce

2 tbsp fresh dill

2 tbsp fresh chives

2 tbsp fresh mint

2 tbsp fresh flat-leaf parsley

7oz (200ml) full-fat crème fraîche

1 cup (200g) full-fat Greek yogurt

1¼ cup (300ml) good mayonnaise

1 tbsp superfine sugar

juice of 1 lemon

SERVES 20

Special equipment *fish poacher*

11–12lb (5–5.5kg) salmon (head on), gutted

small handful of salt

12 black peppercorns

cucumber, sliced into thin ribbons, to garnish

40 cooked North Atlantic shrimp, shelled but heads left on, to garnish

sprigs of parsley or dill, to garnish

For the sauce

4 tbsp fresh dill

4 tbsp fresh chives

4 tbsp fresh mint

4 tbsp fresh flat-leaf parsley

14oz (400ml) full-fat crème fraîche

2 cups (400g) full-fat Greek yogurt

2½ cups (600ml) good mayonnaise

2 tbsp superfine sugar

juice of 2 lemons

1. Put the salmon in the fish poacher and pour in enough cold water from the tap to cover it completely. Remove the fish.

2. Add the salt and peppercorns to the water, then bring to a full rolling boil. Carefully lower the salmon into the water, bring back to a boil, and boil for 1 minute per pound (2 minutes per kilo) and no more. Do not cover with a lid.

3. Remove from the heat and cover with a tight-fitting lid. Set in a cool place (not the fridge) and leave undisturbed for about 8 hours—the salmon will continue to cook as it cools.

4. Transfer the salmon to a cutting board or work surface and carefully peel off the skin while it is still lukewarm. Using two fish spatulas and taking care not to damage the flesh, turn the fish over and peel the skin from the other side, leaving a little over the end of the tail and the head. Cut off the fins with scissors and cut a neat "V" in the tail.

5. To make the sauce, put the herbs into a food processor and process until chopped. Add the rest of the ingredients and season well with salt and pepper. Spoon into a serving dish (not silver as the sauce will discolor), cover, and chill until required.

6. To serve, arrange the salmon on a platter and decorate with cucumber ribbons and shrimp. Finish with the sprigs of parsley or dill. Serve cold with the lemon and herb sauce.

PREPARE AHEAD

The salmon can be poached up to 1 day ahead, then skinned and wrapped tightly in plastic wrap to keep it moist. Garnish to serve. The herb sauce is better made 1 day ahead but can be made up to 3 days ahead. Not suitable for freezing.

SALMON SALSA VERDE EN CROÛTE

The traditional Italian salsa verde sauce gives an amazing flavor and a wonderful green layer.

SERVES 6

For the salsa verde

3 tbsp flat-leaf parsley

2 tbsp fresh basil leaves

2 tbsp fresh mint leaves

1 garlic clove, halved

3 anchovy fillets

2 tbsp Dijon mustard

1 egg yolk

freshly ground black pepper

2 x 12oz (350g) salmon fillets, skinned and bones removed

13oz (375g) all-butter puff pastry

a little all-purpose flour, to dust

1 egg beaten with 1 tbsp milk

For the dressing

2 large firm but ripe tomatoes

salt

2 scallions, finely chopped

2 tsp superfine sugar

2 tbsp white wine vinegar

4 tbsp olive oil

½ tsp Dijon mustard

1 tbsp freshly chopped parsley

SERVES 12

For the salsa verde

2½oz (75g) flat-leaf parsley

scant 1oz (25g) fresh basil leaves

scant 1oz (25g) fresh mint leaves

2 garlic cloves, halved

6 anchovy fillets

4 tbsp Dijon mustard

1 egg

freshly ground black pepper

2 x 1lb 10oz (750g) salmon fillets, skinned and bones removed

17½oz (500g) all-butter puff pastry

a little all-purpose flour, to dust

1 egg beaten with 1 tbsp milk

For the dressing

4 large firm but ripe tomatoes

salt

3 scallions, finely chopped

1 tbsp superfine sugar

4 tbsp white wine vinegar

8 tbsp olive oil

1 tsp Dijon mustard

2 tbsp freshly chopped parsley

1. To make the salsa verde, put the herbs into a food processor and process. Add the garlic, anchovies, mustard, egg yolk (whole egg for 12), and some pepper and process until smooth.

2. Arrange one fillet on a cutting board and spread the salsa verde over in an even layer. Sit the other fillet on top to look like a whole fish.

3. Cut two-thirds of the pastry from the block (freeze the rest for later) and place on a piece of lightly floured parchment paper. Roll it out so it is long enough and wide enough to enclose the fillets completely. Sit the fillets in the center and brush the pastry with the beaten egg (reserving some for later). Fold the ends of the pastry over the fillet and bring the sides up to meet at the top. Pinch the edges together with your fingers. Chill for a minimum of 30 minutes.

4. Preheat the oven to 475°F (240°C) [425°F (220°C) for 12] and put a cookie sheet in to get hot. Brush the en croûte with beaten egg, then coarsely grate the frozen pastry and sprinkle on top.

5. Transfer the en croûte (still on the parchment paper) to the hot cookie sheet and bake for 25–30 minutes (35–40 minutes for 12) or until the pastry is golden and cooked at the top and bottom. Allow to rest at room temperature for about 15 minutes.

6. Meanwhile, make the dressing. Plunge the tomatoes into boiling salted water for 1 minute, then remove with a slotted spoon, plunge into cold water, and drain. Remove the skins, then seed, dice, and put into a bowl. Add the remaining ingredients, season with salt and pepper, and stir to combine.

7. Carve the en croûte into thick slices and serve the dressing alongside in a bowl.

PREPARE AHEAD AND FREEZE

The en croûte can be made up to the end of step 3 up to 12 hours ahead. The dressing can be made up to 2 days ahead. Freeze the uncooked en croûte for up to 2 months.

SALMON FILLET WITH TARRAGON BUTTER SAUCE

The tomato in the vegetable stock gives the sauce a wonderful color. To allow the flavors to infuse, prepare it the day before. You can cook individual salmon fillets if you like, but we prefer doing it this way, as the fish doesn't dry out. Serve with new potatoes and fresh green vegetables or salad.

SERVES 6

1 onion, finely chopped

1 carrot, finely chopped

1 celery stick, finely chopped

1 large tomato, cut in half

1½ cup (360ml) water

1 heaped tbsp freshly chopped tarragon (stalks reserved)

a little olive oil, to grease

salt and freshly ground black pepper

1lb 10oz–2lb (750–900g) side of salmon fillet in one piece, skin on

⅔ cup (150g) cold butter (straight from the fridge), cut into cubes

SERVES 12

2 onions, finely chopped

2 carrots, finely chopped

2 celery sticks, finely chopped

2 large tomatoes, cut in half

3 cups (750ml) water

2 heaped tbsp freshly chopped tarragon (stalks reserved)

a little olive oil, to grease

salt and freshly ground black pepper

4lb (1.8kg) side of salmon or 2 x 1lb 10oz–2lb (750–900g) sides of salmon

1⅓ cup (300g) cold butter (straight from the fridge), cut into cubes

1. Put the onion, carrot, celery, tomato, and water into a saucepan. Add the reserved tarragon stalks and bring to a boil. Cover with a lid and simmer over low heat for 10 minutes. Set aside for a minimum of 1 hour (ideally overnight) for the flavors to infuse.

2. Preheat the oven to 350°F (180°C). Line a cookie sheet with foil, oil it lightly, and sprinkle with salt and pepper.

3. Lay the salmon skin side down on a board. Using a sharp knife, divide it into equal serving portions, cutting through the flesh until the knife touches the skin, but not cutting through it. Lay skin side up on the foil and bake for 20 minutes (25–30 minutes for 12) or until matte pink and just done. The precise timing will depend on the thickness.

4. To make the sauce, strain the vegetable stock into a saucepan, then boil rapidly until it reduces by half. Put the butter into a heatproof bowl, pour over the boiling stock, and process with a handheld blender or in a food processor until smooth.

5. Peel the skin from the fish and discard (if it doesn't peel easily, it isn't quite cooked, so pop it back into the oven for a few minutes). Transfer the fish portions to a platter or plates. Add the tarragon to the hot sauce, pour over the fish, and serve.

PREPARE AHEAD

The sauce can be made up to 2 days ahead. Add the tarragon while reheating. The salmon can be cooked the day before and served cold. Not suitable for freezing.

SALMON AND ASPARAGUS WITH A BASIL SAUCE

SERVES 6

6 x 5½oz (150g) center-cut salmon fillets, skinned

salt and freshly ground black pepper

12 asparagus spears

1¼ cup (300ml) heavy cream

juice of ½ lemon

4 tbsp pesto

SERVES 12

12 x 5½oz (150g) center-cut salmon fillets, skinned

salt and freshly ground black pepper

24 asparagus spears

2½ cups (600ml) heavy cream

juice of 1 lemon

8 tbsp pesto

Salmon fillets, cooked simply and slowly, are complemented by a rich sauce of asparagus, cream, and pesto. Don't be tempted to pile the fillets on top of each other to cook them—bake in a single layer in separate roasting pans. Serve with baby new potatoes.

1. Preheat the oven to 275°F (140°C). Line a roasting pan with a large piece of foil and arrange the salmon fillets on top in a single layer. Season with salt and pepper, then scrunch the sides of the foil at the top so the fillets are enclosed.

2. Cook in the oven for 50 minutes (1 hour for 12) or until the salmon is matte pink and just done. Don't let it overcook or it will become dry.

3. Meanwhile, trim the woody ends from the asparagus spears and discard, then cut off 2in (5cm) from each tip and put to one side. Finely shred the stalks, cutting them diagonally into thin slices.

4. Bring a pan of salted water to a boil, add the asparagus tips and shredded stalks, then bring back to a boil and cook for 3 minutes. Drain, separate the tips from the stalks, and keep warm.

5. Heat the cream, lemon juice, and pesto in a pan until hot. Add the cooked shredded stalks and season with salt and pepper.

6. To serve, arrange the hot salmon fillets on a serving plate. Pour over the sauce and garnish each fillet with two asparagus tips. Serve any leftover sauce separately.

PREPARE AHEAD

The asparagus can be cooked up to 8 hours ahead, then drained, refreshed in cold water, and drained again. Plunge the asparagus tips into boiling water for 30 seconds to warm through. The sauce can be made up 8 hours ahead. Not suitable for freezing.

TROUT FILLETS WITH ROASTED VEGETABLES AND HOT LEMON DRESSING

A wonderful all-in-one dish—new potatoes, onions, and zucchini with lightly cooked trout fillets and a fresh sauce.

SERVES 6

1lb 10oz (750g) baby new potatoes, halved lengthwise

3 medium onions, peeled and cut into 8 wedges

salt and freshly ground black pepper

3 tbsp olive oil

4 small zucchini, thinly sliced

6 trout fillets, skin on

For the sauce

6 tbsp freshly chopped parsley

finely grated zest and juice of 1 large lemon

⅓ cup (85g) butter, melted

SERVES 12

3lb 3oz (1.5kg) baby new potatoes, halved lengthwise

5 large onions, peeled and cut into 8 wedges

salt and freshly ground black pepper

6 tbsp olive oil

8 small zucchini, thinly sliced

12 trout fillets, skin on

For the sauce

large bunch of parsley, chopped

finely grated zest and juice of 2 large lemons

¾ cup (175g) butter, melted

1. Preheat the oven to 400°F (200°C). Put the potatoes and onions in a pan, cover with cold salted water, bring to a boil, and cook for 10 minutes or until just tender.

2. Drain, toss in half the oil, season with pepper, and arrange in a single layer in a large roasting tin or ovenproof dish (two pans or dishes for 12). Roast for 20 minutes (30 minutes for 12) or until the potatoes and onions are just tender.

3. Toss the zucchini in a bowl with the remaining oil and season with salt and pepper.

4. Season the flesh side of the trout with salt and pepper. Stir the contents of the roasting pan, then lay the trout skin side up in a single layer on top of them. Scatter the zucchini around the fish. Return to the oven and cook for 12–15 minutes (20–30 minutes for 12) or until the fish is tender.

5. Meanwhile, make the sauce: mix the parsley, lemon zest, and lemon juice together in a bowl. Stir in the butter and season with salt and pepper.

6. Peel the skin from the fish and discard. If the skin doesn't come off easily, the trout is not quite cooked, so pop it back into the oven for a few minutes. Transfer the fish to a serving plate with the vegetables, then spoon some of the hot sauce over the top. Serve the rest of the sauce separately.

PREPARE AHEAD

The vegetables can be cooked up to the end of step 2 up to 6 hours ahead. The sauce can be made up to 1 day ahead. Not suitable for freezing.

HOT BAKED TROUT WITH TOMATO AND BASIL SALSA

An impressive centerpiece for a dinner party or buffet table. Cooking the trout with the skin on gives it a fresher flavor and keeps it moist.

SERVES 6

a little olive oil

salt and freshly ground black pepper

1lb 10oz (750g) trout fillet, skin on

For the salsa

1lb 2oz (500g) tomatoes

½ cucumber

3 scallions, finely chopped

3 tbsp freshly shredded basil

3 tbsp olive oil

1 tsp superfine sugar

a good dash of Tabasco

1 tbsp lemon juice

SERVES 12

a little olive oil

salt and freshly ground black pepper

3lb (1.35kg) trout fillet or 2 x 1lb 10oz (750g) trout fillets, skin on

For the salsa

2¼lb (1kg) tomatoes

1 cucumber

6 scallions, finely chopped

6 tbsp freshly shredded basil

6 tbsp olive oil

2 tsp superfine sugar

a good dash of Tabasco

2 tbsp lemon juice

1. Preheat the oven to 400°F (200°C). Line a cookie sheet with foil, then brush it with a little olive oil and sprinkle with salt and pepper.

2. Lay the trout skin side down on a board. Using a sharp knife, cut it into equal serving portions, taking care not to cut through the skin. Lay it skin side up on the cookie sheet and bake for 15–20 minutes (30 minutes for 12) or until just cooked.

3. Meanwhile, make the salsa. To skin the tomatoes, place them in boiling water for 20 seconds or until the skin splits, then remove. When cool enough to handle, carefully peel the skin from the tomato with a paring knife. Slice in half, remove the seeds, and dice the flesh. Peel the cucumber with a vegetable peeler, then slice in half lengthwise. Discard the seeds and dice the flesh the size of the tomatoes.

4. Mix the tomatoes, cucumber, scallions, and half the basil in a bowl. Whisk the oil, sugar, Tabasco, lemon juice, and some salt and pepper in a separate bowl, then pour over the vegetables and stir to combine.

5. Peel the skin from the trout and discard (if it does not peel off easily, it is not quite cooked, so pop it back in the oven for a few minutes). Arrange on a serving platter.

6. Spoon the salsa down the center of the fish and sprinkle with the remaining basil. If you have any salsa left over, serve it in a separate bowl. Serve the trout hot or warm with the cold salsa.

PREPARE AHEAD

The salsa can be made up to 8 hours ahead. Not suitable for freezing.

LOCH FYNE HADDOCK BAKE

Named after the area of Scotland famous for its fish and seafood, this pie is quick to make. It's unusual in that the potatoes are in the bake and not mashed on top. Make sure you buy undyed smoked haddock— the dyed fillets are bright yellow and very unnatural-looking. Serve with peas or salad.

SERVES 6

Special equipment *3½ pint (2 liter) shallow, wide-bottomed, ovenproof dish*

12oz (350g) Russet potatoes or other starchy potatoes, peeled and cut into ¾in (2cm) cubes

salt and freshly ground black pepper

1lb 2oz (500g) baby spinach

1 tbsp olive oil

9oz (250g) small button mushrooms, sliced in half

pat of butter, to grease

3 eggs, hardboiled, peeled, and sliced into quarters

1lb 2oz (500g) undyed smoked haddock, skinned and cut into 2in (5cm) pieces

1¼ cup (300ml) heavy cream

2 tsp coarse mustard

2½oz (75g) sharp Cheddar cheese, grated

SERVES 12

Special equipment *2 x 3½ pint (2 liter) shallow, wide-bottomed, ovenproof dishes or 1 x 7 pint (4 liter) dish*

1lb 10oz (750g) Russet potatoes or other starchy potatoes, peeled and cut into ¾in (2cm) cubes

salt and freshly ground black pepper

2¼lb (1kg) baby spinach

2 tbsp olive oil

1lb 2oz (500g) small button mushrooms, sliced in half

pat of butter, to grease

6 eggs, hardboiled, peeled, and sliced into quarters

2¼lb (1kg) undyed smoked haddock, skinned and cut into 2in (5cm) pieces

2½ cups (600ml) heavy cream

4 tsp coarse mustard

6oz (175g) sharp Cheddar cheese, grated

1. Preheat the oven to 400°F (200°C). Meanwhile, put the potatoes into a pan of cold, salted water, cover with a lid, bring to a boil, and cook for 10–15 minutes or until just cooked. Drain well and set aside.

2. Heat a large frying pan, add the spinach, and cook for a few minutes or until just wilted but still holding its shape. Drain well in a colander, squeezing to remove excess liquid, then set aside. You may need to do this in batches.

3. Heat the oil in the frying pan, add the mushrooms, and saute for 3 minutes or until just cooked.

4. Grease the ovenproof dish(es) with the butter, then arrange the potatoes, spinach, and mushrooms in the base. Sprinkle over the eggs and haddock and season with salt and pepper.

5. Mix the cream and mustard in a bowl with some salt and pepper, then pour over the fish mixture, and sprinkle with the cheese.

6. Bake for 20–25 minutes (30–35 minutes for two dishes for 12 or 40–45 minutes for one dish for 12) or until golden on top and cooked through.

PREPARE AHEAD

The bake can be made up to the end of step 4 up to 8 hours ahead. Not suitable for freezing.

TUNA SALADE NIÇOISE

SERVES 6

3½oz (100g) haricot verts, trimmed

salt and freshly ground black pepper

6 eggs

3 small Baby Gem lettuces

6 tomatoes, quartered

8oz (225g) baby new potatoes, cooked and halved lengthwise

14oz (400g) canned tuna in oil, drained

12 canned anchovy fillets, drained

3½oz (100g) pitted black olives, halved lengthwise

1 red onion, finely sliced

For the dressing

4 tbsp good olive oil

2 tbsp coarse mustard

2 tbsp white wine vinegar

2 tsp superfine sugar

juice of 1 lemon

SERVES 12

7oz (200g) haricot verts, trimmed

salt and freshly ground black pepper

12 eggs

6 small Baby Gem lettuces

12 tomatoes, quartered

1lb (450g) baby new potatoes, cooked and halved lengthwise

28oz (800g) canned tuna in oil, drained

24 canned anchovy fillets, drained

8oz (225g) pitted black olives, halved lengthwise

2 red onions, finely sliced

For the dressing

8 tbsp good olive oil

4 tbsp coarse mustard

4 tbsp white wine vinegar

4 tsp superfine sugar

juice of 2 lemons

This is a great entrée for a picnic, but it's also good as a side dish—in which case it will feed more. Serve with fresh crusty bread.

1. Cook the haricot verts in boiling salted water for 4 minutes or until just tender. Drain, refresh in cold water, and set aside.

2. Put the eggs into a saucepan, cover with water, and bring to a boil. Boil for 7 minutes, then drain and cover again with cold water. Peel and slice into quarters.

3. Cut each lettuce into six wedges. Place in a serving bowl with the haricot verts, eggs, tomatoes, potatoes, tuna, anchovies, olives, and onion and mix together. Season with salt and pepper.

4. Mix the ingredients for the dressing in a bowl, pour over the salad, toss gently, and serve.

PREPARE AHEAD

The salad can be prepared up to the end of step 3 up to 6 hours ahead. Dress just before serving. Not suitable for freezing.

MACARONI TUNA BAKE

Guests of all ages will enjoy this tasty tuna, macaroni, and cheese bake—Mary's grandchildren love it! And it really is extremely economical to make. Serve with crusty bread or dressed salad.

SERVES 6

Special equipment *2¾ pint (1.5 liter) shallow, wide-bottomed, ovenproof dish*

12oz (350g) macaroni

salt and freshly ground black pepper

5½oz (150g) frozen peas

⅓ cup (75g) butter

⅔ cup (75g) all-purpose flour

3¾ cups (900ml) hot milk

1 tbsp Dijon mustard

juice of ½ lemon

2½oz (75g) sharp Cheddar cheese, grated

2½oz (75g) Parmesan cheese, freshly grated

13oz (370g) canned tuna in water, drained

4 large tomatoes, cut in quarters, seeded, and coarsely chopped

SERVES 12

Special equipment *4 pint (2.4 liter) shallow, wide-bottomed, ovenproof dish*

1lb 10oz (750g) macaroni

salt and freshly ground black pepper

10oz (300g) frozen peas

¾ cup (175g) butter

1½ cup (175g) all-purpose flour

6 cups (1.7 liters) hot milk

2 tbsp Dijon mustard

juice of 1 lemon

6oz (175g) sharp Cheddar cheese, grated

6oz (175g) Parmesan cheese, freshly grated

26oz (740g) canned tuna in water, drained

8 large tomatoes, cut in quarters, seeded, and coarsely chopped

1. Preheat the oven to 400°F (200°C). Cook the macaroni in boiling salted water according to the package instructions. Add the peas 3 minutes before the end of cooking. Drain, refresh in cold water, and set aside.

2. Melt the butter in a saucepan, add the flour, and stir over the heat for 1 minute. Add the hot milk slowly, whisking until the sauce is smooth and thick.

3. Add the mustard, lemon juice, and two-thirds of each cheese. Add the pasta and peas and lots of salt and pepper. Stir in the tuna and mix together. Spoon into the ovenproof dish, sprinkle over the tomatoes, and sprinkle over the remaining cheese.

4. Bake for 20–25 minutes (30–35 minutes for 12) or until lightly golden and crispy.

PREPARE AHEAD

The dish can be made up to the end of step 3 up to 1 day ahead. Not suitable for freezing.

SEAFOOD LINGUINE

SERVES 6

8oz (225g) dried linguine

salt and freshly ground black pepper

5½oz (150g) (shelled weight) raw tiger shrimp

small pat of butter

5½oz (150g) raw squid, sliced

5½oz (150g) raw sea scallops, sliced in half horizontally

1 large shallot, finely chopped

1 cup (250ml) dry white wine

¾ cup (200ml) heavy cream

juice of 1 large lemon

small bunch of dill, chopped

SERVES 12

1lb (450g) dried linguine

salt and freshly ground black pepper

11oz (300g) (shelled weight) raw tiger shrimp

large pat of butter

11oz (300g) raw squid, sliced

11oz (300g) raw sea scallops, sliced in half horizontally

2 large shallots, finely chopped

2½ cups (600ml) dry white wine

2 cups (450ml) heavy cream

juice of 2 large lemons

large bunch of dill, chopped

We usually buy ready-peeled shrimp for this, but if you can only find them with their shells on, buy a few extra and do it yourself—they're very easy to shell. Serve with dressed salad.

1. Cook the linguine in boiling salted water according to the package instructions. Drain well.

2. Shell the shrimp if needed. Start by pulling off the head of the shrimp, then peel off the shell and legs with your fingers. If the shrimp are large, you may wish to slice along the back and remove the dark intestinal vein.

3. Heat the butter in a large frying pan, add the shrimp, squid, and scallops, and fry for 3–4 minutes or until the shrimp have turned pink and the squid and scallops are just cooked. Remove with a slotted spoon and set aside.

4. Add the shallot and wine to the pan, bring to a boil, and allow to bubble over high heat until the wine has reduced by half. Add the cream and return to a boil.

5. Add the cooked seafood and toss together. Season with salt and pepper, stir in the pasta, lemon juice, and dill, heat through thoroughly, and serve.

SPAGHETTI WITH KING PRAWNS AND TOMATOES

SERVES 6

11oz (300g) spaghetti

salt and freshly ground black pepper

4 tbsp olive oil

1 cup (50g) very fine fresh brown bread crumbs

finely grated zest and juice of 1 lemon

1 large shallot, finely chopped

4 garlic cloves, crushed

1 red chile, halved, seeded, and finely diced

11oz (300g) shelled cooked king prawns

6 large ripe tomatoes, halved, seeded, and coarsely chopped

1 large bunch of flat-leaf parsley, chopped

freshly grated Parmesan cheese, to serve

SERVES 12

1lb 5oz (600g) spaghetti

salt and freshly ground black pepper

7 tbsp olive oil

2 cups (100g) very fine fresh brown bread crumbs

finely grated zest and juice of 2 lemons

2 large shallots, finely chopped

8 garlic cloves, crushed

2 red chiles, halved, seeded, and finely diced

1lb 5oz (600g) shelled cooked king prawns

12 large ripe tomatoes, halved, seeded, and coarsely chopped

1 very large bunch of flat-leaf parsley, chopped

freshly grated Parmesan cheese, to serve

This full-flavored tomato and garlic sauce with a hint of chile is excellent with spaghetti. The bread crumbs give a lovely crispy texture—make sure they are very fine. Serve with dressed salad.

1. Cook the spaghetti in boiling salted water according to the package instructions. Drain well.

2. Heat 1 tablespoon of the oil (1½ tablespoons for 12) in a deep frying pan, add the bread crumbs and lemon zest, and saute for 1 minute or until crispy. Remove with a slotted spoon and set aside.

3. Add the remaining oil to the pan, stir in the shallot, garlic, and chile and saute for 3–4 minutes or until starting to soften.

4. Stir in the prawns and tomatoes, then add the parsley and lemon juice.

5. Stir in the spaghetti, season with salt and pepper, and heat through thoroughly. Stir in the bread crumbs and serve immediately with the Parmesan.

TIGER SHRIMP BALTI

Tiger shrimp are expensive, but this is a great dish for a special occasion. To cut costs, you could use a mixture of tiger shrimp and other cooked seafood, such as mussels and squid. Serve with Pilaf Rice (page 247) or, as part of a buffet, with Vegetable Korma (page 245) and Aromatic Beef Curry (page 152).

SERVES 6

3 tbsp sunflower oil

2 large onions, finely chopped

2 red peppers, halved, seeded, and coarsely chopped

2½in (6cm) piece fresh ginger, peeled and finely grated

3 red chiles, halved, seeded, and coarsely chopped

1 tsp turmeric

2 tsp ground coriander

2 tsp garam masala

1 tsp black mustard seeds

2 x 14½oz (400g) cans diced tomatoes

1¼ cup (300ml) water

4 tbsp tomato paste

4 tsp Indian lime pickle

juice of 1 lime

2 tbsp honey

salt and freshly ground black pepper

2¼lb (1kg) raw shelled tiger shrimp

1 heaped tbsp freshly chopped cilantro, to garnish

SERVES 12

5 tbsp sunflower oil

4 large onions, finely chopped

4 red peppers, halved, seeded, and coarsely chopped

7in (18cm) piece fresh ginger, peeled and finely grated

6 red chiles, halved, seeded, and coarsely chopped

2 tsp turmeric

4 tsp ground coriander

4 tsp garam masala

2 tsp black mustard seeds

4 x 14½oz (400g) cans diced tomatoes

2½ cups (600ml) water

8 tbsp tomato paste

2 heaped tbsp Indian lime pickle

juice of 2 limes

4 tbsp honey

salt and freshly ground black pepper

4½lb (2kg) raw shelled tiger shrimp

2 heaped tbsp freshly chopped cilantro, to garnish

1. Heat the oil in a large frying pan or saucepan, add the onions, peppers, ginger, and chiles and saute over high heat for 2 minutes or until starting to soften.

2. Cover with a lid, then reduce the heat and cook for 10 minutes or until the onions and peppers are nearly soft. Add the spices and stir over high heat to coat the vegetables.

3. Add the tomatoes, water, tomato paste, Indian lime pickle, lime juice, and honey. Bring to a boil and simmer for 10 minutes (15 minutes for 12). Season with salt and pepper, add the shrimp, and cook for 5 minutes (5–10 minutes for 12) or until they turn pink and are cooked through. Garnish with the cilantro and serve immediately.

PREPARE AHEAD AND FREEZE

The sauce can be made up to 1 day ahead. Reheat to serve, adding the shrimp at the end. Freeze the sauce without the shrimp for up to 1 month.

VEGETARIAN ENTRÉES AND VEGETABLE SIDES

Whether at a special dinner, on a buffet table, or at a dinner party, vegetarians will love these entrées. We've also included a selection of potato, rice, and vegetable side dishes which are popular served alongside many of the entrées in this book.

MUSHROOM AND SPINACH CANNELLONI

To make the cannelloni easier to serve, arrange them in neat rows in a rectangular dish. Serve with dressed salad and crusty bread.

SERVES 6

Special equipment *3 pint (1.7 liter) wide-bottomed ovenproof dish*

1 tbsp olive oil

1lb 2oz (500g) mixed mushrooms, such as shiitake, chestnut, and button, coarsely chopped

3 garlic cloves, crushed

8oz (225g) baby spinach, coarsely chopped

salt and freshly ground black pepper

14½oz (400g) can tomatoes, drained and juice discarded

2 tbsp pesto

2½oz (75g) freshly grated Parmesan cheese or vegan alternative

12–14 cannelloni tubes

For the sauce

⅓ cup (75g) butter

⅔ cup (75g) all-purpose flour

3¾ cups (900ml) hot milk

½ cup (100ml) heavy cream

2 heaped tbsp pesto

SERVES 12

Special equipment *2 x 3 pint (1.7 liter) wide-bottomed ovenproof dishes or 1 x 5¼ pint (3 liter) dish*

2 tbsp olive oil

2¼lb (1kg) mixed mushrooms, such as shiitake, chestnut, and button, coarsely chopped

6 garlic cloves, crushed

1lb 2oz (500g) baby spinach, coarsely chopped

salt and freshly ground black pepper

2 x 14½oz (400g) cans tomatoes, drained and juice discarded

4 tbsp pesto

6oz (175g) freshly grated Parmesan cheese or vegan alternative

24–28 cannelloni tubes

For the sauce

¾ cup (175g) butter

1½ cup (175g) all-purpose flour

6 cups (1.7 liters) hot milk

1 cup (200ml) heavy cream

4 heaped tbsp pesto

1. Heat the oil in a frying pan, add the mushrooms, and saute over high heat for 2 minutes or until just cooked. Add the garlic and spinach and toss together until the spinach is just wilted. Season with salt and pepper and set aside to cool.

2. To make the sauce, melt the butter in a saucepan, whisk in the flour, and cook for 1 minute. Whisking all the time, gradually blend in the hot milk and the cream and bring to a boil. Season with salt and pepper, remove from the heat, and stir in the pesto.

3. Put the tomatoes into a mixing bowl, add the cooled mushroom mixture, the pesto, and one-third of the cheese. Stir to combine.

4. Preheat the oven to 400°F (200°C). Meanwhile, fill the cannelloni tubes with the mushroom and spinach filling, dividing it equally among them.

5. Spoon one-third of the sauce into the base of the ovenproof dish and arrange the filled cannelloni on top in neat rows. Pour the remaining sauce over the top and sprinkle with the rest of the cheese.

6. Bake for 30–35 minutes (45 minutes for 12) or until golden brown and bubbling.

PREPARE AHEAD

The cannelloni can be made up to the end of step 5 up to 8 hours ahead. Not suitable for freezing.

MUSHROOMS AND SPINACH EN CROÛTE

Whether it's on a buffet table or at a dinner party, vegetarians will love this. Be sure to buy all-butter puff pastry, as it has a much better flavor than other kinds and is a little softer to handle. If you are serving large numbers, make multiple en croûtes—never make an en croûte larger than for 12, as the pastry may split. Serve with dressed salad leaves.

SERVES 6

1 tbsp olive oil

½ large onion, chopped

1 garlic clove, crushed

5½oz (150g) button mushrooms, sliced

8oz (225g) baby spinach

½ cup (125g) ricotta

2½oz (75g) Gruyère, grated

1 egg yolk

dash of Tabasco

salt and freshly ground black pepper

a little all-purpose flour, to dust

½ x 17oz (500g) package ready-to-bake all-butter puff pastry (freeze the other half for another occasion)

1 egg beaten with 1 tbsp milk

SERVES 12

1 tbsp olive oil

1 large onion, chopped

2 garlic cloves, crushed

9oz (250g) button mushrooms, sliced

1lb (450g) baby spinach

¾ cup (200g) ricotta

6oz (175g) Gruyère, grated

1 egg

dash of Tabasco

salt and freshly ground black pepper

a little all-purpose flour, to dust

13oz (375g) ready-to-bake all-butter puff pastry

1 egg beaten with 1 tbsp milk

1. Preheat the oven to 425°F (220°C) and put a cookie sheet in the oven to get hot. Meanwhile, heat the oil in a nonstick frying pan, add the onion, and saute for 2 minutes. Lower the heat, cover with a lid, and cook for 15 minutes or until soft.

2. Add the garlic, mushrooms, and spinach and cook over high heat for 3 minutes or until the spinach has wilted and the mushrooms have softened. Set aside to cool.

3. Meanwhile, put the ricotta, Gruyère, egg yolk (whole egg for 12), and Tabasco into a bowl, season with salt and pepper, and mix until combined. Stir into the cold spinach mixture.

4. Lay the sheet of pastry on a lightly floured work surface and roll it out into a 11 x 13in (28 x 33cm) rectangle (13 x 15in/ 33 x 38cm rectangle for 12).

5. Pile the spinach mixture into the middle, leaving a 1½in (4cm) gap around the edge. Brush the pastry with the egg mixture, then fold the ends over the filling and bring the sides up so they meet at the top. Crimp the ends together to seal, then brush the pastry with egg.

6. Transfer to the hot cookie sheet and bake for 30 minutes (45 minutes for 12) or until golden all over. Leave to rest at room temperature for 5 minutes, then slice and serve hot.

PREPARE AHEAD

The en croûte can be made up to the end of step 5 up to 8 hours ahead. Not suitable for freezing.

MUSHROOM STROGANOFF

SERVES 6

scant 2 tbsp (25g) butter

1 large onion, thinly sliced

2 garlic cloves, crushed

1 tbsp paprika

1 tbsp all-purpose flour

½ cup (100ml) Marsala

7oz (200g) full-fat crème fraîche

1lb 7oz (650g) mixed mushrooms, such as oyster, button, and portobello, sliced

salt and freshly ground black pepper

juice of ½ lemon

1 tsp tomato paste

1 tsp superfine sugar

1¾oz (50g) cornichons, chopped

SERVES 12

¼ cup (50g) butter

2 large onions, thinly sliced

4 garlic cloves, crushed

2 tbsp paprika

2 tbsp all-purpose flour

¾ cup (200ml) Marsala

14oz (400g) full-fat crème fraîche

2½lb (1.1kg) mixed mushrooms, such as oyster, button, and portobello, sliced

salt and freshly ground black pepper

juice of 1 lemon

2 tsp tomato paste

2 tsp superfine sugar

3½oz (100g) cornichons, chopped

This is great for vegetarians and meat-eaters alike—the mass of tasty mushrooms is delicious and the cornichons (baby gherkins) give a lovely texture and sweetness. If you don't have any Marsala, you can use another fortified wine such as medium sherry or Port. Serve with rice.

1. Melt the butter in a deep frying pan, add the onion, and saute for 1 minute. Lower the heat, cover with a lid, and simmer for 15 minutes or until soft.

2. Stir in the garlic, then sprinkle in the paprika and flour and mix well. Add the Marsala and crème fraîche and stir until thickened slightly.

3. Add the mushrooms, season with salt and pepper, and simmer over low heat for 4 minutes (5–10 minutes for 12) or until the mushrooms are just cooked.

4. Stir in the lemon juice, tomato paste, and sugar and check the seasoning. Sprinkle over the cornichons and serve hot.

PREPARE AHEAD

This is best made and served immediately. Not suitable for freezing.

BUTTERNUT SQUASH LASAGNA

A lasagna with wow factor. The star ingredient is butternut squash. Prepare the dish the day before if you can, so the lasagna noodles have time to soften in the sauce. Serve with salad and crusty bread.

SERVES 6

Special equipment *4 pint (2.4 liter) shallow, wide-bottomed, ovenproof dish*

1 tbsp olive oil

8oz (225g) butternut squash (peeled weight), chopped into small cubes (see page 223)

1 red pepper, halved, seeded, and diced

1 onion, coarsely chopped

2 garlic cloves, crushed

8oz (225g) buttoned mushrooms, sliced

2 x 14½oz (400g) cans diced tomatoes

1 tbsp tomato paste

2 tsp sugar

1 tbsp freshly chopped thyme

salt and freshly ground black pepper

3½oz (100g) spinach, chopped

6–8 lasagna noodles

For the white sauce

⅓ cup (75g) butter

⅔ cup (75g) all-purpose flour

3¾ cups (900ml) hot milk

2 tsp Dijon mustard

3½oz (100g) Gruyère cheese, grated

9oz (250g) mozzarella, chopped into small cubes

SERVES 12

Special equipment *2 x 4 pint (2.4 liter) shallow, wide-bottomed, ovenproof dishes or 1 x 7 pint (4 liter) shallow, wide-bottomed, ovenproof dish*

2 tbsp olive oil

1lb 2oz (500g) butternut squash (peeled weight), chopped into small cubes (see page 223)

2 red peppers, halved, seeded, and diced

2 onions, coarsely chopped

4 garlic cloves, crushed

1lb 2oz (500g) button mushrooms, sliced

4 x 14½oz (400g) cans diced tomatoes

2 tbsp tomato paste

1 heaped tbsp sugar

2 tbsp freshly chopped thyme

salt and freshly ground black pepper

7oz (200g) spinach, chopped

12–16 lasagna noodles

For the white sauce

¾ cup (175g) butter

1½ cup (175g) all-purpose flour

6 cups (1.7 liters) hot milk

1 heaped tbsp Dijon mustard

7oz (200g) Gruyère cheese, grated

1lb 2oz (500g) mozzarella, chopped into small cubes

1. Heat the oil in a large deep frying pan. Add the squash, pepper, onion, and garlic and saute over medium heat for 4–5 minutes or until the onion is starting to soften. Add the mushrooms, tomatoes, tomato paste, sugar, thyme, and some salt and pepper. Cover with a lid and simmer over low heat for 20–30 minutes (35–40 minutes for 12) or until the vegetables are tender. Add the spinach and toss together until just wilted.

2. Meanwhile, make the white sauce. Melt the butter in a saucepan, add the flour, and stir over the heat for 1 minute. Slowly whisk in the hot milk until the sauce is smooth and thick. Season with salt and pepper, then stir in the mustard and half the Gruyère.

3. Spoon one-third of the tomato sauce over the base of the ovenproof dish, then spoon one-third of the white sauce on top. Arrange a single layer of lasagna noodles over the white sauce and sprinkle over half the mozzarella. Spoon half the remaining tomato sauce on top, followed by half the remaining white sauce. Arrange another layer of lasagna noodles on top and sprinkle over the remaining mozzarella. Spread the rest of the tomato sauce on top, followed by the rest of the white sauce, then sprinkle with the remaining Gruyère.

4. Transfer to the fridge for at least 6 hours or overnight so the lasagna noodles start to soften.

5. To serve, preheat the oven to 400°F (200°C), then bake the lasagna for 45 minutes (1–1¼ hours for 12) or until golden brown and bubbling around the edges.

PREPARE AHEAD AND FREEZE

The lasagna can be made up to the end of step 3 up to 2 days ahead. Freeze for up to 2 months.

SPICY ROASTED SQUASH AND FETA SALAD

SERVES 6

1 large butternut squash

1 red onion, thinly sliced

2 tbsp olive oil

salt and freshly ground black pepper

1 tsp ground cumin

3½oz (100g) feta cheese, crumbled

2 tbsp freshly chopped parsley

For the dressing

1 tbsp white wine vinegar

2 tbsp olive oil

1 tsp honey

½ garlic clove, crushed

SERVES 12

2 large butternut squash

2 red onions, thinly sliced

4 tbsp olive oil

salt and freshly ground black pepper

1 tbsp ground cumin

7oz (200g) feta cheese, crumbled

4 tbsp freshly chopped parsley

For the dressing

2 tbsp white wine vinegar

4 tbsp olive oil

2 tsp honey

1 garlic clove, crushed

This unusual salad goes well with grilled meat or fish. To allow the flavors to infuse, make it up to six hours ahead.

1. Preheat the oven to 425°F (220°C). Cut the squash in half lengthwise, then scoop out the seeds and fibers with a spoon and discard. Then cut into sections and use a peeler to remove the skin. You may need a knife for larger squash. Cut the flesh into thin half-moon slices.

2. Sprinkle the squash and onion over the base of a roasting pan. Drizzle with the oil, season with salt and pepper, and toss to combine.

3. Roast for 25–30 minutes (30–35 minutes for 12) or until pale golden and just tender. Transfer to a mixing bowl with a slotted spoon, sprinkle over the cumin, and toss together. Set aside to cool.

4. When completely cool, stir in the feta and parsley. Put the ingredients for the dressing into a clean jam jar, tighten the lid, and shake well.

5. Pour the dressing over the salad and mix together. Transfer to a salad bowl and chill for up to 6 hours before serving.

PREPARE AHEAD

The salad can be made up to 6 hours ahead.
Not suitable for freezing.

BUTTERNUT SQUASH WITH SPINACH AND MUSHROOMS

Half a small butternut squash per person is ideal at lunchtime or even as a main meal. Choose the smallest squash you can find—somewhere between 14oz–1½lb (400–700g) works well. Serve with dressed salad and bread.

SERVES 6

3 x 14oz (400g) butternut squash, halved lengthwise through the stalk and seeds and fibers discarded

2 tbsp olive oil

⅔ cup (150ml) water

salt and freshly ground black pepper

2 leeks, sliced

9oz (250g) button mushrooms, quartered

3½oz (100g) baby spinach

½ cup (100ml) heavy cream

2½oz (75g) Parmesan cheese or vegan alternative, freshly grated

freshly chopped parsley, to garnish

SERVES 12

6 x 14oz (400g) butternut squash, halved lengthwise through the stalk and seeds and fibers discarded

4 tbsp olive oil

⅔ cup (150ml) water

salt and freshly ground black pepper

4 leeks, sliced

1lb 2oz (500g) button mushrooms, quartered

7oz (200g) baby spinach

1 cup (200ml) heavy cream

6oz (175g) Parmesan cheese or vegan alternative, freshly grated

freshly chopped parsley, to garnish

1. Preheat the oven to 400°F (200°C). Put the squash cut side up in a large roasting pan (two pans for 12) and drizzle over the oil. Pour the water around them, season with salt and pepper, and roast in the oven for 45 minutes (1 hour for 12) or until the flesh is soft. Set aside and allow to cool slightly.

2. Meanwhile, put the leeks into a frying pan and cook slowly over medium heat for 10 minutes or until soft. Add the mushrooms and spinach and stir together over high heat for 10 minutes or until the spinach has wilted and the mushrooms are nearly cooked.

3. Remove the pan from the heat and stir in the cream, some salt and pepper, and half the cheese. Scoop out some of the cooked squash, leaving a ¾in (2cm) border inside each squash case, and stir into the spinach mixture. Spoon the mixture into the squash cases and sprinkle over the remaining cheese.

4. Bake for 20–25 minutes (55 minutes for 12) or until golden on top and heated through. Garnish with a sprinkle of parsley and serve.

PREPARE AHEAD

The squash can be prepared up to the end of step 3 up to 1 day ahead. Not suitable for freezing.

RED PEPPER AND EGGPLANT SALAD WITH BASIL DRESSING

SERVES 6

2 red peppers, cut in half and seeded

2 large eggplants, sliced in half lengthwise and cut into ¼in (5mm) slices

2 tbsp olive oil

salt and freshly ground black pepper

3½oz (100g) baby spinach

For the dressing

2 tbsp olive oil

2 tbsp balsamic vinegar

1½ tbsp fresh basil pesto

1¾oz (50g) pine nuts, toasted

1 tbsp chopped basil

SERVES 12

4 red peppers, cut in half and seeded

4 large eggplants, sliced in half lengthwise and cut into ¼in (5mm) slices

4 tbsp olive oil

salt and freshly ground black pepper

7oz (200g) baby spinach

For the dressing

4 tbsp olive oil

4 tbsp balsamic vinegar

3 tbsp fresh basil pesto

2½oz (75g) pine nuts, toasted

2 tbsp chopped basil

Buy the freshest peppers and eggplants you can find, with smooth skins, not wrinkly. Toast the pine nuts in a dry frying pan until golden. Watch them carefully, as they burn quickly. Serve with crusty bread.

1. Preheat the oven to 425°F (220°C). Arrange the pepper halves cut side down in a single layer on one end of a cookie sheet, then lay the eggplant slices in a single layer at the other. (For 12, lay the peppers on one sheet and the eggplants on another sheet.) Drizzle over the oil and season with salt and pepper.

2. Roast for 25–30 minutes or until the peppers are chargrilled and the eggplants tender and golden. Put the hot peppers into a plastic bag, seal tightly, and set aside until cold. This allows them to sweat, which makes it easier to remove the skins.

3. Peel the skin from the peppers and discard. Cut the flesh into thin slices and transfer to a serving bowl. Add the eggplants and spinach and season with salt and pepper.

4. To make the dressing, put the oil, balsamic vinegar, and pesto into a jam jar, seal with a lid, and shake vigorously.

5. To serve, pour the dressing over the salad, toss well, then sprinkle with the pine nuts and the basil. For the flavors to infuse, it is best to do this about an hour before serving.

PREPARE AHEAD

The salad can be made up to the end of step 2 up to 12 hours ahead. The dressing can be made up to 4 days ahead. Not suitable for freezing.

GLOBE ARTICHOKE
AND PUY LENTIL SALAD

Packed with lentils, herbs, and vegetables, this side salad makes a fantastic accompaniment to grilled meats and fish.

SERVES 6

7oz (200g) dried Puy lentils

2 large celery sticks, finely diced

½ small red onion, finely diced

3½ oz (100g) grilled artichoke hearts in oil, drained and sliced into large pieces

2 tbsp freshly chopped flat-leaf parsley

2 tbsp freshly chopped mint

8oz (225g) cherry tomatoes, quartered

For the dressing

2 tbsp white wine vinegar

4 tbsp olive oil

1 garlic clove, crushed

2 tbsp sun-dried tomato paste

1 tbsp balsamic vinegar

salt and freshly ground black pepper

SERVES 12

11oz (400g) dried Puy lentils

4 large celery sticks, finely diced

1 small red onion, finely diced

7oz (195g) grilled artichoke hearts in oil, drained and sliced into large pieces

small bunch of flat-leaf parsley, chopped

small bunch of mint, chopped

1lb 2oz (500g) cherry tomatoes, quartered

For the dressing

4 tbsp white wine vinegar

8 tbsp olive oil

2 garlic cloves, crushed

4 tbsp sun-dried tomato paste

2 tbsp balsamic vinegar

salt and freshly ground black pepper

1. Cook the lentils in boiling water for 15–20 minutes or until tender. Don't add salt or they might not soften. Drain and refresh in cold water.

2. Put the celery, onion, artichokes, herbs, and tomatoes into a large mixing bowl and stir in the lentils.

3. Mix the ingredients for the dressing in a small bowl and pour over the salad.

4. Season well with salt and pepper and chill in the fridge for 1 hour before serving.

PREPARE AHEAD

The salad can be made up to the end of step 2 up to 12 hours ahead. Add the dressing up to 3 hours ahead. Not suitable for freezing.

GRILLED VEGETABLE AND HALLOUMI SKEWERS

SERVES 6

Special equipment 6 metal or wooden skewers (soak wooden skewers in water for 12 hours beforehand to prevent them burning)

2 medium red onions

salt

1 yellow pepper, halved, seeded, and cut into 12 large pieces

1 red pepper, halved, seeded, and cut into 12 large pieces

9oz (250g) halloumi cheese, cut into 18 cubes

12 small cherry tomatoes

2 tbsp olive oil, for frying

For the marinade

2 tbsp soy sauce

1 tbsp honey

1 red chile, halved, seeded, and finely chopped

1 large garlic clove, crushed

SERVES 12

Special equipment 12 metal or wooden skewers (soak wooden skewers in water for 12 hours beforehand to prevent them burning)

4 medium red onions

salt

2 yellow peppers, halved, seeded, and cut into 24 large pieces

2 red peppers, halved, seeded, and cut into 24 large pieces

1lb (450g) halloumi cheese, cut into 36 cubes

24 small cherry tomatoes

4 tbsp olive oil, for frying

For the marinade

4 tbsp soy sauce

2 tbsp honey

2 red chiles, halved, seeded, and finely chopped

2 large garlic cloves, crushed

The sweet marinade for these kebabs helps the vegetables and cheese turn golden. Serve with salad and baked potatoes.

1. Slice each onion into six wedges, leaving the root end intact on each wedge so that the layers stay together during cooking. Bring a pan of salted water to a boil, add the onion wedges, the pieces of yellow pepper and the pieces of red pepper, and bring back to a boil. Boil for 5 minutes, then drain, refresh in cold water, and drain again.

2. In the order of your choice, thread two onion wedges, two pieces of yellow pepper, two pieces of red pepper, three cubes of cheese, and two tomatoes on to each skewer. Place in a shallow dish.

3. Put all the ingredients for the marinade into a small bowl and mix well. Pour over the kebabs and leave to marinate for at least 1 hour and up to 8 hours.

4. Heat the oil in a large frying pan or griddle pan, add the kebabs, and fry for 2–3 minutes on each side or until grilled and brown and the cheese is just soft. You may need to do this in batches. Alternatively, cook under the broiler or on a grill. Serve hot on the skewers.

PREPARE AHEAD

The kebabs can be made up to the end of step 2 up to 1 day ahead. They can be marinated for up to 8 hours. Not suitable for freezing.

EGGPLANT BAKED WITH FETA AND CHICKPEAS

SERVES 6

3 medium eggplants, sliced in half lengthwise

2 tbsp olive oil

salt and freshly ground black pepper

1 large onion, coarsely chopped

2 garlic cloves, crushed

14½oz (400g) can diced tomatoes

14½oz (400g) can chickpeas, drained and rinsed

2 tbsp sun-dried tomato paste

1¾oz (50g) pitted black or green olives, sliced in half

small bunch of fresh mint, chopped

3½oz (100g) feta cheese, crumbled

SERVES 12

6 medium eggplants, sliced in half lengthwise

4 tbsp olive oil

salt and freshly ground black pepper

2 large onions, coarsely chopped

4 garlic cloves, crushed

2 x 14½oz (400g) cans diced tomatoes

2 x 14½oz (400g) cans chickpeas, drained and rinsed

4 tbsp sun-dried tomato paste

3½oz (100g) pitted black or green olives, sliced in half

large bunch of fresh mint, chopped

7oz (200g) feta cheese, crumbled

This is a winning recipe for vegetarians and perfect for a summer lunch with a green salad and crusty bread.

1. Preheat the oven to 400°F (200°C). Put the eggplants cut side up in a roasting pan. Drizzle over half the oil, season with salt and pepper, and bake for 25 minutes (40 minutes for 12) or until the flesh is tender. Remove from the oven and leave to cool.

2. Heat the remaining oil in a frying pan. Add the onion and garlic and saute for 10 minutes or until soft. Add the tomatoes, chickpeas, tomato paste, and olives, and simmer for 5 minutes.

3. Meanwhile, scoop out a little of the flesh from the eggplant halves, leaving a ½in (1cm) border inside the eggplant cases. Add the flesh to the chickpea mixture and mix together. Add the mint and half the feta and season with salt and pepper. Spoon the mixture into the eggplant cases and top with the remaining feta.

4. Bake in the oven for 20 minutes (35 minutes for 12) or until the feta is tinged brown and the eggplants are hot.

PREPARE AHEAD

The dish can be assembled up to the end of step 3 up to 1 day ahead. Not suitable for freezing.

MINI EGGPLANT AND ARUGULA PIZZAS

These look so lovely and the soft-yolked quail eggs on top are an extra treat. You'll find pizza crust in most supermarkets. The uncooked dough comes in packages ready for you to add your choice of topping. Marinated and grilled eggplants are available from the deli counter of the supermarket.

SERVES 6

Special equipment *4in (10cm) biscuit cutter*

2 x 5½oz (150g) pizza crusts

½ cup (100ml) tomato puree

2 tbsp sun-dried tomato paste

salt and freshly ground black pepper

7oz (200g) marinated and grilled eggplants, drained (oil reserved) and sliced

3½oz (100g) Gruyère cheese, grated

6 quail eggs

1¾oz (50g) arugula

SERVES 12

Special equipment *4in (10cm) biscuit cutter*

4 x 5½oz (150g) pizza crusts

1 cup (200ml) tomato puree

4 tbsp sun-dried tomato paste

salt and freshly ground black pepper

14oz (400g) marinated and grilled eggplants, drained (oil reserved) and sliced

8oz (225g) Gruyère cheese, grated

12 quail eggs

3½oz (100g) arugula

1. Preheat the oven to 400°F (200°C). Using a 4in (10cm) biscuit cutter, cut three circles from each pizza crust and arrange on a cookie sheet (two cookie sheets for 12).

2. Put the tomato puree into a bowl, add the sun-dried tomato paste, season with salt and pepper, and mix well. Spread over the base of each dough circle.

3. Arrange the eggplant slices over the pizzas and sprinkle with the cheese. Using the back of a tablespoon, make a well in the center of each pizza, ready for the egg to sit in.

4. Bake for 8 minutes (10 minutes for 12) or until the pizzas are very hot, then carefully crack an egg into the well in each one, keeping the yolk intact. Return to the oven for 3 minutes or until the pizza is lightly golden, the egg white completely cooked, and the yolk just set.

5. Transfer to serving plates, arrange some arugula on top of each pizza, and drizzle with a little of the reserved eggplant oil. Serve at once.

PREPARE AHEAD AND FREEZE

The pizzas can be made up to the end of step 3 up to 8 hours ahead. Freeze at the end of step 3 for up to 2 months.

VEGETARIAN ENTRÉES AND VEGETABLE SIDES 235

GOAT CHEESE, THYME, AND ONION MARMALADE GALETTE

A fantastic vegetarian lunch. Make two separate galettes for 12. If you don't have time to roast the peppers and make the onion marmalade, use store-bought, but buy the best you can. Allow to cool slightly before slicing and serving warm with salad.

SERVES 6

2 red peppers, halved and seeded

1 tbsp olive oil

salt and freshly ground black pepper

a little all-purpose flour, to dust

11oz (320g) ready-to-bake puff pastry

10oz (300g) soft goat cheese

1 tbsp fresh thyme leaves, plus a few sprigs to garnish

1 egg, beaten

For the onion marmalade

2 tbsp olive oil

3 large onions, sliced

1 tbsp superfine sugar

1 tbsp balsamic vinegar

SERVES 12

4 red peppers, halved and seeded

2 tbsp olive oil

salt and freshly ground black pepper

a little all-purpose flour, to dust

22oz (640g) ready-to-bake puff pastry

20oz (600g) soft goat cheese

2 tbsp fresh thyme leaves, plus a few sprigs to garnish

1 egg, beaten

For the onion marmalade

3 tbsp olive oil

6 large onions, sliced

2 tbsp superfine sugar

2 tbsp balsamic vinegar

1. Preheat the oven to 400°F (200°C). Arrange the peppers cut side down on a cookie sheet, drizzle over the oil, and season with salt and pepper. Roast for 25–30 minutes or until blackened. Transfer to a plastic bag, seal, and set aside.

2. Meanwhile, make the onion marmalade. Heat the oil in a nonstick frying pan over high heat, add the onions, and saute for 3 minutes or until starting to soften. Sprinkle in the sugar and balsamic vinegar and season with salt and pepper. Cover with a lid, lower the heat, and cook for 20–30 minutes or until the onions are soft. Set aside to cool.

3. Pop a cookie sheet in the oven to get hot (two sheets for 12). Lightly flour a piece of parchment paper (two pieces for 12) and roll the pastry out into a 9 x 13in (23 x 33cm) rectangle (two rectangles for 12). Prick the base with a fork, leaving a border of 2in (5cm). Spread the cheese inside the border, sprinkle over the thyme, and spoon the onion marmalade on top. Peel the peppers, cut into strips, and sprinkle over the top. Brush the border with beaten egg.

4. Transfer the parchment paper and galette(s) to the cookie sheet and bake for 20–25 minutes (30–35 minutes for 12) or until the pastry is golden. Garnish with thyme sprigs.

PREPARE AHEAD

The galette can be made up to the end of step 3 up to 8 hours ahead. Not suitable for freezing.

PENNE ALLA PARMIGIANA

This is a budget recipe. A sort of upscale macaroni and cheese—perfect for a crowd of hungry teenagers—and one they could very easily cook for themselves. Serve with dressed salad.

SERVES 6

Special equipment
2¾ pint (1.5 liter) shallow, ovenproof dish

12oz (350g) penne

salt and freshly ground black pepper

¼ cup (50g) butter

½ cup (50g) all-purpose flour

4 cups (1.2 liters) hot milk

1 tbsp Dijon mustard

3½oz (100g) sharp Cheddar cheese, grated

3½oz (100g) Parmesan cheese or vegan alternative, freshly grated

6 tomatoes

SERVES 12

Special equipment
4 pint (2.4 liter) shallow, ovenproof dish

1lb 5oz (600g) penne

salt and freshly ground black pepper

½ cup (100g) butter

1 cup (100g) all-purpose flour

6 cups (1.7 liters) hot milk

2 tbsp Dijon mustard

6oz (175g) sharp Cheddar cheese, grated

6oz (175g) Parmesan cheese or vegan alternative, freshly grated

8 large tomatoes

1. Preheat the oven to 400°F (200°C). Cook the penne in boiling salted water according to the package instructions. Drain and refresh in cold water.

2. Melt the butter in a large saucepan, add the flour, and stir over the heat for 1 minute. Gradually add the hot milk, whisking all the time, until the sauce is smooth and thick.

3. Add the mustard and two-thirds of the Cheddar and Parmesan, then add the penne and some salt and pepper.

4. Spoon into the ovenproof dish. To prepare the tomatoes, halve them, loosen the seeds with a teaspoon, then gently squeeze them out into a bowl. Place the seeded tomatoes cut side down on a board and chop. Arrange the chopped tomatoes on top of the pasta, and sprinkle over the remaining cheese.

5. Bake for 20–25 minutes (35–40 minutes for 12) or until lightly golden and crispy.

PREPARE AHEAD

The dish can be made up to the end of step 4 up to 1 day ahead. Not suitable for freezing.

PENNE WITH ASPARAGUS AND DOLCELATTE

Penne is one of our favorite kinds of pasta because sauces cling really well to the quill shape. But you can use spaghetti if you prefer. Serve with dressed salad.

SERVES 6

12oz (350g) asparagus spears

12oz (350g) penne

salt and freshly ground black pepper

1 tbsp olive oil

9oz (250g) small portobello mushrooms, sliced

1 garlic clove, crushed

⅔ cup (150ml) heavy cream

3½oz (100g) dolcelatte cheese, cut into small cubes

small bunch of basil, chopped

SERVES 12

1lb 5oz (600g) asparagus spears

1lb 5oz (600g) penne

salt and freshly ground black pepper

2 tbsp olive oil

1lb 2oz (500g) small portobello mushrooms, sliced

2 garlic cloves, crushed

1¼ cup (300ml) heavy cream

8oz (225g) dolcelatte cheese, cut into small cubes

large bunch of basil, chopped

1. Cut off the tips of the asparagus about 2in (5cm) from the top and set aside. Cut the rest of the spears into small slices.

2. Cook the penne in boiling salted water according to the package instructions. Add the sliced asparagus 5 minutes before the end of cooking. Add the asparagus tips 3 minutes before the end of cooking. Drain and refresh in cold water.

3. Heat the oil in a large frying pan, add the mushrooms and garlic, and saute for 2 minutes. Add the cream and cheese, season with salt and pepper, and stir well.

4. Add the pasta and asparagus to the pan, bring to a boil, and reheat until piping hot. Stir in half the basil and transfer to a serving bowl.

5. Garnish with the remaining basil and serve at once.

PREPARE AHEAD

The penne and asparagus can be cooked up to the end of step 2 up to 6 hours ahead and kept in a colander covered with plastic wrap. Not suitable for freezing.

ROASTED VEGETABLE RISOTTO

Risottos are popular with everyone, and this version, full of flavor and bright healthy vegetables, is great for vegetarians. Serve hot with fresh salad leaves.

SERVES 6

8oz (225g) butternut squash, peeled and cut into ¾in (2cm) cubes

1 onion, coarsely chopped

1 small eggplant, cut into ½in (1cm) cubes

1 small red pepper, halved, seeded, and cut into ½in (1cm) cubes

3 tbsp olive oil

salt and freshly ground black pepper

2 tsp freshly chopped thyme leaves

11oz (300g) risotto rice

8oz (225g) button mushrooms, sliced

4 cups (1.2 liters) hot vegetable stock

1¾oz (50g) Parmesan cheese or vegan alternative, made into small shavings with a vegetable peeler

2 tbsp freshly snipped chives

SERVES 12

1lb (450g) butternut squash, peeled and cut into ¾in (2cm) cubes

2 onions, coarsely chopped

2 small eggplants, cut into ½in (1cm) cubes

2 small red peppers, halved, seeded, and cut ½in into (1cm) cubes

6 tbsp olive oil

salt and freshly ground black pepper

1 heaped tbsp freshly chopped thyme leaves

1lb 5oz (600g) risotto rice

1lb (450g) button mushrooms, sliced

8 cups (2.4 liters) hot vegetable stock

3½oz (100g) Parmesan cheese or vegan alternative, made into small shavings with a vegetable peeler

4 tbsp freshly snipped chives

1. Preheat the oven to 400°F (200°C). Put the squash, onion, eggplant, and pepper into a large roasting pan (two pans for 12) in a single layer.

2. Pour over one-third of the oil and toss well with your hands. Season with salt and pepper, then sprinkle over the thyme.

3. Roast for 30 minutes (35 minutes for 12) or until tender and golden.

4. Heat the remaining oil in a deep saucepan over high heat, add the rice, and stir to coat. Stir in the mushrooms, then gradually add the stock, a ladleful at a time. Stir continuously and only add more when it's been absorbed.

5. When all the stock has been absorbed and the rice is cooked, stir in the roasted vegetables and half the cheese. Transfer to a serving dish and sprinkle with the remaining cheese and the chives.

PREPARE AHEAD

The vegetables can be roasted up to 8 hours ahead. Not suitable for freezing.

VEGETABLE KORMA

SERVES 6

3½oz (100g) haricot verts, sliced into three

salt and freshly ground black pepper

2 tbsp olive oil

1 large onion, coarsely chopped

¾in (2cm) piece fresh ginger, peeled and grated

1 tsp cardamom seeds, crushed

1½ tbsp ground cumin

1½ tbsp ground coriander

1½ tbsp garam masala

1lb (450g) potatoes, peeled and chopped into ⅜in (1½cm) cubes

12oz (350g) carrots, peeled and chopped into ⅜in (1½cm) cubes

12oz (350g) cauliflower, cut into even-sized florets

13½oz (400g) can coconut milk

2 cups (450ml) vegetable stock

3½oz (100g) ground almonds

juice of 1 lemon

2 tbsp mango chutney

SERVES 12

6oz (175g) haricot verts, sliced into three

salt and freshly ground black pepper

3 tbsp olive oil

2 large onions, coarsely chopped

2in (5cm) piece fresh ginger, peeled and grated

2 tsp cardamom seeds, crushed

3 tbsp ground cumin

3 tbsp ground coriander

3 tbsp garam masala

2lb (900g) potatoes, peeled and chopped into ⅜in (1½cm) cubes

1lb 9oz (700g) carrots, peeled and chopped into ⅜in (1½cm) cubes

1lb 9oz (700g) cauliflower, cut into even-sized florets

2 x 13½oz (400g) cans coconut milk

4 cups (900ml) vegetable stock

8oz (225g) ground almonds

juice of 2 lemons

4 tbsp mango chutney

We always try to keep the number of ingredients to a minimum, but by nature a curry has many—it's the blend of spices that give it flavor. Sorry! Serve with naan and Pilaf Rice (pages 246–247).

1. Cook the haricot verts in boiling salted water for 4 minutes or until just cooked. Drain, refresh in cold water, and set aside.

2. Heat the oil in a deep frying pan or casserole dish, add the onion, and saute over high heat for 2 minutes.

3. Add the ginger and spices, stir to coat the onions, and saute for 1 minute. Add all the vegetables except the haricot verts, then stir in the coconut milk and stock. Season well with salt and pepper and bring to a boil.

4. Cover with a lid and simmer over low heat for 25–35 minutes (45 minutes for 12) or until the vegetables are tender.

5. Stir in the ground almonds (they will thicken the sauce), then add the reserved haricot verts, the lemon juice, and chutney. Check the seasoning and serve.

PREPARE AHEAD

The korma can be made up to the end of step 4 up to 12 hours ahead. Not suitable for freezing.

GARLIC AND CILANTRO NAAN

True naan are tricky to make, so these are a bit of a cheat—but a really delicious one! Serve them with any of the curries on pages 121, 152, 210, and 245.

SERVES 6

3 large or 6 small plain naan

scant 2 tbsp (25g) butter, at room temperature

2 garlic cloves, crushed

3 tbsp freshly chopped cilantro

salt and freshly ground black pepper

SERVES 12

6 large or 12 small plain naan

¼ cup (50g) butter, at room temperature

4 garlic cloves, crushed

6 tbsp freshly chopped cilantro

salt and freshly ground black pepper

1. Preheat the oven to 400°F (200°C). Arrange the naan on a cookie sheet without overlapping them.

2. Put the butter, garlic, and cilantro into a bowl and mix until combined. Season with salt and pepper and mix again.

3. Spread evenly over the naan so the whole of each bread is covered.

4. Bake for 5–8 minutes (8 minutes for 12) or until the butter has melted and the bread is crisp.

PREPARE AHEAD AND FREEZE

The naan can be prepared up to the end of step 3 up to 12 hours ahead. Freeze for up to 3 months.

PILAF RICE

Pilaf (sometimes called pilaff or pilau) rice is a dish that originates from the near East. It's the perfect accompaniment to any of the curries on pages 121, 152, 210, and 245.

SERVES 6

8oz (225g) basmati rice

salt and freshly ground black pepper

¼ cup (50g) butter

1 onion, coarsely chopped

4 garlic cloves, crushed

1 red chile, halved, seeded, and finely chopped

8oz (225g) button mushrooms, sliced

1 tsp paprika

juice of 1 lemon

⅓ cup (50g) golden raisins

¼ cup (25g) flaked almonds

3½oz (100g) cooked petits pois

SERVES 12

1lb (450g) basmati rice

salt and freshly ground black pepper

⅓ cup (75g) butter

2 onions, coarsely chopped

6 garlic cloves, crushed

2 red chiles, halved, seeded, and finely chopped

12oz (350g) button mushrooms, sliced

2 tsp paprika

juice of 2 small lemons

⅔ cup (100g) golden raisins

½ cup (50g) flaked almonds

8oz (225g) cooked petits pois

1. Cook the rice in boiling salted water according to the package instructions. Drain, refresh in cold water, and set aside.

2. Meanwhile, melt the butter in a large saucepan, add the onion, garlic, and chile and saute for 2 minutes. Lower the heat, cover with a lid, and simmer for 20 minutes or until the onion is soft.

3. Add the mushrooms, turn up the heat, and saute for 3 minutes or until soft. Sprinkle in the paprika, lemon juice, golden raisins, almonds, and petits pois and saute for a few minutes, stirring. Add the rice and stir until it is piping hot. Season with salt and pepper and serve.

PREPARE AHEAD

The pilaf can be cooked up to 12 hours ahead. To reheat, transfer to a buttered, wide-bottomed, ovenproof dish, cover with buttered foil, and place in an oven preheated to 400°F (200°C) for 15 minutes (25 minutes for 12) or until piping hot. Not suitable for freezing.

THAI GREEN RICE

This brightly colored side dish is full of flavor. It is the perfect accompaniment to our Thai Beef with Lime and Chile on page 138.

SERVES 6

24 asparagus spears

3½oz (100g) baby corn

salt

8oz (225g) frozen petits pois

3½oz (100g) easy cook long-grain rice

4 scallions, finely sliced

2 tbsp soy sauce

2 tbsp sweet chili dipping sauce

a little olive oil, to fry

SERVES 12

48 asparagus spears

7oz (200g) baby corn

salt

1lb (450g) frozen petits pois

7oz (200g) easy cook long-grain rice

8 scallions, finely sliced

4 tbsp soy sauce

4 tbsp sweet chili dipping sauce

a little olive oil, to fry

1. Trim the tough ends from the asparagus spears diagonally and discard, then cut the stalks into diagonal slices and set the tips to one side. Cut the corn into 3–4 diagonal slices, depending on their size.

2. Cook the asparagus stalks and corn in boiling salted water for 4 minutes or until just cooked, then drain and refresh in cold water.

3. Cook the asparagus tips and petits pois in boiling salted water for 2 minutes, then drain and refresh in cold water. Cook the rice in boiling salted water according to the package instructions, then drain.

4. Mix the rice with the cooked vegetables and scallions, then toss with the soy sauce and sweet chili dipping sauce.

5. Heat the olive oil in a wok or nonstick frying pan and stir-fry the rice for 5 minutes or until hot. Serve at once—if kept hot, the vegetables will lose their vibrant green color.

PREPARE AHEAD

The rice can be prepared up to the end of step 4 up to 12 hours ahead. Not suitable for freezing.

ROAST POTATOES WITH CHILE AND THYME

SERVES 6

6 large potatoes, peeled and cut into 2in (5cm) cubes

salt and freshly ground black pepper

3 tbsp olive oil

juice of ½ lemon

2 tsp freshly chopped thyme leaves

2–3 garlic cloves, crushed

1–2 red chiles (depending on preference), seeded and finely chopped

2 tbsp freshly chopped parsley

SERVES 12

12 large potatoes, peeled and cut into 2in (5cm) cubes

salt and freshly ground black pepper

6 tbsp olive oil

juice of 1 lemon

4 tsp freshly chopped thyme leaves

5 fat garlic cloves, crushed

2–3 red chiles (depending on preference), seeded and finely chopped

4 tbsp freshly chopped parsley

These are great all year round, but are especially good in the summer months when the flavor of fresh thyme is at its best. Serve with grilled meats or fish.

1. Preheat the oven to 425°F (220°C). Meanwhile, cook the potatoes in boiling salted water for 4–5 minutes or until they are just soft around the edges but still have a little bite in the middle. Drain and transfer to a bowl.

2. Put all the other ingredients except the parsley into a small bowl and lightly whisk to combine. Pour over the potatoes and season with salt and pepper.

3. Pop a roasting pan (two pans for 12) into the oven for a few minutes to get very hot. Spoon the potatoes into the pan(s) and roast for 25–30 minutes (45–55 minutes for 12) or until golden and crispy. Garnish with the parsley and serve.

PREPARE AHEAD

The potatoes can be prepared up to the end of step 2 up to 1 day ahead. Not suitable for freezing.

HEAVENLY POTATO GRATIN

This is one Mary's favorite ways of serving potatoes. She's been cooking them for over 25 years and they're as popular now as they were then. Make sure you use an ovenproof dish that's wide and shallow, so you get more of the delicious crispy golden crust. Serve with chops, grilled meat, or fish.

SERVES 6

Special equipment *1¾ pint (1 liter) shallow, ovenproof dish, buttered*

2lb (900g) even-sized waxy potatoes, such as Désirée

1 tsp salt

freshly ground black pepper

¼ cup (45g) butter, melted, plus a little extra to grease

⅔ cup (150ml) light cream

SERVES 12

Special equipment *3½ pint (2 liter) shallow, ovenproof dish, buttered*

4lb (1.8kg) even-sized waxy potatoes, such as Désirée

1 tsp salt

freshly ground black pepper

⅓ cup (75g) butter, melted, plus a little extra to grease

1¼ cup (300ml) light cream

1. Preheat the oven to 400°F (220°C). Rub off any excess dirt from the potatoes and put them unpeeled into a pan. Cover with cold water and add the salt. Cover with a lid, bring to a boil, and cook until just tender. The timing will depend on their size, but they should be soft around the edges and slightly firm in the center. Set aside for them to cool completely.

2. Peel the skins from the potatoes and discard. Using a coarse grater, grate the potatoes into the buttered dish, seasoning between the layers with salt and pepper. Do not press down—they should be light and fluffy.

3. Pour over the melted butter and cream and bake for 20–25 minutes (40 minutes for 12) or until crisp and golden brown.

PREPARE AHEAD

The potatoes can be made up to the end of step 2 up to 1 day ahead. Not suitable for freezing.

CHEESE-TOPPED DAUPHINOIS POTATOES

These are best prepared a day ahead. Make more than you need and freeze them for another occasion—they're great when there are just two or four of you. Serve with chops, grilled meat, or fish.

SERVES 6

Special equipment *7in (18cm) square, shallow, metal pan lined with parchment paper and greased*

1lb 10oz (750g) large Russet potatoes or other starchy potatoes

⅔ cup (150ml) chicken stock or vegetable stock

½ cup (100ml) heavy cream

salt and freshly ground black pepper

pat of butter

scant 1oz (25g) sharp Cheddar cheese, grated

SERVES 12

Special equipment *9 x 12in (23 x 30cm) roasting pan lined with parchment paper and greased*

3lb (1.35kg) large Russet potatoes or other starchy potatoes

1¼ cup (300ml) chicken stock or vegetable stock

⅔ cup (150ml) heavy cream

salt and freshly ground black pepper

scant 2 tbsp (25g) butter

1¾oz (50g) sharp Cheddar cheese, grated

1. Preheat the oven to 425°F (220°C). Peel the potatoes and rinse under cold water, then dry and slice very thinly by hand or with the slicer attachment on a food processor. Put the stock into a large jug and mix with the cream.

2. Arrange a layer of potato on the bottom of the pan, season with salt and pepper, then pour over a little of the stock mixture. Continue in the same way until the potato and liquid are used up. Dot the butter over the top and cover tightly with foil.

3. Bake for 30 minutes (45 minutes for 12) or until soft around the edges but still firm in the middle. Remove the foil and cook for a further 25–30 minutes (35–45 minutes for 12) or until golden and tender. Leave to cool, then chill—overnight is best.

4. Choose a lipped cutting board or tray that's bigger than the roasting pan (so it will catch any juices). Place on top of the pan and carefully turn it upside down so that the board is on the bottom. Remove the pan and parchment paper. Cut the potatoes into even-sized servings, arrange on a parchment paper–lined baking sheet, and sprinkle the cheese on top.

5. Reheat in an oven preheated to 400°F (200°C) for 25–30 minutes (35 minutes for 12) or until golden and piping hot.

PREPARE AHEAD AND FREEZE

The dish can be made up to the end of step 3 up to 1 day ahead or up to the end of step 4 up to 8 hours ahead. Freeze for up to 2 months.

ORANGE-GLAZED CARROTS

We love recipes that you can do much of the preparation for up to a day ahead and that require little last-minute attention. These carrots can be popped into the oven while you're doing the roast.

SERVES 6

2¼lb (1kg) carrots, sliced thickly diagonally

salt and freshly ground black pepper

scant 2 tbsp (25g) butter, melted

½ orange

freshly chopped parsley, to garnish

SERVES 12

4½lb (2kg) carrots, sliced thickly diagonally

salt and freshly ground black pepper

¼ cup (50g) butter, melted

1 orange

freshly chopped parsley, to garnish

1. Preheat the oven to 400°F (200°C). Immerse the carrots in a pan of boiling salted water for 4 minutes to blanch them, then drain and refresh in cold water.

2. Pour over the melted butter, season with salt and pepper, and stir to coat well.

3. Arrange in a roasting pan or ovenproof dish. Squeeze over the juice from the orange and pop the shell in the pan for extra flavor.

4. Cover with foil and bake for 30 minutes (40 minutes for 12) or until tender.

5. To serve, remove the orange shell and discard. Sprinkle over the parsley and toss lightly.

PREPARE AHEAD

The carrots can be blanched up to 1 day ahead. Coat in the butter and orange juice and roast to serve. Not suitable for freezing.

ROASTED ENDIVE WITH GARLIC BUTTER

SERVES 6

salt and freshly ground black pepper

12 endive heads, sliced in half lengthwise

scant 2 tbsp (25g) butter

2 garlic cloves, crushed

1¾oz (50g) sharp Cheddar cheese, grated

a little paprika, to dust

SERVES 12

salt and freshly ground black pepper

24 endive heads, sliced in half lengthwise

¼ cup (50g) butter

4 garlic cloves, crushed

3½oz (100g) sharp Cheddar cheese, grated

a little paprika, to dust

This is an unusual vegetable dish, best served alongside more conventional vegetables such as broccoli or runner beans. Serve as an accompaniment to meat or fish.

1. Preheat the oven to 425°F (220°C). Bring a pan of cold salted water to a boil, add the endive, and bring back up to a rolling boil. Cook for 3 minutes, then drain. Arrange the endive in a single layer in an ovenproof dish.

2. Add the butter and garlic to the empty pan and melt over the heat. Spoon the melted butter over the endive in the dish and season with salt and pepper. Sprinkle over the cheese and a light dusting of paprika.

3. Bake for 15–20 minutes (25–30 minutes for 12) or until lightly golden.

PREPARE AHEAD

The endive can be prepared up to the end of step 1 up to 6 hours ahead. Not suitable for freezing.

ROASTED CAULIFLOWER AND CARROTS

SERVES 4

1 large cauliflower

2 tbsp olive oil

1 lb (500g) large carrots, peeled and sliced into thick batons

salt and freshly ground black pepper

juice and zest of ½ lemon

2 tbsp parsley, chopped

This is a wonderful change to the more traditional roasted potatoes or root vegetables. It makes a great accompaniment for the Highland Game Pie on page 130.

1. Preheat the oven to 400°F (220°). To prepare the cauliflower, remove the leaves and discard. Break the florets from the stalk into small pieces.

2. Pour the oil into a large roasting pan and place in the oven for 5 minutes to get hot. Add the carrots and cauliflower and season with salt and pepper. Toss in the hot oil to coat, then roast in the oven for about 15 minutes or until nearly tender.

3. Add the lemon juice and zest and return to the oven for another 5 minutes or until golden.

4. Sprinkle with the parsley and serve piping hot.

SWEET CHILI COLESLAW

Coleslaw should be light and fresh rather than rich and sloppy. This recipe comes from our lovely friend Joanna. Look for sweet chili dipping sauce in the world food section of the supermarket. It gives coleslaw a sweet kick and stops the sauce being too thick.

SERVES 6

11oz (300g) white cabbage

1 small white onion

2 celery sticks

2 carrots, coarsely grated

salt and freshly ground black pepper

3 tbsp cider vinegar

2 tsp Dijon mustard

8 tbsp mayonnaise

5 tbsp sweet chili dipping sauce

SERVES 12

1lb 5oz (600g) white cabbage

1 large white onion

4 celery sticks

4 carrots, coarsely grated

salt and freshly ground black pepper

6 tbsp cider vinegar

1 heaped tbsp Dijon mustard

1 cup (250ml) mayonnaise

⅔ cup (150ml) sweet chili dipping sauce

1. Slice the cabbage, onion, and celery in a food processor, using the slicing blade. If you have a mandolin, use the thin blade. Alternatively, slice them very finely by hand.

2. Transfer to a bowl, add the carrots, and season with salt and pepper.

3. Put the vinegar, mustard, mayonnaise, and sweet chili dipping sauce into a jam jar. Seal with a lid and shake vigorously to combine.

4. Pour over the dressing and toss well. Transfer to the fridge for a minimum of 3 hours. Serve chilled or at room temperature.

PREPARE AHEAD

The dressing can be made and kept in the jar for up to 4 days. The coleslaw can be made up to 1 day ahead. The flavors improve, in fact. Not suitable for freezing.

ROASTED MEDITERRANEAN VEGETABLES

Roasted vegetables make a wonderful side dish for so many meats and fish. The secret is to cook the vegetables in a single layer, so they roast rather than steaming and becoming soggy. If you have any vegetables left over, toss them with a little balsamic vinegar and some olive oil and serve them as a salad.

SERVES 6

2 tbsp olive oil

1 small eggplant, sliced into 2in (5cm) chunks

2 small zucchini, thickly sliced

1 red pepper, halved, seeded, and cut into 2in (5cm) chunks

1 onion, quartered

3 garlic cloves (unpeeled)

2 sprigs of fresh rosemary

3 sprigs of fresh thyme

salt and freshly ground black pepper

SERVES 12

4 tbsp olive oil

2 small eggplants, sliced into 2in (5cm) chunks

4 small zucchini, thickly sliced

2 red peppers, halved, seeded, and cut into 2in (5cm) chunks

2 onions, quartered

6 garlic cloves (unpeeled)

4 sprigs of fresh rosemary

6 sprigs of fresh thyme

salt and freshly ground black pepper

1. Preheat the oven to 425°F (220°C). Put the oil into a large roasting pan (two pans for 12) and pop in the oven for a few minutes to get hot.

2. Add the vegetables and toss in the hot oil. Sprinkle over the garlic and herbs.

3. Roast for 40–45 minutes (1 hour for 12) or until tender and golden. Turn halfway through cooking.

4. Transfer to a serving bowl with a slotted spoon. Squeeze the garlic from their skins and mix in with the vegetables. Discard the herbs if woody. Season with salt and pepper, toss, and serve.

PREPARE AHEAD

The vegetables can be prepared up to the end of step 4 up to 1 day ahead. Not suitable for freezing.

OUR FAVORITE DESSERTS

Even if it's only one sumptuous dessert plus a fruit salad, we always serve a choice of desserts at any gathering of eight people or more. In general, we'll serve one dessert that's rich and indulgent, and another that's light and fruity—fruit compotes are always popular.

APRICOT AND ALMOND GALETTE

MAKES 1 (SERVES 6)

a little all-purpose flour, to dust

6½oz (185g) all-butter puff pastry

a little milk

15oz (400g) can apricots in natural juices, drained

5½oz (150g) golden marzipan, coarsely grated

1 tbsp apricot jam

1 tsp water

MAKES 2 (SERVES 12)

a little all-purpose flour, to dust

13oz (375g) all-butter puff pastry

a little milk

2 x 15oz (400g) cans apricots in natural juices, drained

9oz (250g) golden marzipan, coarsely grated

2 tbsp apricot jam

2 tsp water

This is also very good made with thinly sliced unpeeled eating apples instead of apricots. Use about three per galette. Take the pastry and marzipan straight from the fridge—they are easier to handle when cold. If you're not using all the pastry immediately, freeze any left over until needed. Serve the galette warm with cream.

1. Preheat the oven to 425°F (220°C). Pop a cookie sheet in the oven to get hot. Lightly flour a piece of parchment paper and roll the pastry out into a 5 x 12in (12.5 x 30cm) rectangle. For 12, roll it out into a 10 x 12in (25 x 30cm) rectangle, cut it in half lengthwise to make two strips, then arrange them neatly side by side.

2. With a knife, score a ½in (1cm) border around the rectangle(s), taking care not to cut all the way through—this allows the strip to rise up around the apricots and stops any liquid or fruit leaking out. Brush the border(s) with a little milk.

3. Slice each apricot into four slices and arrange them in rows inside the borders. Sprinkle over the marzipan.

4. Slide the paper on to the hot cookie sheet and bake for 20 minutes (20–25 minutes for two galettes) or until golden brown. Check halfway through cooking and, if they are getting too brown, cover loosely with foil.

5. Heat the apricot jam in a pan with the water, whisking until smooth. Brush the apricots with a thin layer to glaze them. Serve warm.

PREPARE AHEAD AND FREEZE

The galette(s) can be made up to 2 days ahead. Freeze for up to 1 month.

MINI APPLE, APRICOT, AND HAZELNUT CRUMBLES

SERVES 6

Special equipment *6 x size 1 (5fl oz/150ml) ramekins*

2lb (900g) Granny Smith apples, peeled and cut into ½in (1cm) cubes

6oz (175g) ready-to-eat dried apricots, snipped into small pieces

½ cup (100ml) apple juice

½ cup (100g) Turbinado sugar

¾ cup (100g) all-purpose flour

¼ cup (50g) cold butter, cubed

1oz (30g) hazelnuts, chopped

SERVES 12

Special equipment *12 x size 1 (5fl oz/150ml) ramekins*

4lb (1.8kg) Granny Smith apples, peeled and cut into ½in (1cm) cubes

12oz (350g) ready-to-eat dried apricots, snipped into small pieces

1 cup (200ml) apple juice

1 cup (200g) Turbinado sugar

1⅔ cup (200g) all-purpose flour

½ cup (100g) cold butter, cubed

1¾oz (50g) hazelnuts, chopped

These individual crumbles are scrumptious and so easy to make. You could also make one large crumble—use a 2 pint (1.2 liter) ovenproof dish for 6 or a 4 pint (2.4 liter) dish for 12, and bake for 30 minutes (45 minutes for 12). Serve with cream, crème fraîche, or warm custard.

1. Preheat the oven to 400°F (200°C). Put the apples, apricots, apple juice, and all but 1 heaped tablespoon (3 level tablespoons for 12) of the Turbinado sugar into a saucepan. Bring to a boil, cover with a lid, and simmer for 5–7 minutes or until the apples are just soft. Remove from the heat and divide among the ramekins.

2. Put the flour and butter into a mixing bowl. Using the tips of your fingers, rub the cold butter into the flour until the mixture resembles bread crumbs. Add the remaining sugar and the hazelnuts and mix together.

3. Sprinkle the crumble topping over the apples in the ramekins, then place on a cookie sheet and bake for 15 minutes or until the crumble is light golden brown and the fruit is bubbling around the edges.

PREPARE AHEAD AND FREEZE

The crumbles can be made up to 2 days ahead. Freeze for up to 1 month.

APRICOT CUSTARD CRUMBLE PIE

MAKES AN 11IN
(28CM) PIE
(SERVES 8–10)

Special equipment *11in (28cm) round tart pan with a removable base*

1½ cup (175g) all-purpose flour, plus a little extra to dust

⅓ cup (75g) butter

2 tbsp superfine sugar

1 egg

For the filling

⅔ cup (150ml) full-fat sour cream

3 egg yolks

1 tsp vanilla extract

1⅔ cup (200g) superfine sugar

¼ cup (25g) all-purpose flour

2 x 15oz (400g) cans apricot halves in natural juices, drained and each apricot cut into three

For the crumble topping

¼ cup (50g) butter

⅔ cup (75g) all-purpose flour

½ cup (50g) superfine sugar

What makes this crumble so unusual is the layer of creamy custard in the middle. Serve it as it is or with a little more cream.

1. Preheat the oven to 400°F (200°C). Put a cookie sheet in to get hot. Meanwhile, make the pastry. Put the flour and butter into a food processor and process until the mixture resembles bread crumbs. Add the sugar and egg and process again to form a ball.

2. Place the base of the tart pan on a work surface. Lightly dust the base of the tart pan and the work surface with flour. To line the tart pan, place the ball of pastry in the middle of the base of the pan and roll into a circle 2in (5cm) bigger than the base. Carefully fold in the edges all around. Return the base of the pan to the surround, then unfold the edge of the pastry and neaten. Prick the disk of pastry all over with a fork.

3. Line the pastry with parchment paper and fill with dried beans or pie weights, then bake for 15 minutes. Remove the weights and paper and bake for a further 5 minutes.

4. To make the filling, put the sour cream, egg yolks, vanilla extract, sugar, and flour into a mixing bowl and whisk by hand until smooth.

5. Arrange the apricots over the base of the pastry case and pour the custard filling over the top. Sit the pie on the hot cookie sheet and bake for 35–40 minutes or until the filling is just beginning to set.

6. Meanwhile, make the crumble topping. Put the butter, flour, and sugar into a mixing bowl and rub with your fingertips until the mixture resembles coarse bread crumbs.

7. Sprinkle the crumble topping over the just-set custard. Return to the oven and bake for a further 15 minutes or until golden and the custard is completely set. If the crumble topping starts to get too brown, cover with foil. Serve warm or cold.

PREPARE AHEAD

The pie can be made the day before and gently reheated. Not suitable for freezing.

MELT-IN-THE-MOUTH APPLE PIE

MAKES A 9½IN
(24CM) PIE
(SERVES 8)

Special equipment *2in
(5cm) deep round pie dish
with a 7½in (19cm) base
and a 9½in (24cm) top*

2 cups (225g) all-purpose
flour, plus a little extra
to dust

⅔ cup (150g) cold butter,
cubed

scant ¼ cup (25g) superfine
sugar, plus a little extra
to decorate

1 egg, beaten

1–2 tbsp water

For the filling

3lb (1.35kg) Granny Smith
apples, peeled, cored, and
thinly sliced

1½ cups (175g) superfine
sugar

½ tsp ground cinnamon

1 egg, beaten, to glaze

*Crisp, piecrust packed with fruit—this apple pie
is perfect for a special Sunday lunch. Serve warm
with custard, cream, or ice cream.*

1. Preheat the oven to 400°F (200°C). Meanwhile, put the flour,
butter, and sugar into a food processor and process until the
mixture resembles bread crumbs. Add the egg and water and
process again until it forms a ball. The dough will weigh about 1lb
(450g). Divide it into a 9oz (250g) piece and a 7oz (200g) piece.

2. Lightly flour a work surface and roll the larger piece out very
thinly, then use it to line the inside of the dish, leaving a little hanging
over at the sides.

3. To make the filling, put the apples, sugar, and cinnamon into
a bowl, mix well, then spoon into the base of the dish. The apples
will be higher than the pastry, but they will sink down as they cook.

4. Lightly flour the work surface and roll the remaining pastry out
slightly larger than the surface of the dish. Brush the top of the
pastry rim in the dish with water, then sit the pastry circle on top
and gently push down to seal the edges. Using a small, sharp knife,
trim off any excess pastry and crimp the edges together with your
fingertips. Brush the pie with the beaten egg.

5. Bake for 45–50 minutes or until golden brown and crisp. Allow
to cool slightly, then sprinkle with a little extra superfine sugar
and serve.

PREPARE AHEAD AND FREEZE

*The pie can be made up to the end of step 4
up to 1 day ahead. Freeze for up to 2 months.*

TWICE-BAKED LEMON SOUFFLÉS

These individual soufflés look impressive and, despite their rather complicated-sounding name, are extremely simple to make.

SERVES 6

Special equipment *6 x size 1 (5fl oz/150ml) ramekins, greased and bottom lined with a disk of parchment paper*

3 eggs, separated

1½ cup (175g) superfine sugar

3 tbsp (25g) cornstarch

finely grated zest of 2 large lemons

juice of 1 large lemon

9oz (250g) half-fat cream cheese

1 large tbsp luxury lemon curd

For the lemon sauce

1¼ cup (300ml) heavy cream

1 tbsp luxury lemon curd

finely grated zest and juice of 1 lemon

SERVES 12

Special equipment *12 x size 1 (5fl oz/150ml) ramekins, greased and bottom lined with a disk of parchment paper*

6 eggs, separated

3 cups (350g) superfine sugar

⅓ cup (50g) cornstarch

finely grated zest of 4 large lemons

juice of 2 large lemons

1lb 2oz (500g) half-fat cream cheese

2 large tbsp luxury lemon curd

For the lemon sauce

2½ cups (600ml) heavy cream

2 tbsp luxury lemon curd

finely grated zest and juice of 2 lemons

1. Preheat the oven to 375°F (190°C). Put the egg yolks and half the sugar into a mixing bowl and whisk with a mixer until pale, thick, and frothy.

2. Mix the cornstarch, lemon zest, and lemon juice in a bowl until smooth. Fold in the egg-yolk mixture, then beat in the cream cheese and lemon curd with a spatula.

3. Whisk the egg whites with a mixer until they resemble clouds. Whisking constantly, add the remaining sugar a teaspoon at a time until the whites are stiff and shiny.

4. Carefully fold the egg-white mixture into the mixing bowl, then spoon into the ramekins. Run a knife around the edge of each one to ensure they rise evenly. Sit the ramekins snugly in a roasting pan, then pour in enough boiling water to come halfway up the sides of the tin.

5. Bake for 15–20 minutes or until the soufflés have risen well and are just cooked. Set aside to cool completely.

6. Turn the soufflés out of the ramekins, remove the paper bases, and arrange snugly in one layer in an ovenproof dish.

7. Preheat the oven to 400°F (200°C). To make the sauce, put all the ingredients into a mixing bowl and whisk until smooth. Pour the sauce around the soufflés in the dish, then bake for 10 minutes (20–25 minutes for 12). Serve at once.

PREPARE AHEAD

The soufflés can be made up to the end of step 6 and the sauce poured around them up to 8 hours ahead. Not suitable for freezing.

LEMON MERINGUE PIE

MAKES AN 11IN
(28CM) PIE
(SERVES 8–10)

Special equipment *11in
(28cm) fluted loose-
bottomed tart pan*

*1¾ cup (225g) all-purpose
flour, plus a little extra
to dust*

*¾ cup (175g) cold butter,
cubed*

*⅓ cup (45g) powdered
sugar*

1 large egg, beaten

1 tbsp water

For the lemon filling

*finely grated zest and juice
of 6 lemons*

½ cup (65g) cornstarch

2 cups (450ml) water

*2 cups (250g) superfine
sugar*

6 egg yolks

For the topping

4 egg whites

*1¾ cup (225g) superfine
sugar*

2 level tsp cornstarch

*This is a truly wonderful LMP. It takes a bit of time
to make but, for a really special occasion, it's worth
it. Serve warm or cold, but not hot, as the pie will be
too soft to cut.*

1. Put the flour and butter into a food processor and process until
the mixture resembles bread crumbs. Add the powdered sugar, egg,
and water and process until it forms a ball. Transfer to a lightly floured
work surface and roll the dough out thinly until slightly larger than the
pan, then use to line the pan. Cover with plastic wrap and chill for
about an hour.

2. Preheat the oven to 400°F (200°C). Line the pastry case with
parchment paper, fill with dried beans or pie weights, and bake for
15 minutes. Remove the weights and parchment and return to the
oven for 5 minutes to dry out, then remove from the oven and set
aside. Reduce the oven temperature to 350°F (180°C).

3. To make the filling, mix the lemon zest, lemon juice, and
cornstarch to a smooth paste in a small bowl. Bring the water to a
boil in a pan, add the lemon mixture, and stir over the heat until
thickened, then boil for 1 minute. Mix the sugar and yolks in a bowl
and carefully add to the pan. Stir over medium heat until you have a
thick custard. Set aside to cool slightly, then pour into the pastry case.

4. To make the topping, whisk the egg whites with a mixer until
they look like clouds. Gradually add the superfine sugar, whisking
on maximum speed until the whites are stiff and glossy. Add the
cornstarch and whisk to combine.

5. Spoon the meringue on top of the lemon filling, spreading to cover
it completely and swirling the top. Bake for 30 minutes or until the
filling is completely set and the meringue is lightly golden and crisp.

PREPARE AHEAD

*The pastry case can be made up to 2 days
ahead. The pie can be made completely up
to 1 day ahead. Not suitable for freezing.*

TOFFEE PUDDING WITH WARM TOFFEE SAUCE

This is similar to sticky toffee pudding and it's truly scrumptious. If you're serving 12–16, bake the pudding in two pans.

SERVES 6–8

Special equipment *9 x 13in (23 x 33cm) baking pan, greased, lined with parchment paper, and greased*

½ cup (100g) butter, at room temperature

¾ cup (175g) light brown sugar, packed

2 eggs

1¾ cup (225g) self-raising flour

2 tbsp molasses

⅔ cup (150ml) milk

1¾oz (50g) walnuts, chopped

For the toffee sauce

⅔ cup (150g) light brown sugar, packed

½ cup (150g) golden syrup

¼ cup (50g) butter

5oz (170g) can evaporated milk

SERVES 12–16

Special equipment *Two 9 x 13in (23 x 33cm) baking pans, greased, lined with parchment paper, and greased*

1 cup (225g) butter, at room temperature

1½ cup (350g) light brown sugar, packed

4 eggs

3⅔ cups (450g) self-raising flour

4 tbsp molasses

1¼ cup (300ml) milk

3½oz (100g) walnuts, chopped

For the toffee sauce

1⅓ cup (300g) light brown sugar, packed

1 cup (300g) golden syrup

½ cup (100g) butter

2 x 5oz (170g) cans evaporated milk

1. Preheat the oven to 350°F (180°C). Put the butter, sugar, eggs, flour, and molasses into a bowl and whisk with a mixer until combined. Slowly add the milk, whisking until smooth. Pour into the lined pan and sprinkle with the walnuts.

2. Bake for 30–35 minutes (40 minutes for two puddings) or until well risen, just firm in the middle, and lightly golden brown. Keep warm.

3. To make the sauce, put the sugar, golden syrup, and butter into a saucepan and stir over low heat until the sugar has dissolved, the butter has melted, and all the ingredients are combined. Simmer for 5 minutes, then remove from the heat and stir in the evaporated milk.

4. Cut the pudding into squares and serve warm with the warm toffee sauce.

PREPARE AHEAD AND FREEZE

The pudding can be made up to 1 day ahead. Freeze for up to 2 months. The sauce can be made up to 3 days ahead. Not suitable for freezing.

WHITE CHOCOLATE
AND ORANGE MOUSSES

SERVES 6

Special equipment 6 x
2¾in (7cm) round metal
cooking rings

2½oz (75g) graham
crackers, crushed

¼ cup (45g) butter, melted

1 tbsp Turbinado sugar

For the mousse

3½oz (100g) full-fat cream
cheese

⅔ cup (150ml) heavy cream

5½oz (150g) Belgian or
continental 100 percent
white chocolate

1 tbsp Cointreau

1 large orange

SERVES 12

Special equipment 12 x
2¾in (7cm) round metal
cooking rings

6oz (175g) graham crackers,
crushed

⅓ cup (75g) butter, melted

1½ tbsp Turbinado sugar

For the mousse

9oz (250g) full-fat cream
cheese

1¼ cup (300ml) heavy
cream

11oz (300g) Belgian or
continental 100 percent
white chocolate

3 tbsp Cointreau

2 large oranges

*This recipe was given to us by Becca, a great friend
of ours. She has her own catering company and has
given us invaluable advice on cooking for numbers.
If you don't have cooking rings, you can make one
large mousse—follow the recipe for 12 and spoon the
mousse into an 8in (20cm) round springform pan.*

1. Put the graham crackers into a mixing bowl, add the butter
and sugar, and mix to combine.

2. Line a cookie sheet with plastic wrap and sit the rings on top.
Spoon the graham cracker mixture evenly into the rings and level
the tops with the back of a teaspoon. Transfer to the fridge to chill
while you make the mousse.

3. Put the cream cheese and cream into a mixing bowl and whisk
with a mixer until thick and holding its shape.

4. Gently melt the chocolate in a bowl set over a pan of just-
simmering water until smooth. Allow to cool.

5. Add the chocolate to the cream mixture and stir in the Cointreau.
Finely grate the zest of the orange and add to the mousse.

6. Spoon the mousse into the rings and level the tops. Chill for a
minimum of 4 hours to firm up. Meanwhile, peel the orange with
a small knife. Cut the segments free and place in a bowl. Squeeze
over the juice from the peel.

7. Remove the rings and serve the mousses with the orange
segments arranged on top. Garnish with grated white chocolate.

PREPARE AHEAD

*You can make the mousses up to 12 hours ahead.
Not suitable for freezing.*

CRÈME BRÛLÉE AND CHOCOLATE POTS

This is so impressive—two small desserts on one plate, served with some glazed summer berries. To serve fewer than 12 people, make just one of these special desserts— cut the crème brûlée into six servings, and make the chocolate pots in six 5fl oz (150ml) ramekins or glasses. Serve with or without the glazed berries.

SERVES 12

For the crème brûlée

Special equipment
7in (18cm) square cake pan, greased

2½ cups (600ml) heavy cream

4 egg yolks

¼ cup (25g) superfine sugar

½ tsp vanilla extract

½ cup (100g) Turbinado sugar

For the chocolate pots
Special equipment *12 shot glasses, about 2½fl oz (75ml) in capacity*

11oz (300g) dark chocolate

1¼ cup (300ml) heavy cream

7oz (200ml) full-fat crème fraîche

1. **To make the crème brûlée**, preheat the oven to 275°F (140°C). Heat the heavy cream gently in a saucepan until hand hot. Put the egg yolks, superfine sugar, and vanilla extract into a bowl and whisk until combined. Pour the hot cream onto the mixture and whisk until smooth. Transfer to a jug, then strain into the cake pan.

2. Sit the cake pan in a roasting pan, pour enough boiling water into the roasting pan to come halfway up the sides of the cake pan, then transfer to the oven and bake for 35–40 minutes or until the cream mixture has just set. Set aside to cool.

3. Once cold, sprinkle the Turbinado sugar on top and slide under a hot broiler until the sugar dissolves and becomes caramel-colored. Set aside to firm up in the fridge for at least 1 hour and up to 5 hours.

4. **To make the chocolate pots**, reserve two squares of chocolate for decoration, then put the rest in a bowl set over a pan of simmering water. Add ¾ cup (200ml) of the cream and stir until the chocolate has melted. Set aside to cool slightly.

5. Stir in the crème fraîche, then pour into the shot glasses. Leave to set in the fridge for at least 2 hours.

6. Once set, pour the remaining heavy cream over the top. Coarsely grate the reserved chocolate and sprinkle on top.

7. When ready to serve, cut the crème brûlée into even-sized squares with a fish spatula. Arrange a crème brûlée, a chocolate pot, and a few of the glazed summer berries on a plate and dust with powdered sugar.

FOR THE GLAZED SUMMER BERRIES

Place 9oz (250g) small strawberries (hulled and halved), 9oz (250g) raspberries, and 3½oz (100g) blueberries in a large mixing bowl and mix gently. Sift 3 tsp powdered sugar over the top and gently combine. Cover and chill in the fridge for up to 4 hours. The sugar will dissolve in the strawberry juices to form a shimmering glaze.

PREPARE AHEAD

The custard for the crème brûlée can be made up to 2 days ahead. Add the topping up to 5 hours before serving. The chocolate pots can be made up to 2 days ahead. The berries can be prepared up to 4 hours ahead. Not suitable for freezing.

RHUBARB AND LEMON POTS

SERVES 6

1lb 10oz (750g) rhubarb, sliced into 1¾in (4cm) pieces

finely grated zest of ½ orange, plus 2 tbsp orange juice

¼ cup (25g) superfine sugar

For the lemon topping

1¼ cup (300ml) heavy cream

½ cup (50g) superfine sugar

finely grated zest and juice of 1½ lemons

6 mint leaves, to decorate

SERVES 12

3lb 3oz (1.5kg) rhubarb, sliced into 1¾in (4cm) pieces

finely grated zest of 1 orange, plus 4 tbsp orange juice

½ cup (50g) superfine sugar

For the lemon topping

2½ cups (600ml) heavy cream

1 cup (100g) superfine sugar

finely grated zest and juice of 3 lemons

12 mint leaves, to decorate

The combination of rhubarb and lemon is delicious. This dessert looks particularly pretty made with young pink rhubarb, which is available in stores toward the end of winter.

1. Put the rhubarb, orange zest, orange juice, and sugar into a saucepan. Stir over high heat for 2 minutes, cover with a lid, lower the heat, and simmer for 10 minutes (15 minutes for 12) or until the rhubarb is just tender. Set aside to cool.

2. To make the topping, put the cream, sugar, and lemon zest into a pan. Heat gently over low heat until the sugar dissolves and the mixture reaches simmering point. Remove from the heat, stir in the lemon juice, and set aside to cool slightly.

3. Spoon the rhubarb and a little of the liquid into the bottom of some pretty glasses or tumblers. Pour the lemon topping on top, then transfer to the fridge for a minimum of 4 hours to set.

4. Serve chilled, decorated with mint leaves.

PREPARE AHEAD

The pots can be made up to 12 hours ahead. Not suitable for freezing.

INDIVIDUAL TIRAMISUS

SERVES 6

1½ tsp instant coffee granules

½ cup (120ml) boiling water

3 tbsp Baileys Irish Cream

2 eggs

⅔ cup (75g) superfine sugar

1¼ cup (300ml) heavy cream

8oz (250g) full-fat mascarpone

3 sponge cake cups

2½oz (75g) semisweet chocolate, coarsely grated

SERVES 12

1 tbsp instant coffee granules

1¼ cup (300ml) boiling water

6 tbsp Baileys Irish Cream

4 eggs

1¼ cup (75g) superfine sugar

2½ cups (600ml) heavy cream

16oz (500g) full-fat mascarpone

6 sponge cake cups

5½oz (150g) semisweet chocolate, coarsely grated

We all love tiramisu. This version is served individually, with the added decadence of a splash of Baileys Irish Cream—if you don't have any, you can replace it with the same quantity of brandy. Serve the tiramisus in tumblers or wine, martini, or champagne glasses.

1. Put the coffee granules and boiling water into a jug and stir to dissolve. Allow to cool slightly, then stir in the Baileys.

2. Break the eggs into a mixing bowl, add the sugar, and whisk with a mixer until pale, thick, and frothy and the whisk leaves a trail on the surface when lifted.

3. Whip the cream till just lightly whipped and holding its shape.

4. Put the mascarpone into a bowl, stir in 2 tablespoons of the whipped cream, and mix with a spatula. Gently fold in the rest of the whipped cream, followed by the egg mixture, taking care not to knock out any of the air.

5. Cut the sponge cakes in half horizontally and then in half diagonally. Push a piece into the bottom of each tumbler or glass, drizzle over half the coffee mixture, then spoon over half the cream mixture. Repeat to give another layer of sponge, coffee, and cream. Finish with a sprinkling of the grated chocolate.

6. Cover and chill in the fridge for a minimum of 4 hours.

PREPARE AHEAD AND FREEZE

The tiramisus can be made up to 12 hours ahead. Freeze for up to 1 month.

CHOCOLATE TRUFFLE CHEESECAKE

SERVES 12

Special equipment 7½in (19cm) square pan or a 7in (18cm) round springform pan, lined with plastic wrap

7oz (200g) dark chocolate

2 eggs, separated

½ cup (50g) superfine sugar

6oz (175g) full-fat cream cheese

½ tsp vanilla extract

⅔ cup (150ml) heavy cream, lightly whipped

6oz (175g) chocolate graham crackers, crushed

⅓ cup (75g) butter, melted

A rich, indulgent cheesecake that requires no gelatin—ideal for vegetarians. Serve on its own or with light cream and fresh summer fruits such as raspberries and strawberries.

1. Break the chocolate into small pieces into a bowl. Sit the bowl over a pan of hot water on low heat and stir until melted. Take care not to allow the chocolate to get too hot or it will lose its shine and become too thick.

2. Put the egg yolks and sugar into a large bowl and whisk with a mixer until light and thick and a trail is left when the whisks are lifted from the bowl.

3. Mix the cream cheese and vanilla extract in a bowl, then stir in the melted chocolate. Fold in the whisked egg yolks and sugar, taking care not to knock out any air. Fold in the whipped cream.

4. Whisk the egg whites with a hand mixer until like clouds. Fold a spoonful of egg whites into the chocolate mixture with a spatula. Cut and fold (but do not mix) until no whites are visible. Add the rest of the egg white and fold in until smooth.

5. Spoon into the prepared pan and level the top. Transfer to the fridge for 1 hour or until just set.

6. Mix the graham crackers and butter together until combined. Carefully press on top of the cheesecake in an even layer. Return to the fridge for a minimum of 6 hours.

7. To serve, turn the cheesecake upside down onto a board or plate and cut into 12 fingers or wedges. Dust with cocoa powder.

PREPARE AHEAD AND FREEZE

The cheesecake can be made up to the end of step 6 up to 2 days ahead. Freeze for up to 3 months.

CHOCOLATE AND HAZELNUT BOOZY ROULADE

MAKES A 13IN (33CM)
ROULADE
(SERVES 8-10)

Special equipment *9 x 13in (23 x 33cm) Swiss roll pan, greased and lined with nonstick parchment paper*

6oz (175g) semisweet chocolate, broken into pieces

6 eggs, separated

1½ cup (175g) superfine sugar

2 level tbsp cocoa, sifted

1¾oz (50g) chopped and roasted hazelnuts

For the filling

1¼ cup (300ml) heavy cream

2–3 tbsp Baileys Irish Cream

For the hazelnut praline

½ cup (100g) granulated sugar

1¾oz (50g) whole blanched hazelnuts, halved

powdered sugar, to dust

The perfect celebratory dessert for any special occasion, especially Christmas. If you don't have time to make praline, top with a coarsely crushed bought praline bar.

1. Preheat the oven to 350°F (180°C). Melt the chocolate slowly in a bowl over a pan of hot water. Allow to cool slightly until warm but still runny.

2. Whisk the egg whites in a large mixing bowl until stiff but not dry. Put the sugar and egg yolks into a separate large bowl and whisk until light, thick, and creamy. Add the melted chocolate and stir until blended.

3. Gently stir two large spoonfuls of the egg whites into the mixture, then fold in the remaining egg whites, followed by the cocoa. Stir in the hazelnuts. Pour into the prepared pan and gently level the surface. Bake for 20–25 minutes or until risen.

4. Remove the cake from the oven and set aside to cool in the pan.

5. For the filling, whip the cream into soft peaks and stir in the Baileys. Dust a large piece of nonstick parchment paper with powdered sugar. Turn the cake out onto the paper and peel off the lining paper, then spread with the whipped cream. Make a cut part way through the roulade along the short edge nearest to you, about ¾in (2cm) in. Roll up the cake, tightly to start with and using the paper to help. Don't worry if it cracks—that is quite normal and part of its charm! Place on a long plate.

6. To make the praline, put the sugar and 3 tablespoons of water into a stainless steel saucepan. Stir over low heat until the sugar has dissolved. When clear, bring up to a boil. Boil until a medium straw color. Add the hazelnuts, then pour quickly onto a cookie sheet lined with nonstick paper. Leave to cool slightly, then use a teaspoon to carefully group together small clusters of nuts. Leave to cool and become hard. When set, break into pieces and arrange on the top of the roulade. Sprinkle with powdered sugar to serve.

PREPARE AHEAD AND FREEZE

The roulade can be assembled up to 6 hours ahead. Freezes well filled.

HEAVENLY LEMON CHEESECAKE ON A GINGER CRUST

MAKES AN 8IN
(20CM) CHEESECAKE
(SERVES 8)

Special equipment *8in
(20cm) round loose-
bottomed cake pan,
greased and bottom lined
with parchment paper*

*3½oz (100g) ginger snaps,
crushed*

¼ cup (50g) butter, melted

*18oz (500g) full-fat
mascarpone*

*10oz (325g) jar luxury lemon
curd*

juice of 1 small lemon

*fresh raspberries and
blueberries, to decorate*

powdered sugar, to dust

*This was the favorite dessert at a charity buffet for
40 that Mary was a guest at—it went like lightning.
The other good news is that once you've collected the
ingredients together, it only takes 10 minutes to make.
You can make up to three of these cheesecakes at once
(but take care not to overbeat the mixture at step 2).
If you're making more cheesecakes than that, prepare
them in separate batches.*

1. Mix the cookies with the butter in a bowl, then press into the
bottom of the tin (but not up the sides).

2. Put the mascarpone, lemon curd, and lemon juice in a bowl and
beat with a spatula until smooth.

3. Spoon onto the cookie base and level the top. Chill in the fridge
for at least 4 hours and up to 24 hours to firm up.

4. To serve, remove the cheesecake from the pan, peel off the
parchment paper, and arrange on a platter. Decorate with the fruit
and dust with powdered sugar.

PREPARE AHEAD

*The cheesecake can be made up to the end
of step 3 up to 1 day ahead. Not suitable for
freezing.*

CHILLED MARBLED RASPBERRY CHEESECAKE

MAKES A 9IN (23CM)
CHEESECAKE
(SERVES 8)

Special equipment *9in
(23cm) round springform
pan, greased and bottom
lined with parchment paper*

*3½oz (100g) graham
crackers, crushed*

¼ cup (50g) butter, melted

*2 tbsp (25g) Turbinado
sugar*

For the raspberry filling

*1lb 2oz (500g) fresh
raspberries*

2 tsp powdered gelatin

2 tbsp water

2 tbsp framboise liqueur

For the creamy filling

3 tsp powdered gelatin

3 tbsp water

*9oz (250g) full-fat cream
cheese, at room
temperature*

2 eggs, separated

*7oz (200g) half-fat crème
fraîche*

*¾ cup (100g) superfine
sugar*

*This unusual chilled cheesecake has a delicious
raspberry-ripple filling. If we don't have any framboise
raspberry liqueur on hand, we make a cherry-ripple
cheesecake, using kirsch instead.*

1. Mix the graham crackers, butter, and sugar together in a bowl and press into the bottom of the pan. Transfer to the fridge to chill.

2. Meanwhile, make the raspberry filling. Process the raspberries in a food processor until smooth, then push through a sieve into a bowl. Put the gelatin into another bowl and add the water. Allow to soak until the gelatin becomes spongy, then stand the bowl in a saucepan of hot water until it dissolves. Once dissolved, add the framboise liqueur, then pour into the raspberry puree. Stir and set aside.

3. To make the creamy filling, prepare the gelatin and water as above. Put the cream cheese, egg yolks, and crème fraîche into a bowl and stir to combine.

4. Spoon 2 tablespoons of the creamy mixture into the liquid gelatin and mix, then pour it all into the creamy mixture and stir until smooth.

5. Whisk the egg whites with a hand mixer until they look like clouds, then add the sugar a teaspoon at a time, whisking constantly until the mixture is stiff and glossy. Fold the egg whites into the creamy mixture until smooth.

6. Carefully fold the raspberry filling into the creamy mixture to give a ripple effect.

7. Spoon into the pan and chill in the fridge for a minimum of 6 hours or until firm.

8. To serve, remove from the pan, discard the disk of paper, and cut into slices.

PREPARE AHEAD AND FREEZE

*The cheesecake can be made up to the end
of step 7 up to 2 days ahead. Freeze for up
to 3 months.*

RUM AND RAISIN ICE CREAM

SERVES 10–12

Special equipment 2¾ pint
(1.5 liter) freezerproof
container

6oz (175g) lexia raisins

5 tbsp dark rum

4 eggs, separated

¾ cup (100g) superfine
sugar

1¼ cup (300ml) heavy
cream

One of the great things about this ice cream (apart from its flavor) is that you don't need an ice-cream maker. It's made with raw meringue, which means it doesn't need whisking as it freezes. Large, plump lexia raisins are lovely in ice cream—if you can't find them, you can use any other kind of raisin.

1. Put the raisins into a bowl and add the rum. Leave to soak—ideally overnight.

2. Put the egg yolks into a small bowl and whisk with a fork until blended.

3. Whisk the egg whites with a mixer until they look like clouds. Whisking on maximum speed, add the sugar a teaspoon at a time until the mixture is stiff and glossy.

4. Whip the cream until soft peaks form, then fold into the egg-white mixture until smooth. Stir in the egg yolks and soaked raisins. If there is any rum left in the bowl, add this, too.

5. Transfer to the freezerproof container and freeze for a minimum of 24 hours.

6. Remove from the freezer 10 minutes before serving to make scooping easier.

PREPARE AHEAD AND FREEZE

Freeze for up to 2 months.

EXOTIC FRUIT SALAD

SERVES 6

½ large cantaloupe melon

1 large mango, stone removed and flesh cut into cubes

3 passion fruit

3 oranges

1 grapefruit

8oz (225g) black seedless grapes

4 tbsp Cointreau or Grand Marnier (optional)

SERVES 12

1 large cantaloupe melon, cut in half

2 large mangoes, stones removed and flesh cut into cubes

6 passion fruit

6 oranges

2 grapefruits

1lb 2oz (500g) black seedless grapes

8 tbsp Cointreau or Grand Marnier (optional)

This is a lovely refreshing fruit salad and any left over is a real treat for breakfast the next day. Raspberries and strawberries are also good in a fruit salad, but add them at the last minute or they will bleed into the other fruits and turn mushy. Bananas will go soft after a while, too. Avoid apples, pears, and peaches, as they discolor. Serve the fruit salad on its own or with cream.

1. Scoop the seeds from the melon and discard. Using a sharp knife, cut into wedges and remove the skin. Slice the flesh into 1in (2.5cm) chunks and put into a serving bowl with the mango cubes.

2. Slice the passion fruit in half and scoop the seeds into the bowl.

3. Segment the oranges and grapefruit by cutting a piece from the top and base, then slicing down around the flesh, removing skin and pith. Slide the knife down one side of each segment, then cut down the other side and pull it free, making sure you catch the juices. Add to the bowl.

4. Slice the grapes in half and add to the bowl.

5. Add the Cointreau or Grand Marnier, if using, and mix lightly together, then chill in the fridge until you are ready to serve.

PREPARE AHEAD

The salad can be made up to 12 hours ahead. Not suitable for freezing.

POACHED PEARS WITH BLACKBERRY SAUCE

SERVES 6

1¾ cup (350g) granulated sugar

4 cups (1.2 liters) water

a few strips of lemon zest

6 pears, peeled, but stalk left on

For the blackberry sauce

1lb (450g) blackberries

½ cup (100g) granulated sugar

SERVES 12

3½ cups (700g) granulated sugar

9 cups (2.5 liters) water

a few strips of lemon zest

12 pears, peeled, but stalk left on

For the blackberry sauce

2lb (900g) blackberries

1 cup (200g) granulated sugar

A fruit-based dessert is so welcome after a rich entrée and these poached pears make a great change from fruit salad. The sauce for them is vivid and vibrant in color. Make the dessert extra special by adding 1 tablespoon of crème de cassis to the puree.

1. Put the sugar, water, and lemon zest into a saucepan just large enough to take the pears upright in a single layer.

2. Heat gently, stirring until the sugar has dissolved, then boil rapidly for 2 minutes.

3. Place the pears in the hot syrup, cover with a wet sheet of parchment paper (this ensures the top of the pears do not dry out), and bring to a boil. Cover with a lid and simmer gently for 30–45 minutes (50 minutes for 12) or until the pears are just tender. Set aside to cool.

4. To make the sauce, put the blackberries and sugar into a pan and cook for 5 minutes or until the juices start to run. Push through a sieve into a bowl to get a thickish puree.

5. When the pears are cold, remove them from the syrup and pat dry with paper towel.

6. Serve one pear per person or cut each one in half lengthwise through the stem, remove the core, and serve two halves. Drizzle over the sauce.

PREPARE AHEAD AND FREEZE

The pears can be poached up to 12 hours ahead and kept in the syrup until ready to serve. The sauce can be made up to 3 days ahead. Freeze the sauce for up to 2 months.

MAGENTA FRUIT COMPOTE WITH WHITE CHOCOLATE SAUCE

SERVES 6

¼ cup (30g) superfine sugar

*2 tbsp crème de cassis
or blackcurrant liqueur*

2 tbsp water

8oz (225g) blueberries

5½oz (150g) raspberries

*8oz (225g) strawberries,
quartered*

*3½oz (100g) Belgian or
continental 100 percent
white chocolate*

¾ cup (200ml) heavy cream

SERVES 12

½ cup (50g) superfine sugar

*4 tbsp crème de cassis
or blackcurrant liqueur*

4 tbsp water

1lb 2oz (500g) blueberries

10oz (300g) raspberries

*1lb 2oz (500g) strawberries,
quartered*

*7oz (200g) Belgian or
continental 100 percent
white chocolate*

*1⅔ cup (400ml) heavy
cream*

*One of the quickest, most delicious desserts you'll
ever make! Serve with shortbread cookies to make
it extra special.*

1. Put the sugar, crème de cassis, and water into a shallow saucepan. Gently heat, then add the blueberries and simmer for a few minutes or until just starting to soften. Remove from the heat and add the raspberries and strawberries. Mix together and leave in the pan to cool completely.

2. Put the chocolate and cream into a bowl set over a pan of just-simmering water and stir until runny. Take care not to overheat the chocolate or it will lose its shine and split. Leave to cool and thicken slightly.

3. Divide the fruit among wine or cocktail glasses. Pour the white chocolate sauce over the top, then place in the fridge for 2 hours to set slightly.

PREPARE AHEAD

*The fruit can be prepared up to 2 days ahead
and the desserts assembled up to 12 hours
ahead. Not suitable for freezing.*

PARTY CRÈME BRÛLÉE

SERVES 12–16

Special equipment *4 pint (2.4 liter) shallow, wide-bottomed, ovenproof dish, greased*

¾ cup (85g) superfine sugar

12 egg yolks

3 tsp vanilla extract

2 pints (1.2 liters) heavy cream

1½ cup (300ml) light cream

1 cup (225g) Turbinado sugar

3½oz (100g) raspberries, to decorate

mint leaves, to decorate

A classic dessert that's brilliant for serving numbers. For a recipe for six, turn to page 278. This is delicious served with soft summer fruits such as raspberries or a fruit coulis.

1. Preheat the oven to 325°F (160°C). Meanwhile, put the superfine sugar, egg yolks, and vanilla extract into a large mixing bowl and whisk together by hand.

2. Put the heavy cream and light cream into a saucepan and heat until just below boiling point (just hot enough to put your finger in).

3. Pour the hot cream into the egg yolk mixture, whisking quickly until combined.

4. Pour the custard through a sieve into the prepared ovenproof dish.

5. Put the dish into a large roasting pan and pour enough boiling water into the pan so that it comes halfway up the sides of the dish.

6. Carefully slide into the oven and cook for 35–45 minutes or until set but with a slight jiggle in the middle. Check after 30 minutes to see how it's doing.

7. Remove from the oven and leave to cool in the roasting pan, then place in the fridge and chill until stone cold.

8. Sprinkle over the Turbinado sugar, then pop under a hot broiler, watching it very carefully, for 20–25 minutes or until melted and golden brown. You could also use a blowtorch to do this. To give the topping time to soften slightly, chill in the fridge for at least 5 hours and up to 10 hours, but no more or it will turn to liquid.

9. To serve, cut into portions with a fish spatula and decorate with raspberries and mint leaves.

PREPARE AHEAD

The custard can be made up to the end of step 7 up to 2 days ahead. Not suitable for freezing.

PEAR AND GINGER PAVLOVA

Pear and ginger is one of our all-time favorite combinations. This pavlova is sprinkled with pomegranate seeds just before serving—they look so pretty and glisten like little gems.

SERVES 6

3 egg whites

1½ cup (175g) superfine sugar

1 level tsp cornstarch

1 tsp white wine vinegar

For the topping

5 fairly ripe pears, peeled, cored, and chopped into chunky slices

juice of ½ lemon

½ cup (50g) superfine sugar

1¼ cup (300ml) heavy cream, whipped

6 bulbs stem ginger (from a jar), drained and coarsely chopped

1 small pomegranate

powdered sugar, to dust

SERVES 12

6 egg whites

3 cups (350g) superfine sugar

2 level tsp cornstarch

2 tsp white wine vinegar

For the topping

10 fairly ripe pears, peeled, cored, and chopped into chunky slices

juice of 1 lemon

¾ cup (100g) superfine sugar

2½ cups (600ml) heavy cream, whipped

12 bulbs stem ginger (from a jar), drained and coarsely chopped

2 small pomegranates

powdered sugar, to dust

1. Preheat the oven to 325°F (160°C). Whisk the egg whites with a mixer until they look like clouds. Gradually add the sugar a little at a time, whisking on maximum speed until the whites are stiff and glossy. Mix the cornstarch and vinegar in a cup until smooth, then stir into the meringue mixture.

2. Line a cookie sheet with parchment paper and draw a 8 x 12in (20 x 30cm) rectangle on it (two rectangles side by side for 12). Spread the meringue mixture out into the rectangle(s) with a knife, then create a well in the middle by building up the sides.

3. Slide the cookie sheet into the oven, immediately reduce the temperature to 300°F (150°C), and bake for 1 hour. Turn the oven off and leave the meringue in the oven for a further hour to dry out.

4. To make the topping, put the pears, lemon juice, and sugar into a small pan and barely cover with water from the tap. Simmer gently over low heat for 10 minutes or until the pears are just tender. Leave in the liquid until needed, then drain. Slice half of the pears into thin slices and reserve for decoration. Chop the remaining pears and stir into the whipped cream with the ginger.

5. Arrange the pavlova on a serving plate, spoon the cream into the well, and decorate with the reserved pears. Cut the pomegranate in half, pick out the seeds, and sprinkle over the top. Serve at room temperature, dusted with powdered sugar.

PREPARE AHEAD AND FREEZE

The pavlova can be made up to the end of step 3 up to 1 month ahead. Wrap in plastic wrap and then foil and keep in a cool place. The pears can be poached up to 8 hours ahead. The pavlova can be assembled up to 4 hours ahead. Freeze the meringue without the topping for up to 6 months.

PARTY PAVLOVA PYRAMID

SERVES 35–40

2 x 6 egg whites

2 x 3 cups (350g) superfine sugar

2 x 1 tsp white wine vinegar

2 x 1 tsp cornstarch

For the filling

3 pints (1.7 liters) heavy cream

20oz (500g) full-fat Greek yogurt

2lb (900g) strawberries, hulled

1lb 10oz (750g) raspberries

1lb (450g) blueberries

a few mint leaves, to decorate (optional)

You don't get successful meringues if you use more than six egg whites at a time, which is why we make them in two batches for this party pyramid. It is the most spectacular dessert you'll ever make. To make a larger pyramid, add another layer as opposed to making larger meringues.

1. Preheat the oven to 325°F (160°C). To make the first batch of meringue, put six egg whites into a bowl and whisk with a mixer until they look like clouds. Add the sugar a little at a time, whisking on maximum speed until the mixture is stiff and glossy. Mix the vinegar and cornstarch in a cup until smooth, then stir into the bowl.

2. Line a cookie sheet with parchment paper and spread the meringue mixture out—it should be about 12in (30cm) in diameter and about 2in (5cm) thick. This will be the base for the pyramid.

3. Slide into the oven, then immediately reduce the temperature to 300°F (150°C) and bake for 1 hour. Turn the oven off and leave the meringue inside for 1 hour or overnight to dry.

4. Prepare a second batch of mixture. Use to make one meringue measuring 10in (25cm) in diameter, another measuring 8in (20cm) in diameter, and a third that is 5in (12cm) in diameter. The smallest can be fairly thin and should fit on a cookie sheet with the 8in (20cm) one.

5. Cook in the same way: put the 10in (25cm) meringue in the oven and bake for 15 minutes, then pop the two smaller meringues in as well and bake for a further 45 minutes. Switch off the oven and leave to dry out for 1 hour or overnight.

6. To assemble, whip the cream until stiff and mix with the yogurt. Put the largest meringue on a sturdy foil-covered board or tray. Cover with cream and half the fruit, ensuring the fruit can be seen at the edges.

7. Place the next-largest meringue on top and cover with cream and fruit. Continue in the same way with the other meringues. Finish with the last of the cream and a pretty arrangement of fruit and mint leaves on top, if using. To serve, cut in wedges, starting from the top.

PREPARE AHEAD AND FREEZE

The meringues can be made up to 1 month ahead and stored (see page 302). Freeze for up to 6 months. The pyramid can be assembled up to 4 hours ahead. This is best done in situ, so you don't need to move it.

HAZELNUT MERINGUE ROULADE WITH RASPBERRIES

MAKES A 13IN (33CM)
ROULADE
(SERVES 8–10)

Special equipment *9 x 13in
(23 x 33cm) Swiss roll pan,
greased and lined with
parchment paper*

4 egg whites

*1¾ cup (225g) superfine
sugar*

*1¾oz (50g) roasted
hazelnuts, chopped*

*1¼ cup (300ml) heavy
cream, whipped*

7oz (200g) fresh raspberries

*Meringue roulade is such a classic dessert. As a twist,
we've added chopped roasted hazelnuts to give a lovely
nutty flavor that goes sublimely well with raspberries
and cream. If you are serving a larger crowd, prepare
individual roulades rather than multiplying the
quantities and making a big one, and bake one at a time.
If your meringues crumble beyond repair, make Eton
mess instead—see below left.*

1. Preheat the oven to 400°F (200°C). Meanwhile, put the egg
whites into a large clean bowl and whisk with a mixer until very
stiff. With the whisk still on full speed, gradually add the sugar a
teaspoon at a time, whisking well between each addition. The
meringue is ready when it is glossy and very, very stiff.

2. Spread the mixture into the prepared pan and sprinkle with the
hazelnuts. Bake for 8 minutes or until lightly golden. Reduce the
temperature to 325°F (160°C) and bake for a further 20 minutes.

3. Remove the meringue from the oven and turn hazelnut side
down onto a sheet of parchment paper. Remove the paper from
the bottom of the meringue and allow to cool for 10 minutes.

4. Spread the whipped cream over the meringue and sprinkle over
the raspberries. Using the parchment to help you, roll the meringue
up fairly tightly from one of the long ends to form a roulade. Wrap
in parchment paper and chill well before serving.

5. To serve, unwrap and cut into slices.

ETON MESS

*To serve six, crush 3½oz (100g) meringue into
grape-sized pieces. Whip 1¼ cup (300ml) heavy
cream until it just holds its shape, and process
3½oz (100g) of your chosen fruit in a food
processor to make a smooth puree. Carefully
fold the fruit puree, 3½oz (100g) chopped fruit,
scant ¼ cup (25g) powdered sugar, and the
crushed meringue into the whipped cream.
Serve chilled. For 12, double all the quantities.
The cream can be whipped and folded with all
the ingredients except the meringues up to 12
hours ahead. Fold in the meringues a maximum
of 6 hours ahead. Not suitable for freezing.*

PREPARE AHEAD AND FREEZE

*The roulade can be made up to 12 hours ahead.
Freeze without the raspberries for up to 2 months.
Serve with the raspberries on the side.*

LEMON AND LIME POSSETS

SERVES 6

1 pint (600ml) heavy cream

1¼ cup (150g) superfine sugar

finely grated zest and juice of 2 lemons

finely grated zest and juice of 2 limes

lime zest, sprigs of mint, or borage flowers, to decorate

SERVES 12

2 pints (1.2 liters) heavy cream

2½ cups (300g) superfine sugar

finely grated zest and juice of 4 lemons

finely grated zest and juice of 4 limes

lime zest, sprigs of mint, or borage flowers, to decorate

These creamy desserts are one of those foolproof ones you'll go back to time and again, and all your friends will ask for the recipe.

1. Put the cream, sugar, lemon zest, and lime zest into a wide-bottomed saucepan.

2. Heat gently over low heat, stirring until the sugar has dissolved and the cream is just under scalding point (just hot enough to touch).

3. Remove from the heat and stir in the lemon juice and lime juice.

4. Pour into small coffee cups or shot glasses and leave to set in the fridge for at least 6 hours.

5. Serve chilled, decorated with lime zest, sprigs of mint, or borage flowers.

PREPARE AHEAD

The possets can be made up to the end of step 4 up to 2 days ahead. Not suitable for freezing.

SUMMER BERRY TART

MAKES AN 11IN
(28CM) TART
(SERVES 8–10)

Special equipment *11in
(28cm) loose-bottomed,
fluted tart pan*

1¾ cup (225g) all-purpose
flour, plus a little extra to
dust

½ cup (100g) cold butter,
cubed

scant ¼ cup (25g)
powdered sugar

1 egg

2 tbsp water

For the crème pâtissière

3 eggs

⅔ cup (75g) superfine sugar

1 tsp vanilla extract

½ cup (50g) all-purpose
flour

1⅔ cup (400ml) milk

For the topping

10oz (300g) strawberries,
hulled and quartered

4½oz (125g) raspberries

4½oz (125g) blueberries

6–8 tbsp red currant jelly

1 tbsp water

*This looks stunning and makes the most of all the lovely
summer fruits. It's a favorite of Lucy's.*

1. Preheat the oven to 400°F (200°C). Put the flour, butter, and
powdered sugar into a food processer and process until the
mixture resembles bread crumbs. Add the egg and water and
process again until it forms a smooth dough. Lightly dust a work
surface with flour and knead the dough for a few minutes or until it
forms a smooth ball. Roll it out and use to line the tart pan (see page
267). Chill while you make the crème pâtissière.

2. Put the eggs, sugar, vanilla extract, and flour into a mixing bowl
and mix with a wooden spoon until smooth. Add 2 tablespoons of
the milk and stir again. Heat the remaining milk until just below
boiling, then pour into the mixing bowl and whisk until smooth.
Return to the pan and gently heat, whisking until thick and nearly
simmering, but don't let it boil. Set aside to cool.

3. Cut a circle of parchment paper just larger than the pan, then
fold into a triangle and snip the edge. Line the pastry case with the
parchment paper, pushing it into the rim, and fill with dried beans
or pie weights. Bake the pastry case blind for 20 minutes, then
remove the weights and paper. The pastry will be partially cooked
and won't go soggy when the filling is added. Lower the oven
temperature to 325°F (160°C) and return the tart case to the oven
for 10 minutes to dry out. Set aside to cool.

4. Pour the crème pâtissière into the tart case and arrange the fruit
in circles on top—strawberries on the outside, then a circle of
raspberries, and the blueberries in the center.

5. Heat the red currant jelly and water together in a pan over gentle
heat, whisking until smooth. Brush this glaze over the fruit, then
place the tart in the fridge and serve chilled.

PREPARE AHEAD

*The pastry case can be baked up to 2 days ahead.
The crème pâtissière can be made up to 1 day
ahead. The tart can be assembled up to 8 hours
ahead. Not suitable for freezing.*

TEA FOR A CROWD

Plates of neatly cut sandwiches, tiers of homemade cakes—it's everyone's idea of a traditional English tea. Keep the food small, and offer a selection of individual items such as cupcakes and muffins, cookies and scones, which are simple to eat as you stand and chat.

SANDWICHES

MAKES 24 (SERVES 6)

soft butter

12 slices bread from a thin-cut or medium-cut white or brown loaf

the filling(s) of your choice (see below)

salt and freshly ground black pepper

Fillings you can add 1 day ahead

Rare roast beef with horseradish sauce and arugula

Egg salad with lots of mustard cress

Smoked salmon and cream cheese

Hummus, olive, and grated carrot

Ham and English mustard

Cream cheese, mango chutney, and watercress

Gravlax and mustard mayonnaise (see page 72)

Sharp Cheddar, pickle, and watercress

Goat cheese, arugula, and sun-dried tomato paste

Thin strips of pan-fried steak and mustard

Crispy bacon with egg salad

Fillings to add on the day

Shrimp with lemon mayonnaise

Feta cheese, sun-dried tomato paste, and cucumber

Cucumber and black pepper

Sardine, mayonnaise, and lemon

Fresh salmon and cucumber

Avocado and bacon

Crab and avocado with lime mayonnaise

Pastrami and sweet dill pickle with cream cheese and horseradish sauce

Tomato, basil, and mozzarella

Smoked mackerel, tomato, and aioli

At teatime, sandwiches should be small. Some fillings can be added up to 10 hours ahead. Others can be added up to one day ahead with no compromise on freshness or taste. Fillings containing cucumber or tomato should only ever be added on the day. To stop the bread going soggy, you also need to remove the seeds from the vegetables. Slice the cucumber in half lengthwise and scoop out the seeds with a teaspoon. To seed tomatoes, see page 238.

1. Butter the bread on one side, top half the slices with the filling(s) of your choice, and sandwich together. Leave the crusts on.

2. Arrange the sandwiches in piles of four on a large tray (check first that it will fit in your fridge). Cover with a layer of damp paper towel, then cover tightly with plastic wrap, and place the tray in the fridge.

3. Two hours before serving, slice off the crusts and cut the sandwiches into fingers or quarters—either triangles or squares. Cover with plastic wrap and keep at room temperature until ready to serve. They will taste as fresh as the moment you made them.

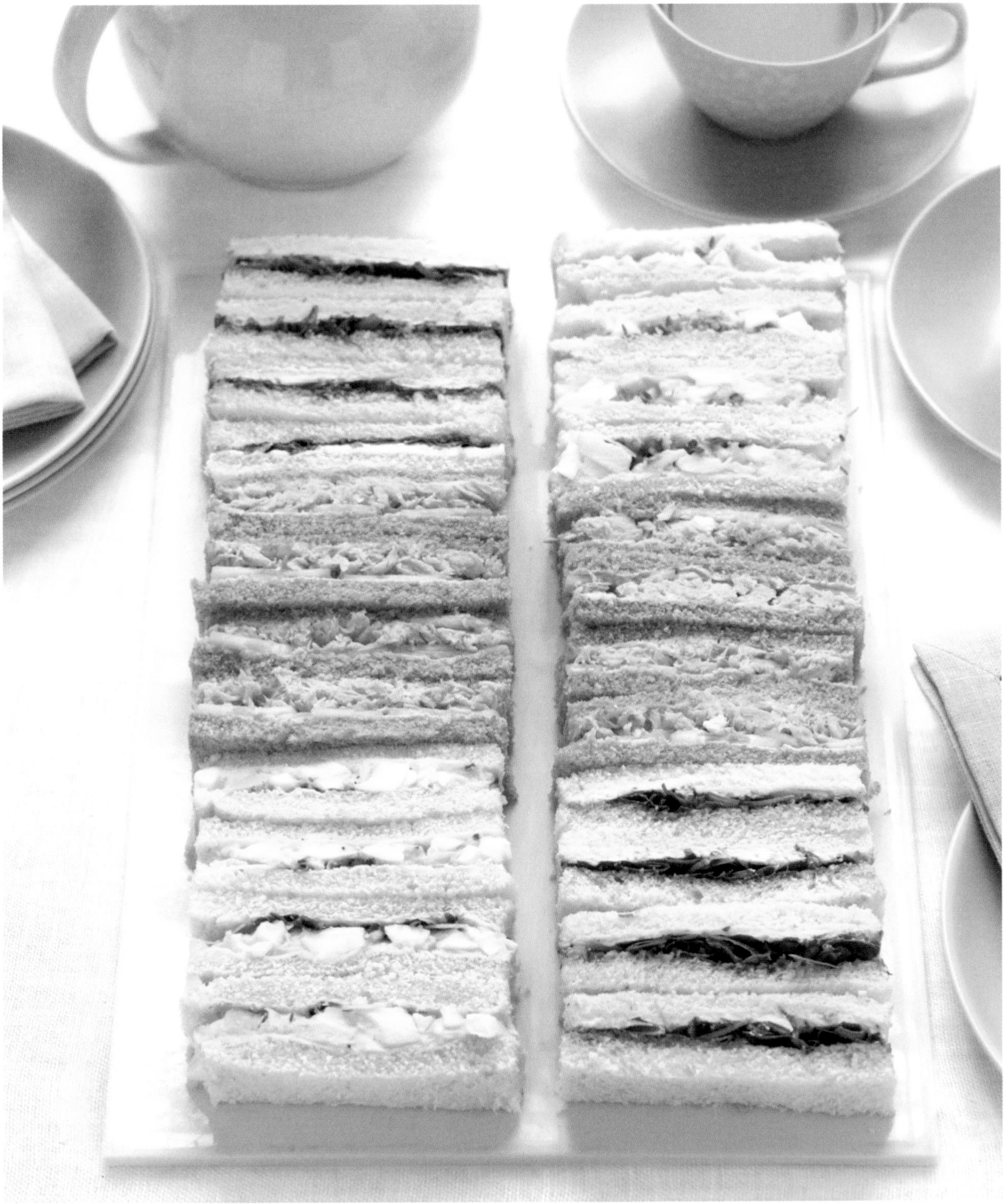

LIME MARMALADE CAKE

CUTS INTO 12 SQUARES

Special equipment *9 x 12in (23 x 30cm) sheet cake pan, lined with foil and greased*

1 cup (225g) butter, at room temperature

1¾ cup (225g) superfine sugar

2½ cups (300g) self-raising flour

4 eggs

1 tsp baking powder

finely grated zest of 1 lime, plus 2 tbsp lime juice

2 tbsp lime marmalade

For the icing

3 cups (350g) powdered sugar

3½oz (100g) full-fat cream cheese

¼ cup (50g) butter, at room temperature

2 tbsp lime marmalade

juice and finely grated zest of 1 small lime

Cut into squares, sheet cakes are great at large gatherings. This unusual recipe has a wonderful zesty taste. See the variation below for another deliciously citrusy cake.

1. Preheat the oven to 350°F (180°C). Put all the ingredients for the cake into a mixing bowl and beat by hand or with a mixer until combined and smooth.

2. Spoon into the sheet cake pan and level the top.

3. Bake for 30–35 minutes or until risen and golden. Set aside to cool completely.

4. To make the icing, sift the powdered sugar into a mixing bowl, add all the other ingredients, and beat with a wooden spoon or a mixer until well combined and smooth.

5. Spread the icing over the cake, making a pretty pattern on it with a palette knife. Cut into 12 squares and serve.

ICED ORANGE AND LEMON CAKE

For orange and lemon cake, follow the recipe above, omitting the lime zest, juice, and marmalade, and adding 4 tbsp milk to the cake mixture. Stir the grated zest of ½ lemon and ½ small orange into the mixture at the end of step 1, then bake for the same length of time. To make the icing, mix 1¾ cup (225g) powdered sugar, 1 tbsp lemon juice, and 2 tbsp orange juice. Sprinkle over the grated zest of ½ lemon and ½ small orange.

PREPARE AHEAD AND FREEZE

The cake can be made up to 1 day ahead and iced on the day. Freeze without the icing for up to 3 months.

ALMOND COOKIES

MAKES 30–35

Special equipment *2in (5cm) fluted biscuit cutter*

½ cup (100g) butter, at room temperature

⅔ cup (75g) superfine sugar

¾ cup (100g) all-purpose flour, plus a little extra to dust

¾ cup (75g) ground almonds

½ tsp almond extract

¼ cup (25g) flaked almonds

These are as delicious with a cup of coffee as they are at teatime. If you're preparing them ahead, stop them going soggy by storing them in a tin with pieces of paper towel between the layers.

1. Put the butter and sugar into a mixing bowl and whisk with a mixer until light and fluffy. Add the flour, ground almonds, and almond extract and whisk again until smooth.

2. Lightly dust a work surface with flour and knead the dough for a few minutes until smooth.

3. Preheat the oven to 325°F (180°C). Grease two cookie sheets or line with parchment paper. Lightly flour the work surface again and roll the dough out until it is ¼in (5mm) thick. Using a 2in (5cm) fluted biscuit cutter, cut out 30–35 rounds.

4. Transfer to the cookie sheets with a palette knife. Sprinkle a few flaked almonds on top of each cookie and press them down gently so they stick to the dough. Chill for 30 minutes.

5. Bake for 12–15 minutes (checking after 10 minutes) or until lightly golden. Leave to cool slightly, then transfer to a wire rack to cool completely.

PREPARE AHEAD AND FREEZE
The cookies can be made up to 4 days ahead and stored, layered with paper towel, in a cookie tin. Freeze for up to 3 months.

PECAN AND CHOCOLATE CHIP COOKIES

MAKES 24

¼ cup (100g) butter, at room temperature

½ cup (50g) superfine sugar

1¼ cup (150g) self-raising flour, plus a little extra to dust

½ tsp vanilla extract

⅓ cup (50g) milk chocolate chips

½ cup (50g) pecan nuts, chopped

Everyone loves cookies. And no one will be able to resist this deliciously gooey combination of pecan nuts and chocolate. The cookies keep well in a tin for a couple of days.

1. Preheat the oven to 350°F (180°C). Put the butter and sugar into a bowl and mix together with a wooden spoon until light and fluffy. Stir in the flour, then add the vanilla extract, chocolate chips, and pecans and mix to a soft dough.

2. Knead the dough lightly on a floured work surface, then divide into 24 balls. Flatten the balls with the palm of your hand and arrange on two cookie sheets lined with parchment paper. Space them out so they have room to spread.

3. Bake for 20–25 minutes or until lightly golden. Transfer to a wire rack to cool.

PREPARE AHEAD AND FREEZE

The cookies can be made up to 2 days ahead and kept in a sealed container. Freeze the dough or the baked cookies for up to 2 months.

COFFEE AND WALNUT CUPCAKES

MAKES 12

Special equipment *12-cup muffin pan lined with 12 paper muffin liners*

1 tbsp instant coffee granules

1 tbsp boiling water

½ cup (115g) butter, softened

1 cup (140g) self-raising flour

1 cup (140g) superfine sugar

2 tbsp milk

2 large eggs

¼ cup (25g) walnuts, chopped

For the coffee icing

2 tsp instant coffee granules

2 tsp boiling water

½ cup (100g) butter, at room temperature

1¾ cup (225g) powdered sugar

12 walnut halves, to decorate

Cupcakes are the cake of the moment, with some shops specializing in just them. These are made in muffin pans, which are fairly large, but make them in bun tins if you wish—you should get 18 smaller cakes. A dozen cupcakes arranged on a tiered cake stand make a spectacular centerpiece for any tea party.

1. Preheat the oven to 350°F (180°C). Put the coffee granules and water into a mixing bowl and stir until smooth. Add the butter, flour, sugar, milk, and eggs to the mixing bowl and mix with a mixer until smooth. Stir in the walnuts, then spoon into the muffin cases.

2. Bake in the center of the oven for 20–25 minutes or until risen and golden brown. Transfer to a wire rack until stone cold.

3. To make the icing, put the coffee granules and boiling water into a bowl and stir until smooth. Add the butter, sift in the powdered sugar, and stir until smooth and free of streaks.

4. Spoon onto the cupcakes, then decorate each one with a walnut half.

PREPARE AHEAD AND FREEZE

The cupcakes can be made and iced up to 1 day ahead. Freeze without the icing for up to 1 month.

FAIRY CAKES

MAKES 24

Special equipment *2 x 12-cup bun tins, greased or lined with paper liners*

⅔ cup (150g) butter, softened

1¼ cup (150g) superfine sugar

1¼ cup (150g) self-raising flour

1½ tsp baking powder

1½ tsp vanilla extract

3 eggs

For the icing

1¼ cup (150g) powdered sugar

about 3 tbsp lemon juice

To decorate

candies of your choice

Fairy cakes are always so popular. These are a basic vanilla cake mix with lemon icing, but you can make whichever flavor you like—see our variations, below left. Decorate them with creative flair. We like to use gum drops and malted milk balls.

1. Preheat the oven to 350°F (180°C). Put all the ingredients for the cakes into a large mixing bowl and beat with a mixer until smooth. Spoon evenly into the pans.

2. Bake for 12–15 minutes or until risen and pale golden brown. Set aside to cool, then remove the cakes from the pans.

3. To make the icing, sift the powdered sugar into a bowl and add enough lemon juice to make a fairly stiff paste. Spoon a circle of the icing on the top of each cake. While the icing is still soft, decorate with the candies of your choice.

FAIRY CAKE VARIATIONS

For chocolate chip fairy cakes, add scant ¼ cup (25g) dark chocolate chips to the basic cake mix. For lemon fairy cakes, add the grated zest of 1 lemon to the basic mix. For orange fairy cakes, add the grated zest of 1 orange to the basic cake mix, and for the icing, use orange juice or orange blossom water instead of lemon juice. For rosewater fairy cakes, make the icing with 2 tbsp rosewater and 1 tbsp water instead of the lemon juice.

PREPARE AHEAD AND FREEZE

The cakes can be made and iced up to 1 day ahead. Freeze without icing for up to 2 months.

CHOCOLATE AND ORANGE MOUSSE CAKE

MAKES 24

Special equipment *9in (23cm) springform pan, greased and bottom lined*

6oz (180g) dark chocolate

6 eggs, separated

⅔ cup (75g) superfine sugar

2–3 tbsp Cointreau

2 level tbsp cocoa powder

For the topping

3½oz (100g) orange milk chocolate, coarsely grated

1–2 tbsp Cointreau

¾ cup (200ml) heavy cream, lightly whipped

cocoa powder, to dust

This lovely cake has no flour—just cocoa powder—so it is as light as a feather. For children, replace the Cointreau with orange juice. Bake it at Easter and decorate with mini eggs.

1. Preheat the oven to 350°F (180°C). Meanwhile, break the chocolate into pieces and place in a small heatproof bowl. Sit the bowl over a pan of hot water and stir until the chocolate has melted. Set aside to cool slightly. To line the bottom of the pan, put parchment paper over the bottom of the pan, clip the ring in place, and trim the parchment with scissors.

2. Whisk the egg whites with a mixer until stiff. Put the egg yolks and sugar into a separate bowl and whisk until light and creamy.

3. Pour the melted chocolate into the egg-yolk mixture, add the Cointreau, and gently fold together, taking care not to knock out any of the air. Add the egg whites and gently fold to combine. Sift in the cocoa powder and fold until combined. Spoon evenly into the pan.

4. Bake for 40 minutes or until risen, shrinking away from the sides of the pan, and just firm to the touch in the center. Leave to cool, then remove from the pan.

5. For the topping, stir half the chocolate and the Cointreau into the cream. Spread over the top of the cake and sprinkle with the remaining chocolate. Sift the cocoa powder on top.

PREPARE AHEAD AND FREEZE

The cake can be made up to the end of step 4 up to 1 day ahead. Add the topping on the day of serving. Freeze without the topping for up to 2 months.

FIGGY SEED BITES

**MAKES 12 BARS
OR 24 BITES**

Special equipment *7in
(18cm) square, shallow pan,
lined with parchment paper
and greased*

⅓ cup (75g) butter

2½ tbsp (50g) corn syrup

*¾ cup (100g) superfine
sugar*

*1 cup (175g) old-fashioned
oats*

*scant ¼ cup (25g) sunflower
seeds*

*scant ¼ cup (25g) pumpkin
seeds*

¼ cup (25g) flaked coconut

*3½oz (100g) dried figs,
snipped into tiny pieces*

*1¾oz (50g) dried apricots,
snipped into tiny pieces*

*Seed bars are extremely popular in stores. They are
also healthier than a slice of cake, so why not make
your own. When we were testing these, the whole batch
disappeared quickly!*

1. Preheat the oven to 350°F (180°C). Heat the butter, corn syrup,
and sugar in a saucepan over a gentle heat, stirring until melted
and dissolved.

2. Put the remaining ingredients into a large mixing bowl, add
the melted butter mixture, and stir well. Pour into the pan and
level the top.

3. Bake for 30–35 minutes or until lightly golden and firm in the
middle. Leave to cool slightly, then cut into 12 rectangles or 24
squares. Leave in the pan to harden, then transfer to a wire rack
to cool completely.

PREPARE AHEAD

*The bites can be made up to 3 days ahead and
kept in a cool place. Not suitable for freezing.*

WHITE CHOCOLATE AND STRAWBERRY MUFFINS

MAKES 12

Special equipment *12-cup muffin pan lined with paper muffin liners*

2½ cups (300g) self-raising flour

1 tsp baking powder

1½ cup (175g) superfine sugar

2 eggs

1 cup (225ml) milk

½ cup (100g) butter, melted

2 tsp vanilla extract

½ cup (100g) white chocolate chips

12 tsp strawberry jam

powdered sugar, to dust

These are perfect for a children's tea party. For a slightly more sophisticated touch, replace the white chocolate chips with dark chocolate chips.

1. Preheat the oven to 400°F (200°C). Put all the ingredients except the chocolate chips and jam into a large bowl and whisk with a mixer until smooth. Stir in the chocolate chips.

2. Divide half the mixture evenly between the cups, spoon 1 teaspoon of jam on top of each one, then spoon the remaining mixture on top.

3. Bake for 25–30 minutes or until well risen and lightly golden brown.

4. Dust with a little powdered sugar and serve warm or cold.

PREPARE AHEAD AND FREEZE

The muffins can be made up to 2 days ahead. Freeze for up to 1 month.

MINCEMEAT BUNS

MAKES 21

Special equipment 2 x 12-cup bun tins, lined with paper liners

⅔ cup (150g) butter, softened

1¼ cup (150g) superfine sugar

1¾ cup (225g) self-raising flour

2 eggs

2 tbsp milk

3½oz (100g) currants

3½oz (100g) mincemeat

¼ cup (25g) flaked almonds

Mincemeat buns are traditional at Christmas, but there's no reason why you shouldn't make them at any time of year. Use vegetarian mincemeat if you don't eat meat.

1. Preheat the oven to 350°F (180°C). Put all the ingredients except the almonds into a bowl and beat well with a wooden spoon to combine.

2. Spoon the mixture into the paper liners, level the tops, and make sure there are no drips over the sides of the liners. Sprinkle with the almonds.

3. Bake for 15 minutes or until well risen and lightly golden.

4. Leave the buns in the pans for a few minutes, then transfer them to a cooling rack and leave to cool completely.

PREPARE AHEAD AND FREEZE

The buns can be made up to 1 day ahead and kept in the fridge. Freeze for up to 2 months.

ALMOND CRUMBLE–TOPPED MINCE PIES

Classic mince pies with a delicious almond crumble topping. They are best served warm.

MAKES 24

Special equipment *2 × 12-cup bun tins*

3in (7.5cm) fluted pastry cutter

1½ cup (175g) all-purpose flour, plus extra to dust

½ cup (100g) chilled butter

2 tbsp powdered sugar, plus extra to dust

1 egg, beaten

14¼oz (410g) luxury mincemeat

For the almond crumble topping

⅔ cup (75g) all-purpose flour

2½ tbsp (25g) old-fashioned oats

2 tbsp (25g) Turbinado sugar

scant 3 tbsp (25g) chopped blanched almonds

¼ cup (50g) butter, at room temperature, cubed

1. Preheat the oven to 400°F (200°C). Measure the flour and butter into a food processor and process for a few minutes until the mixture resembles bread crumbs. Add the powdered sugar and egg and process again until the mixture forms a smooth ball.

2. Roll the pastry out on a floured work surface until thin. Using the fluted cutter, cut out 24 disks. You may need to gather and re-roll the pastry.

3. Line the bun tins with the disks of pastry. Prick the bases with a fork and chill for 10 minutes.

4. To make the almond crumble topping, measure all the ingredients into a bowl and use your fingers to rub them together to make a crumble mixture.

5. Spoon mincemeat into the bottom of each pastry case, then top with the crumble topping.

6. Bake for 20–25 minutes until golden. Serve warm, dusted with powdered sugar.

PREPARE AHEAD AND FREEZE

The mince pies freeze well. Wrap well once cooked and reheat to serve.

APRICOT AND CHERRY LOAF CAKES

MAKES 2

Special equipment 2 x 1lb (450g) loaf pans, greased and the bottoms and sides lined with parchment paper

1½ cup (175g) self-raising flour

½ cup (115g) butter, softened

1 cup (115g) superfine sugar

3 large eggs, beaten

5½oz (150g) dried apricots, snipped into small pieces

⅓ cup (50g) raisins

1½oz (50g) Maraschino cherries, snipped into small pieces

Small loaf cakes are always lovely to make and are quicker to bake than large ones. This recipe makes two. If you don't need both right away, you can eat one and freeze the other.

1. Preheat the oven to 180°C (350°F). Put the flour, butter, sugar, and eggs into a mixing bowl and whisk with a mixer until combined. Stir in the dried fruit and cherries, then spoon into the pans and level the tops.

2. Bake for 45–50 minutes or until golden brown and well risen. Transfer to a wire rack to cool completely.

PREPARE AHEAD AND FREEZE

The cakes can be baked up to 2 days ahead, although they are best made and eaten on the same day. Freeze for up to 3 months.

ASHBURTON CARROT CAKE

MAKES A 9IN (23CM) CAKE (SERVES 8)

Special equipment *2 x 9in (23cm) round cake pans, greased and lined with a disk of parchment paper*

1⅔ cup (200g) self-raising flour

1½ cup (300g) granulated sugar

1 tsp baking powder

1½ tsp ground cinnamon

¾ cup (175ml) sunflower oil

2 eggs, lightly beaten

1 tsp vanilla extract

3½oz (100g) raw carrots, grated

¾ cup (100g) chopped walnuts

¾ cup (60g) desiccated coconut

8oz (220g) can pineapple slices, drained, chopped, and dried thoroughly

For the icing

7oz (200g) full-fat cream cheese

½ cup (100g) butter, softened

1⅔ cup (200g) powdered sugar

1 tsp vanilla extract

Passing through the village of Ashburton, in Devon, Mary stopped at a tea shop and had a piece of wonderful carrot cake. The owner kindly gave Mary the recipe and it's loved by one and all.

1. Preheat the oven to 350°F (180°C). To line the bottom of the pans, stand each on parchment paper, draw around the base with a pencil, then cut the disk out and place it in the bottom of the greased pan. Put the flour into a large mixing bowl, add the sugar, baking powder, and cinnamon and stir together.

2. Add the oil, eggs, and vanilla extract and beat well with a wooden spoon or spatula. Fold in the carrots, walnuts, coconut, and pineapple and beat until smooth.

3. Spoon evenly into the pans and bake for 45–50 minutes or until well risen and golden brown. To check that the cakes are cooked in the middle, insert a skewer into the center—if it comes out clean, they are done. Transfer to a wire rack and leave to cool.

4. To make the icing, put the cream cheese and butter into a bowl, sift in the powdered sugar, add the vanilla extract, and whisk with a mixer until smooth.

5. Remove the cakes from the pans and peel off the parchment paper. Turn one cake upside down onto a serving plate and spread with half the icing. Sit the other cake on top and spread the remaining icing over the top.

PREPARE AHEAD AND FREEZE

The cake can be made up to 1 day ahead, although it is best made on the day.
Freeze without the icing for up to 2 months.

BUTTERY SCONES

MAKES 12

Special equipment *3in (7.5cm) biscuit cutter*

1¾ cup (225g) self-raising flour, plus a little extra to dust

2 tsp baking powder

¼ cup (45g) butter, at room temperature

scant ¼ cup (25g) superfine sugar

1 egg

about ⅔ cup (150ml) milk

Scones are so quintessentially English and a traditional part of tea. For success every time, make sure the dough is good and sticky rather than dry. Be careful not to twist the cutter when cutting the scones out or they won't rise evenly during baking. Serve warm with clotted cream and strawberry jam.

1. Preheat the oven to 400°F (200°C). Put the flour, baking powder, and butter into a food processor and process until the mixture resembles bread crumbs. Add the sugar.

2. Break the egg into a measuring jug and beat with a fork, then pour in enough of the milk to make just over 5oz (150ml). Beat again to mix.

3. Turn the food processor on and gradually pour in the milk and egg mixture, leaving about 1 tablespoon in the jug for glazing. Process until combined—the mixture should be slightly sticky. Add a little more milk if it isn't.

4. Transfer the dough to a lightly floured work surface and knead until smooth, then roll it out until it is ½in (1cm) thick. Using a 3in (7.5cm) biscuit cutter, cut out 12 scones, re-rolling the dough until it is all used up.

5. Arrange on a greased cookie sheet and brush the tops with the remaining milk and egg mixture to glaze.

6. Bake for 15–20 minutes or until well risen and golden.

PREPARE AHEAD AND FREEZE

The scones can be made up to 1 day ahead. Freeze for up to 3 months.

BEST-EVER BROWNIES

MAKES 12

Special equipment *9 x 13in
(23 x 33cm) baking pan,
lined with parchment
paper and well greased*

*1 cup (225g) butter,
softened*

12oz (350g) milk chocolate

4 eggs

1lb (450g) light brown sugar

⅔ cup (150ml) milk

*1¾ cup (225g) self-raising
flour*

*Most brownies are dense and dark, but we use milk
chocolate so ours are very light in color and texture,
with gooey pieces of melted chocolate. Simply delicious.*

1. Preheat the oven to 350°F (180°C). Melt the butter and 8oz (225g)
of the chocolate in a bowl set over a pan of hot water until the
mixture is smooth and glossy.

2. Break the eggs into a mixing bowl, add the sugar, milk, and
the melted chocolate mixture, and beat with a wooden spoon
to combine. Sift in the flour and mix until smooth.

3. Coarsely chop the remaining chocolate then stir into the
mixture. Pour into the pan and bake for 45–50 minutes or
until well risen and cooked in the middle. Leave to cool,
then cut into 12 squares.

PREPARE AHEAD AND FREEZE

*The brownies can be made up to 2 days ahead.
Freeze for up to 3 months.*

INDEX

Penguin
Random
House

Editor Megan Lea
Senior art editor Sara Robin
US editor Megan Douglass
Jacket designer Saffron Stocker
Jackets co-ordinator Lucy Philpott
Producer, pre-production Heather Blagden
Senior producer, pre-production Tony Phipps
Producer Francesca Sturiale
Creative technical support Tom Morse
Senior DTP designer Tarun Sharma
DTP designer Umesh Singh Rawat
Pre-production manager Sunil Sharma
Managing editor Dawn Henderson
Managing art editor Marianne Markham
Art director Maxine Pedliham
Publishing director Mary-Clare Jerram

Photographer Georgia Glynn Smith
Photography art direction Sara Robin

NOTE: The author and publisher advocate sustainable food choices, and every effort has been made to include only sustainable foods in this book. Food sustainability is, however, a shifting landscape, and so we encourage readers to keep up to date with advice on this subject, so that they are equipped to make their own ethical choices.

Previously published in 2014 as Cook Up a Feast
This American edition 2020
First American edition 2010
Published in the United States by DK Publishing
1450 Broadway, Suite 801, New York, NY 10018

Text copyright © 2010, 2014, 2019 Mary Berry
Copyright © 2010, 2014, 2019 Dorling Kindersley Limited
DK, a Division of Penguin Random House LLC
20 21 22 23 24 10 9 8 7 6 5 4 3 2 1
002–315230–March/2020

Published in Great Britain by Dorling Kindersley Limited.
A catalog record for this book is available
from the Library of Congress.
ISBN 978-1-4654-8935-7

Printed and bound in China

AUTHORS' ACKNOWLEDGMENTS

Firstly, a huge thank you to the lovely Lucinda McCord, who was an essential part of the team that created the recipes with us for this book. Lucinda, thank you for your dedication, passion for your work, and friendship. We could not do what we do without you.

Thank you, too, to Mary-Clare Jerram at DK, who commissioned us to write this book and could see our vision for it. She has worked closely with us at every stage and always with a smile.

And a huge thank you to Dawn Henderson and Megan Lea, who edited the book with such dedication and commitment, and great understanding. It has been a joy to work with you.

Thank you to home economist lovely Lisa Harrison who made our recipes for the shoots, and to Georgia Glynn Smith for the stunning photography.

We would also like to thank our agents, Felicity Bryan and Michele Topham, who never seem to worry about our problems, but just sort them out fast!

Finally, thank you to you our readers for your amazing support.

PUBLISHER'S ACKNOWLEDGMENTS

For the 2019 edition, DK would like to thank Alice Horne for project editing; Georgia Glynn Smith for photography; Lisa Harrison and Evie Harbury for the beautiful food styling; Hannah Wilkinson and Rob Merrett for prop styling; Sara Robin for photography art direction; Steve Crozier for image retouching; Tessa Wright for wardrobe styling; Jo Penford for hair and makeup; Vanessa Bird for providing the index; and Corinne Masciocchi for proofreading.

For the 2014 edition thanks are due to the following people: Project editors Michael Fullalove and Andrew Roff; photographer William Reavell; Managing editor Angela Wilkes; Managing art editor Christine Keilty; and in DK India: Head of publishing Arpana Sharma; Managing art editor Romi Chakraborty; Senior editor Saloni Talwar.

A WORLD OF IDEAS:
SEE ALL THERE IS TO KNOW

www.dk.com